HOW DOES ONE DRESS
TO BUY DRAGONFRUIT?

TRUE STORIES OF EXPAT WOMEN IN ASIA

Praise for *How Does One Dress to Buy Dragonfruit: True Stories of Expat Women in Asia*:

How Does One Dress to Buy Dragonfruit is an eclectic, soulful collection of stories by badass women who have adventured far out of their comfort zones. Full of candid observations about travel, language, food, self, and other, it's a book for anyone who has ever felt peripheral, upside down, culturally shocked, or inspired. In other words, a book for all of us.

—Rachel DeWoskin, author of *Foreign Babes in Beijing, Repeat after Me, Big Girl Small*, and *Blind*.

A unique and inspiring collection of voices that calls up all the wonder, fascination, challenges, disorientation, and delights faced by women expats throughout Asia. I was moved by the breadth of experiences included in this anthology at the same time that I fell in love with one thread running throughout: how the expatriate journey takes us away from ourselves and then ultimately delivers us back, richer, wiser, and even more aware of how our own identities fit within our wide, wide world.

—Tracy Slater, author of *The Good Shufu: A Wife in Search of a Life between East and West*

How Does One Dress to Buy Dragonfruit?

True Stories of Expat Women in Asia

Edited by

Shannon Young

Signal 8 Press
Hong Kong

How Does One Dress to Buy Dragonfruit:
True Stories of Expat Women in Asia
Edited by Shannon Young
Published by Signal 8 Press
An imprint of Typhoon Media Ltd
Copyright 2014 Shannon Young
ISBN: 978-988-12195-2-7

Typhoon Media Ltd:
Signal 8 Press | BookCyclone | Lightning Originals
Whirlwind Book Consultancy
Hong Kong
www.typhoon-media.com

Cover design: Justin Kowalczuk
Editor photo: Joanna Suen

For Donna Young
And for all the women who inspire us in our lives abroad

CONTENTS

EDITOR'S FOREWORD

THERE *are rules to how one dresses to buy dragonfruit.* The first time I read Shannon Dunlap's essay "Forwarding Addresses," this sentence resonated. It echoed an unspoken question that appeared again and again in the stories of the 86 expatriate women who submitted their work for consideration in this collection. It is a question I tackled when I moved to Asia four years ago, when I started my first expat job, when I married into a local family. It is, of course, not a question about shopping, nor is it about clothes.

It is a question of balance.

How can I be respectful of the rules of this new culture? When do I choose *not* to adhere to the norms of my adopted home? Should I assimilate? Should I be independent? Or accommodating? Where is the point of equilibrium for a modern woman navigating a new culture?

From everyday occurrences like shopping and taking the bus, to dealing with loss and infertility far from home, the expat life is full of tension. Despite the enthralling stories resulting from this tension, too often expat women's voices go unheard. We are labeled and dismissed, tagalong characters in someone else's adventure. But if the scores of submissions I read for this work are any indication, there's a lot more to the story.

In Asia especially, expat men have long held the spotlight. They arrive, tall and privileged, and find a life that is charmed, exotic. Sometimes, they bring along wives who may not be able to find work, no matter how educated and accomplished they were back home. The women's voices are confined to coffee mornings and emails to the folks back home. You will find those voices in this collection. But there are as many kinds of stories as there are expat women. Some feel freer, safer, and more valued in East Asia than in their home countries. They innovate and take control in a way they couldn't in a more stagnant environment. They trail their ambitions here. They thrive. They make their voices heard.

The twenty-six women in this collection will show you what it's like to be an outsider. Some of them came to Asia alone, striking out to find a new life. Some took risks on a job, a lover, a whim. Some look, on the outside, as if they should blend in, women with Asian faces and other cultures who strongly identify as expatriates. They feel their otherness but are expected to be fluent in the language and the culture and the way one dresses to buy dragonfruit.

These twenty-six women built spaces for themselves between the skyscrapers of China, the markets of Cambodia, the streets of Vietnam, and the art galleries of Japan. You will find them struggling to fit in and fighting to stand out. Just like any other women, they study, they work, they fall in love; they bear children and lose them; they wander; and they wonder where and what home is. You will find memories of childhood and confrontations with mortality, the furious uncertainty of youth and the emerging maturity of women who have found their place in the world—for now.

As you read these stories, put yourself in their shoes, their dresses, their motorcycle boots. These women are making choices every day. They must ask: *Who am I in this culture, this place?* Follow along as they explore the balance they've found in themselves and in their homes abroad.

Shannon Young
Hong Kong
February 2014

FORWARDING ADDRESSES

By Shannon Dunlap

Wet Season: What I Look Like Here

DEAR Mignon,

Even after twenty hours on a plane, flying away from you, there are few people I can imagine in more vivid detail. Perhaps it is because we have always looked so completely different. As a teenager, it was both a torment and a comfort to be the inconspicuous one, to take shelter behind your glossy golden-ness and know that watching eyes were directed elsewhere. Ever since, I have had a gift for vanishing, for flattening myself against the backdrop. In Cambodia, it is different.

I have become suddenly, glaringly visible. I am aware of things I never thought about much in New York: my height, my weight, my clothes. There, I could have worn a Halloween costume and marched through the park playing an accordion and would have attracted only a passing interest. You know this as well as I do—it is a city in which you have to work to be noticed.

But on my first full day in Phnom Penh, I stepped around the corner to the market and into a cultural pothole. There are rules to how one dresses to buy dragonfruit. How could I have known that Kate, in her spangled leggings and movie-star sunglasses, was within the boundaries of decorum, but I, in a plain tank top and shorts with my pale knees exposed, was not? I'm not sure why I didn't ask her before I left the house instead of after, when I could see all over her face that no, it was not okay. "Everyone was looking at you," Jason said, and I am such an oaf that I didn't even notice.

He is my partner here, more clearly my other half than ever, out of both love and necessity. But together we are otherness squared, the combination of us drawing infinitely more eyes. Two days ago, at a waterfall outside of Sihanoukville, a group of giggling little boys stuffed wads of pink toilet paper up their noses and made faces at us, posing spontaneously and eagerly when we pulled out a camera. But as they continued to trail us, watching with rapt attention as we walked, as we waded into the stream, as we clumsily put on our lace-up shoes, there was no ambivalence about who was the object, about who really belonged in front of the lens.

Even when we are separated, Jason tells me more about what I look like than the mirror does. On the other side of a window at a roadside bus station in rural Thailand, he seemed the center of a complex diorama—the only non-native, all pale skin and hiking boots, staring dumbfounded at the steaming pots of unidentifiable food. Slumped in the bus seat, an undetected observer, I reflexively thought, *God help us.*

Don't misunderstand. I am not some poor little white girl; I chose to come here knowing that I would be a foreigner, an outsider. This is their country, not mine, and they have every right to notice the strangers among them. I certainly notice the smattering of other white people and find myself disliking them—for their loudness, for their rotundity, for their ugly socks and tourists' T-shirts. Given this, I find it remarkable that no one here seems to shower me with the same disdain that I feel for the other foreigners; it is rare that a Khmer person looks at me with anything besides a mixture of kindness and curiosity.

Even so, that curiosity is new to me. I find myself staring at the ground sometimes as I walk, a version of peek-a-boo in which I convince myself that if I'm not looking at anyone, no one is looking at me. But we learn as infants that we don't disappear when we close our eyes. These anonymous watchers, what are they seeing? What are they thinking? And how have *you* managed to live your whole life under everyone else's gaze?

The last time you visited me in New York, the waitress at the pancake house asked us if we were sisters and insisted that we looked so much alike, which we found strange and laughable. Here, they would probably say the same thing, our similarities much more salient in these surroundings than our differences. But maybe there is more to it than that. What could the waitress see, as we sat there sipping our coffee? Maybe it is a little like spotting two people in love, the way it is visible in their faces, on their bodies. Maybe that waitress could tell how we grew up together, how infrequently we get to see each other now, how dear you are to me, and somehow all of that translated in her brain to one fact—that we looked just the same.

And if that is true, I wonder what it means for the way I look at Cambodia and for the way it looks back. Maybe there will come a moment when this place and I will develop enough fondness for each other that we'll take a long hard look and find nothing strange there at all.

With much love,

S

Cool Season: Native Tongue

Dear Mme. Dahlberg,

I do not want you to feel wholly responsible for the fact that I am miserably monolingual. After all, it could not have been easy to be the sole high school French teacher in Lexington, Ohio, the only local expert in a language not your own, the lone Francophile amidst the fields of corn. But I do not think I am being merely modest when I say that I came out of four years of French class lacking the ability to speak any French. Half of the expats in Siem Reap are French, but I would rather feign mental retardation when I meet one of them than try to strike up a conversation in my pidgin français. And if I can't speak even a fairly common Romance language with any fluency, how will I ever be able to tackle Khmer?

Mind you, learning Khmer is hardly a prerequisite for living in Cambodia. Everyone here, from the tuk-tuk drivers to the wealthy businessmen, can speak English, and one's fluency is usually a good indication of one's affluence. ESL textbooks and workbooks are everywhere (though I've yet to find similar ones that teach Khmer). Children and young adults love to test out their English skills on us with stilted but spirited conversations. We have been told that American accents are especially respected, and when I see Obama and McCain orating from every television screen, I understand why. Unwittingly, and through pure luck and happenstance, I have been fluent in the language of influence and power for over twenty years. For a monolinguist, it is the most fortuitous possible position, and I can't help but feel some guilt for stumbling into it.

Maybe because of this guilt, it is important to me to be able to speak at least some semblance of the local language. I refuse to look like a tourist for the next year, unable to pronounce even the blandest pleasantries correctly. Let the record show that I tried, in advance, to prevent this from happening by purchasing "Talk Khmer Now!" for my computer, which features two decidedly Anglo-looking people whose lip movements do not match the words they are supposedly saying. But a single CD-ROM gave me little insight into a language so complex that it's difficult to pronounce even the *name* of the language correctly (despite being spelled "Khmer," it's pronounced, inexplicably, more like "k'mai"), and while the software was marginally successful in teaching me a few single words, I am still incapable of stringing them into sentences ("Rice yes meat no please thanks big-big!")

Since the intricacies of Khmer grammar seem to be something only a real teacher can convey, Jason and I went in search of one at the local monastery, Wat Bo. A monk named Savuth was convinced to take us on as students, though he usually teaches English and seemed a little nervous about the prospect of teaching Khmer. Nonetheless, he told us we could come as often as we want, and when we mentioned the subject of formal payment, he looked embarrassed and said something supremely monkish, such as, "If you will learn to speak the Khmer language, this will make me happy." Savuth's request seems like an exceedingly modest one, but I worry that making him happy will be a little harder than scoring an A in French IV.

Apparently, the sight of crazy white people wandering around the monastery is not an everyday occurrence, and two other monks showed up at our first lesson, counting on the potential entertainment value of the event. Savuth got right down to business, trying to teach us how to say *I*. This sounds simple enough, but the way you say *I* varies widely depending upon whether you're talking to your grandmother or to a monk or to the King of Cambodia. A simple *k'nyom* will do if I'm talking to Jason, for instance, but for the king it's *knyom prea-ang meh cha*, and God only knows what would happen if I had to speak to both of them at once. If I wanted to say something to Savuth, like "I think I might feel faint if I have to look at any more of the absurdly complicated Khmer alphabet," I would have to say, "*K'nyom prea-cah ro nah...*" or something of the sort, just to express that initial pronoun, at which point I would have forgotten the rest of the sentence.

After an exhausting assortment of *I*s, we moved on to telling someone your name. "Listen," Savuth said. "*Cheameuooioereh*," or some other combination of vowels I have never heard before. "*K'nyom cheameuooioereh* Savuth."

"*Chamore?*" I said hopefully.

"*Cheameuooioereh,*" Savuth said, moving his mouth in a way that I cannot hope to replicate.

"*Shamoo?*" I said, feeling smaller and smaller. This went back and forth for a while, until Savuth settled back to drink some Coca-Cola and compose himself. I slumped dejectedly while one of the monk audience members told me, "Clever student! Clever student!" in a way that I found extremely kind but unduly optimistic.

The lesson ended with Savuth trying valiantly to teach us how to say, "See you Monday!" and then waving goodbye as we sputtered gibberish back at him.

Mme. Dahlberg, where did we go wrong? Am I really such a dullard that acquisition of a foreign language is beyond my reach? Or did all that time in the middle of an enormous and powerful country muffle all the other voices of the world? Keep fighting the good fight, Mme. Dahlberg—we need people who can talk to each other, and Savuth and the rest of the international community deserve better than a one-trick pony like me.

Best wishes,

Shannon Dunlap

Hot Season: Tea and Indifference

Dear Kent,

This morning, I was making tea, and I read the name on the tea canister—the Thai company Phuc Long—and I didn't even smirk, didn't even think about making a joke about it. And that's one indication that perhaps I have been living here too long. Here's another:

Yesterday, I was walking down the street, and the guy with no arms who sells books out of a box hanging around his neck asked me for some money. I wasn't carrying my moto helmet under my arm (as I usually do, marking me as an expat rather than a tourist), and he didn't recognize me at first. And then he remembered me from around town, and gave a sort of shrug and a not unfriendly smile, as if to say, "Sorry! You're a regular here. Of course you're not going to give me anything." And then we both sort of chuckled and walked past each other, and it wasn't until I was about half a block away that I got a sickening chill at my own indifference.

Has living in Cambodia made me less capable of sympathy? Even after close to a year here, it's hard to know the "right" way to behave in the face of other people's poverty and trauma. Feel it too much and you'll be incapacitated; feel it too little and you'll be some sort of Marie Antoinette ("Let them drink Angkor Beer if they have no potable drinking water!"). To feel as if you belong here at all, you have to become a little inured to the realities of landmine victims and grubby children, and to act otherwise is to be viewed as a sap by both Khmer and expats. Once, I went into the local Mexican restaurant and two expat women were sitting there with a little Khmer boy for whom they had purchased dinner. They seemed a little sheepish, though, because after they had ordered, they noticed that, unlike most of the kids hanging around Pub Street at night, this guy had new tennis shoes, went to a government school reserved for the solidly middle class, and had a mother who was keeping an eye on him while chatting with her friends across the street. Of course, there are far worse things than buying a child, any child, a Coke and a quesadilla, but they felt as if they'd been duped, giving help to someone who might not need it the most. It was such a tourist thing to do. And we roll our eyes at tourists, the people who swoop in for a week or two and throw money at the first problem they see, regardless of whether it will do any lasting good. (Then again, at least they're doing something. What am I doing? Has anyone in Cambodia benefited from my writing so far?)

And if I'm sometimes less sympathetic than I should be toward Khmer, you should hear my internal monologue about Westerners and their problems. Woe to the person whom I overhear complaining about heat, insects, potential bacteria in the water, or uncomfortable bus seats; they will be silently excoriated by me. Firstly, haven't they ever opened a guidebook about any Southeast Asian country? And there's another level to my reaction, the part of me that has always considered myself sort of a wimp. "If I can handle this," this part of myself says disdainfully, "then you must be the lowliest of pansies."

What's worse, I actually like this tougher side of myself sometimes. It makes me feel hearty and resilient and less likely to feel sorry for myself. It's not as if I've forgotten about the fact that, should I fall into penury tomorrow and die a slow death of starvation, I still will have lived a more comfortable life than ninety-nine percent of Cambodian citizens. But sometimes it is an asset to be able to witness the misfortunes of others and, instead of feeling crushing depression at the state of the world, feel sort of…well, lucky. And yet…

I was talking to my monk friend Savuth about how, in the Buddhist view of things, human love is a kind of suffering, just like hate is. It is hard, having been raised amidst Western ideas, to wrap my head around this. To a Westerner, the Buddhist ideal of "detachment" sounds suspiciously like indifference. But I think what Savuth was talking about was achieving a philosophical equanimity—you should feel sympathy and pity for wealthy crooks and beggar children alike, because they are both suffering as part of the human condition. My friend Elizabeth long ago told me something similar in a different way: "Just because root canals exist, doesn't mean that getting a paper cut isn't painful."

But isn't that just like me, to look at a problem cerebrally instead of dealing with the sticky business of how to feel? I am confessing all of this to you because of the horror on your face when we had dinner in New York and I told you about the Big-Headed Baby, the monstrously deformed infant whose mother takes him to all large festivals, where she begs for money, a container for change placed on the corner of his dirty blanket. Who wouldn't feel sympathy for the child? But I have a hard time feeling pity for the mother, when she must be aware of the glut of nonprofit organizations in Cambodia who could possibly help her child; it is simply more profitable to parade him around like a circus act. Even so, you looked a little taken aback by my callousness when I said this. And maybe you should have been. I cannot conflate my own attitude with Savuth's universal sympathy—nothing proves this more than my very disparate feelings toward the Big-Headed Baby and his mother.

So where does this leave me? Vainly hoping that I can force myself to feel for both the root canal patient and the paper cut victim? Cambodia never provides any easy answers; it only makes it harder to ignore the questions. Perhaps that means that I have not lived here long enough.

xoxo,

S

Wet Season: Learning to Fly

Dear Dad,

Perhaps you have wondered why I have not written to you sooner. But actually, I have been writing this letter in my head for many months now, maybe for years, even, and waiting to commit it to the page until it was finally the truth. I rode a bicycle yesterday.

You should not feel concerned or guilty that it took me this long. I offer this reassurance only because when you found out that I could not ride a bicycle about a year ago, you looked shocked, as though you had forgotten something important, and responded by gamely running down the sidewalk and holding up the back of a bike as your twenty-seven-year-old daughter wobbled ineptly through the streets of Westerville and demonstrated little to no signs of improvement. Most people master this skill before they have lost all their baby teeth, but then, if anyone understands that I am not like most people, it is you, who have borne my eccentricities and stubbornness for many years now. For one, let us not forget that I was far from an athletic child, finding solace only in books, and you responded by trying to be as excited about Academic Challenge meets as you would naturally have been about basketball games. Also, I was not always receptive to help, as witnessed by my disturbing meltdown in the parking lot of the school when you tried to teach me to parallel park a car. Anyway, it was in no way your fault that you did not personally usher me over this particular milestone.

I will admit, however, that it might have been a less humbling experience if I had learned when I was six like everyone else. There were many aborted attempts. There was the time I went with my friend Kent (another non-biker) to practice in a park in Brooklyn, but we could not figure out how to adjust the seat, so we gave up and drank margaritas instead. There was the time you tried to help me in Ohio, and though I think all those avid cyclists in spandex shorts were trying to be encouraging by giving me waves and thumbs-up as they whizzed past, it was a little humiliating. And then, of course, there was Cambodia, where not only are biking conditions far from optimal, but also where advanced knowledge of two-wheel vehicles is taken to be much more of a given than most of my skills. One evening, soon after we moved to Siem Reap, I was practicing in a hotel parking lot, providing the local tuk-tuk drivers with some novel entertainment, and one of them walked over to where Jason was watching. "No," he said, pointing to me and sadly shaking his head. "Cannot. Is impossible." Later I would recognize that that is a favorite English phrase around here, but at the time, it felt like a good summation of my public shame. I should admit that I did not handle these failures with very much grace or patience.

Given these setbacks, it was a revelation to finally feel my feet pedaling steadily under the blue fluorescent lights of the Royal Empire Hotel last night, weaving around parked tour buses, waving at the baffled-looking drivers. There was no reason that this attempt was any different than the rest, except that this time, for some reason, it worked.

"Bah! Bah!" the tuk-tuk drivers yelled, finally. "Yes!" I felt victorious, much as when, right before I moved to New York, you looked at me proudly. "If living in Chicago has taught you anything," you said, (what would follow? A reference to my college GPA? The degree you shelled out thousands for? My first real job? None of the above…) "it's how to parallel park."

Maybe it would be an exaggeration to say that the most important thing I have learned in Cambodia is how to ride a bike, but then again, maybe not. After all, is it not the small obstacles that surprise us, that cause us to stumble, that embarrass us, and consequently, that teach us the most about ourselves? Yes, I learned something about my shortcomings. But there was something else there, too, something about perseverance and propensity for change, something that reminded me of you and of many of the people I have come to know here in Siem Reap.

Keep the bicycle chains oiled for me. We will go on a ride together, even if it is frozen and icy by the time I make it back to Ohio.

With love,
Shannon

Shannon Dunlap is a writer of fiction and creative nonfiction. While living in Cambodia, she was a regular columnist for The Phnom Penh Post and created the blog Forwarding Addresses (www.

forwardingaddresses.blogspot.com) with Jason Leahey. They now edit the blog PitchKnives & ButterForks (www.pitchknives.com), telling stories of food from the seed to the platter. Shannon *currently lives in Brooklyn and is working on a novel for young adults.*

THE WEIGHT OF BEAUTY

By Dorcas Cheng-Tozun

"**I**F you went running every day, you could lose some weight." A maintenance worker with a receding hairline squinted at me as the elevator in our apartment building rose far too slowly. This was the first time I had ever interacted with this man. Unfortunately, he was speaking Cantonese, which meant that I understood him perfectly.

"Mmm…" I responded, avoiding his eyes.

"Really. If you ran every day, you could lose some weight," he repeated, concerned that I had not given him a proper reply.

I flashed him a tight smile, but I did not trust myself to say anything else before he stepped out of the elevator. As I watched his stooped, retreating back, I tried to remember how I was considered "petite" and "tiny" by my American friends. But the US was, literally, half a world away.

When my husband and I moved to China in the summer of 2008, my body's relative mass seemed to triple during the time it took us to cross the Pacific Ocean. From my first day living in the industrial city of Shenzhen, my weight was a favorite conversation topic of friends, colleagues, and acquaintances alike. "You're rather fat," I would often hear. Or, "Did you gain weight? You look fatter." If I stepped into a shop, sales clerks would rush forward, stopping my progress with wild gesticulations communicating that they had no merchandise remotely close to my size.

My figure was not the only thing wrong with me in the Middle

Kingdom. I had grown up speaking Cantonese in the United States, but I knew barely any Mandarin. And judging by the reaction of the locals, my lack of language skills was by far my greater sin. Restaurant waitresses turned up their noses at me; grocery store cashiers clucked their tongues at me; taxi drivers quizzed me endlessly about my deficiency in Mandarin. My life in China at times felt like a series of one-act plays in which characters emerged with the sole purpose of telling me how stupid, fat, and just plain *wrong* I was.

"Ignore them," my husband Ned, whose Turkish and Jewish roots had combined to make him look generically Caucasian, urged me.

"How can I?" I protested. "They're everywhere."

"But their opinions don't matter. They don't know you."

That was the problem: they thought they knew me. I was a Chinese woman living in urban China, so knowing how to speak Mandarin was the minimum criterion for proving my sentience. It was equal to a blonde, blue-eyed woman in a cowboy hat and boots in rural Texas barely comprehending a word of English. It just wasn't supposed to happen.

In exasperating contrast, the locals regarded Ned like a creature with magical properties. They were entranced by his height and broad shoulders, his light hair and green eyes, and they immediately set the bar for cultural competence at zero. All he had to do was say, "*Ni hao*," and the same individuals who had been glaring at me as if I had insulted their ancestors as far back as the Tang Dynasty would glow with beatific smiles and tell Ned how amazing his Mandarin was. *Ni hao* was Ned's universal password to obtain what would forever be denied to me: respect, attentive service, automatic entry into heavily guarded buildings, and a mysterious fount of Chinese joy and happiness that seemed to emerge only at the white man's touch.

"He's so handsome," Chinese women would tell me, glancing at him through fluttering eyelashes. "Is he your boyfriend?"

"He's my husband" was a Mandarin phrase I quickly learned to say.

Under the daily barrage of insults and sneers, my former life in the United States as an independent, competent, well-adjusted young woman began to recede from memory. It was as if that old version of me had never existed, as if I had always been the overweight, bumbling idiot that 1.3 billion people seemed to think I was.

I learned to wear an I-don't-care-what-you-think expression on my face, but in reality, my defenses were only shadows of battlements. I felt as if I was constantly under siege; even the most innocuous encounter could become a surprise assault.

One day I greeted a deliveryman at the door of the office where Ned and I worked. I had done this several times before, and the routine was easy. All I had to do was say "Ni hao," take the package, and sign for it.

But this time, when I handed the clipboard back to the deliveryman, he scrutinized my signature before eyeing me suspiciously. "Why don't you have a Chinese signature?" he asked in Mandarin, a stony expression on his face.

"I'm American. I only have an English name." I spoke slowly and gave him a small, apologetic smile.

"Why don't you have a Chinese signature?" he repeated stubbornly, red blotches blooming across his forehead.

"I was born in the US I only have an English name," I repeated just as stubbornly, all traces of the smile gone.

I didn't understand any of the words he spat at me after that; he was speaking too fast and I was too shocked at his venomous tone. Knowing that I had just been deeply insulted, I refused to give him a response. We faced off in silence for a few tense moments before he turned on his heel, continuing to mutter vitriol under his breath as he walked away.

At that moment, learning Mandarin became my top priority. I contacted a company called New Concept Mandarin, which focused on teaching conversational survival Mandarin. They promptly responded, offering to send a company representative to my office the following day. When I told Ned about it, he asked to join in on the meeting to see if the classes were right for him as well.

The next afternoon, when I heard a knock at the office door, I jumped up from my desk. "I'll get it," I announced to the office in general.

Easing the door open, I called a cheery *"Ni hao"* into the dimly lit hallway. Then I froze.

"Ni hao," responded the supermodel standing in the doorway.

I couldn't stop the thought from entering my mind: *If this woman isn't from New Concept Mandarin, she must be a high-class prostitute.* My eyes locked first on her dress, a body-hugging, black-and-white-striped mini that revealed every impeccable curve on her petite form. The shine of her straight, long black hair, which she casually tossed behind one shoulder, mesmerized me; her wide almond-shaped brown eyes, her thin upturned nose, and her closed-lip smile left me in awe.

As I stared at her, I remembered how I had barely brushed my hair that morning; how I had a grease stain on my blouse from lunch; how I had an angry zit on my forehead that was probably doubling in size at that very moment.

"Are you from New Concept Mandarin?" I asked in a squeaky voice.

"Yes," the vision said confidently, with only a trace of a Chinese accent. "My name is Joanna." She held out a tiny hand adorned by a French manicure.

Feeling oafish, I extended my sweaty, un-manicured hand and awkwardly shook hers. "Please come in."

I shuffled to the conference table in the middle of the office, conscious that five pairs of eyes followed our progress. The room suddenly felt too open, too public. I didn't want all my colleagues—and certainly not my husband—seeing what I saw: this epitome of Chinese beauty in juxtaposition with the ungainly, unkempt Chinese American who actually liked to eat.

I invited Joanna to sit in a black swivel chair. She descended gracefully into the seat and crossed her slender legs. I attempted to imitate her movements, but instead I had to steady myself on the armrests when I nearly missed my seat. Clearing my throat to hide my embarrassment, I asked Ned to join us.

As we waited, I tried to look into Joanna's blemish-free face without flinching. "Are you from Shenzhen?" I asked casually.

"No." She shook her head, her obsidian hair dancing in synchronized waves. "I come from Jianxi Province. And you? Where are you from?" She gave me another smile, her lips opening this time to show me two rows of unevenly spaced and slightly yellowed teeth.

At the sight, my shoulders relaxed a bit. Perhaps Joanna was human, after all.

I smiled widely, showing off my orthodontically perfected teeth. "I'm from California, in the US" As Ned eased into a seat next to me, I added, "This is my husband, Ned."

"Nice to meet you," he said, giving Joanna a neutral smile and shaking her hand briefly before turning his full attention to me, waiting for me to move the conversation forward.

I sent him a happy *thank you* with my eyes before asking Joanna to proceed.

She spent the next twenty minutes explaining the various classes that New Concept Mandarin offered. I tried hard to concentrate, but

I kept marveling at her flawless figure and shining hair. Whenever I felt myself becoming overwhelmed with envy, I would angle my head to catch another glimpse of Joanna's teeth.

Was she one of the teachers? I couldn't resist asking.

She shook her head. No, her focus was recruitment and sales.

I began breathing a little easier.

As she neared the end of her presentation, Ned began tapping his foot, his mind wandering back to all the work he had to do. I hastily thanked Joanna and promised we would be in touch.

I had just returned from walking her to the door when Ana, a Chinese American colleague, bustled up to my desk. I only had to see the gleam in her eye to know that she was about to offer commentary about the impossibly gorgeous Mandarin program representative with the imperfect teeth.

"You know," Ana began in a conspiratorial tone. Amanda, a Chinese national colleague from the freezing northern city of Harbin, looked up and leaned in to listen. "They probably thought you were a guy."

I wasn't quite sure where Ana was headed with that comment. "Well, my name is pretty unusual," I hedged.

"That's why they sent *her*." She nodded in the direction of the door.

I glanced furtively behind me, as if Joanna might suddenly reappear in a blaze of light, accompanied by a full orchestral soundtrack. "You really think that's why?"

"Oh, definitely," Ana said. "To seduce you into signing up for their classes."

Amanda made a small sound of dismay, the corners of her eyes turning down. I knew she was hurt by the accusation that a fellow Chinese woman would resort to such measures to make a sale, but even she couldn't deny it. My eyes slid over to Ned, who was fully absorbed in his work and had clearly already forgotten what Joanna looked like.

One week later I signed up for New Concept Mandarin's first level of Survival Mandarin. When Ana raised her eyebrows at my decision, I cited their excellent curriculum materials, the flexible class schedules, and the extra online training they offered. It didn't hurt that Ned had decided to forego taking Mandarin classes and would never need to encounter Joanna again.

The Mandarin teacher for my one-on-one lessons was a young woman aptly named Sunny, who was generous with both her praise and her smiles. Unlike Joanna, Sunny wore simple blouses and skirts, no makeup, and a ponytail. Each week Sunny would marvel at how quickly I was learning and how good my pronunciation was. Thanks to my foundational knowledge in Cantonese, we flew through the curriculum.

Not only was my Mandarin improving, but so was my self-esteem. I could learn Mandarin, I assured myself, and I could find kind, genuine locals with whom to build relationships.

But a few weeks later, I entered the New Concept Mandarin office to find Joanna, in another body-hugging outfit and looking as manicured as ever, sitting in my classroom.

"Hello," I said cautiously, trying to hide my surprise as I sat down across from her.

"Hi." Joanna's smile was strained, her voice bitter. "Sunny no longer works for us. So I'll be your teacher now."

"Oh, okay." I tried to muster enthusiasm in my tone, but I was not particularly successful.

She continued as if she hadn't heard me. "She found another job at a TV station. A better-paying one."

I murmured something unintelligible, unsure whether I should be offering congratulations or condolences.

"Sunny was a great teacher, but New Concept Mandarin doesn't pay enough to keep people like her." When I didn't respond, Joanna gave me a hard look. "Don't you think? Isn't it worth it to pay more for good teachers?"

"Yes, sure." At least I knew the right response to that question.

Joanna sighed heavily and shook her glowing tresses. "Let's look at your last homework assignment."

I squirmed in my seat, anxious about displaying my language inadequacies to a woman who outshone me in so many ways. That first class, our interactions were stilted, but we both plowed ahead, determined to fulfill our obligations.

As the weeks continued, I began to suspect that my stunningly beautiful Mandarin teacher was nowhere near as polished on the inside. In fact, she seemed lonely and even a bit miserable. I could never tell if it was calculated on her part or if it was just her way of making conversation, but she increasingly found ways to insert details about her personal life into our interactions during class.

"I have a two-year-old daughter," she told me one day as we practiced Mandarin phrases for asking others about their family members.

"Really?" I exclaimed, my surprise immediately giving way to admiration. Given how amazing she looked, I would never have suspected she was a mother.

"*Dui,*" she confirmed, then switched to English. "But I don't get to see her much."

I nodded, thinking of Shenzhen's many migrant workers who lived far from their children, most of whom were being raised by their grandparents.

"Her father won't let me." Her almond eyes flashed with anger.

Unsure how to respond, I remained silent.

With each sentence she spoke, Joanna's life unfolded like a

sordid soap opera. She and her husband had divorced soon after the baby was born. He and his mother had conspired to keep the child from her. Even now, when she went to visit, they would hide the young girl from her mother. They told the girl that this woman trying to see her wasn't her mother but someone who was trying to snatch her away.

I was riveted, despite the fact that my expensive Mandarin class was devolving into an English-language therapy session. Each week, the proportion of English we used to communicate increased as Joanna recited her former mother-in-law's most recent insults or relayed her latest efforts to get custody of her daughter.

I listened, made sympathetic noises, and occasionally glanced at my Mandarin textbook as a subtle reminder of our original purpose. The irony of our cultural exchange was not lost on me: Joanna regularly dominated our conversations and had limited personal boundaries; I, in turn, was resorting to subtle cues and indirect communication in hopes of helping her save face.

The one bright spot in Joanna's life was her Australian boyfriend, a former student who promised to bring her to Australia one day. Her eyes alight, she told me how much kinder he was than her ex-husband and how he was trying to help her gain custody of her daughter.

I kept my expression neutral, but I had seen enough shady relationships between expatriate men and Chinese women in Shenzhen—usually involving promises of visas and marriage in exchange for sexual favors—to be deeply skeptical of the Australian man's intentions. Whenever I heard Joanna talking to him on the phone, calling him "darling" and asking him what he wanted her to cook for dinner that night, I tried not to cringe. I was sure this relationship would end badly for her as soon as he decided to move back to Australia.

Toward the end of our second-to-last class, as Joanna wrapped up the weekly update on her drama-filled life, she looked me in the eye and said, "You're really nice."

"Uh, thanks." I wasn't sure how to take the compliment.

"You really are," she emphasized. "Your smile is so kind and you always listen to me. You're much nicer than other people in Shenzhen."

I smiled at her. "Thanks. That's very nice of you to say."

Her words stayed with me as I took the subway home that evening. I couldn't remember doing anything for Joanna beyond listening and offering her my sympathy—hardly actions that should generate such effusive praise. I wondered if her stunning beauty was actually a handicap that lured in treacherous men and caused other women to shun her. Perhaps this was why she had chosen to share intimate details of her life with a captive student who was just a stranger passing briefly through her life.

At the beginning of our last class together, I noticed a diamond ring on Joanna's left hand. Unable to resist, I asked pointedly, "Is that a new ring?"

"Yes!" Her smile was electric as she showed off her sparkling rock. "Matt and I are engaged."

"Congratulations!" I felt a burst of hope for her. Sketchy expats, as I liked to call them, didn't usually invest in expensive jewelry to symbolize their empty promises.

"We'll move to Australia when we get married." A shadow crossed her flawless face. "I hope I can bring my daughter with me, but I'm not sure if I can."

At the end of the class, we embraced stiffly. I congratulated her again and wished her well in her upcoming marriage. With one last brilliant smile and a toss of her perfect hair, she encouraged me to continue practicing my Mandarin.

As I rode the elevator down to the ground floor of the New Concept Mandarin office, I thought how Joanna had been the perfect foil to highlight many of my shortcomings: my poor language skills, my cultural incompetence, my imperfect complexion, and my waist that wasn't as thin as I wanted it to be. But my impossibly beautiful Mandarin teacher with the crooked teeth and the sad almond eyes had also reminded me—in broad, bright strokes—what I did have: an adoring husband, an affectionate family, and an email inbox full of messages from friends living thousands of miles away.

The elevator reached the ground floor, warbled a weak chime, and opened its doors. As I walked through the lobby, the security guard in the lobby eyed me with disdain. I ignored him and stepped lightly onto the sidewalk, breathing in a measured cadence through the suffocating, smoggy night air.

Dorcas Cheng-Tozun is a writer, blogger, and editor whose personal essays and short stories have been published in Hong Kong, the UK, and the US. She is particularly passionate about telling true stories of the messiness and beauty of human connections, of sustainable social change, and of the unexpected ways in which we experience the sacred. She has written a full-length memoir about her experiences as a Chinese American living in the industrial city of Shenzhen, China, and is represented by Carrie Pestritto of Prospect Agency. www.cheng-tozun.com

BANGKOK THROUGH THE EYES OF AN INDIAN GIRL

By Neha Mehta

IT'S 7:30 in the evening. I finished my work a bit late due to a last-minute meeting. I come out of my office and decide to take a bus to my home. By the time the bus arrives, it's already 8 pm. The bus is jam-packed with Thai people. I can see I am the only foreigner—or should I say, the only Indian girl—in the bus. This feeling of being the odd one out has always made me nervous. I manage to handle my nervousness and look for a place to sit in the bus. I have to stand because there is no space, and as the crowded bus makes several stops, more and more people board. I remain the odd one out. I am standing in the middle.

There are men standing in front of me. There are men standing behind me. They look strange because of their unique Thai features. A lady conductor comes to me for the ticket. Since I am already sandwiched between people, I struggle to open my handbag, find my wallet, and hand over money for the ticket. The men realize my discomfort, create some room even though there is virtually no space, and let me find my money easily. After forty minutes, I press the 'stop' button. The driver struggles to stop at my bus stand in such heavy traffic. He gives the indicator, and all the cars slow down, giving him his due space. The bus driver, equipped with a screen near his seat attached to a CCTV camera on the exit and entrance

ge, opens the door and waits until his screen shows no more
engers exiting the bus.

No, I do not fall from the running bus, nor do I have to get down in the middle of the crowded road. I get down safe and secure. That's quite an experience for an Indian girl. In India, where I originally belong, one can never be so comfortable on the bus, especially when you are a girl sandwiched between strange-looking men. And getting down from the bus takes an athlete's legs as the buses never stop at the bus stand, nor do they care to use indicators. Had I been living in India, I would never have opted for a local bus to my home.

In India, bus rides are quite adventurous. It's the things you have to face and people you have to bear that make it an adventure. First, the stinking smell inside the bus gives you nausea. And when you can't hold it any longer, you end up throwing up on the road in the moving bus with no tissues or water to clean yourself. Second, the seats are often broken. If you are a person with regular back pain, a bus ride is not for you in India. That's the first advice doctors give to back patients.

Apart from cleanliness, which has always been out of question in Indian buses, the people on the bus add to your fury. Men stare at ladies traveling on the bus irrespective of their age, status, or looks. Some daring chaps even go to the extent of touching. When you object, they get infuriated and suddenly they are no longer human. They will try to slap you, tear off your clothes to embarrass you, or grope your genitals. Some daring ones follow you when you get down from the bus and harass you in an unexpected manner.

Even when there are more ladies on the bus than men, the discomfort persists. They will sit as if they have paid for two seats, not for one. Their heavy handbags will leave you with no space to sit, and if they are with a child, they won't pay for an extra ticket. They will place the child between the seats, causing utter distress to fellow passengers. Then we have some ill-mannered youths who sit on the seats reserved for elderly people. Knowing all this, riding a bus is the last thing I would do in India. But in Bangkok, it's not the same.

It's 9 pm. My home is still far from the bus stop. I will have to walk for another fifteen minutes before I finally reach the door of my house. I walk past an empty, isolated road, a shortcut to my home. I see some men crossing the street, but they don't look at me. For my own safety, I pretend that I am talking on the phone with some friend who is coming to pick me up in a moment. But the men do not notice. They seem to be completely ignorant that there is a girl walking alone. There are a few abandoned shops on the street with weird symbols made with graffiti art. There is a thick growth of bushes and wild trees that suggests the land has been deserted for many years. And the absence of streetlights adds to its scary look. I take this road every day and manage to cross this area safely.

My husband is already home. I reach our door and knock. He opens it with a smile and asks me how the meeting was. I take a glass of water and discuss the minutes of the meeting with him.

No, he doesn't show any sign of worry. No, I don't discuss with him how the men in the bus were rubbing against my body. No, I do not tell him that the men I saw on the isolated road tried to molest or harass me. And I certainly do not tell him how scared I feel every time I cross the desolate road that leads me to my home. I do not discuss any of these things because they did not happen. In fact, those things never happen to me in Thailand. Although I am a foreigner, men never chase me, molest me, comment on me, or do anything repulsive. I could walk up to the nearest grocery shop even in the middle of night, taking the abandoned routes, without fearing men on the road.

Traveling safely and comfortably in a bus and walking through abandoned streets that are usually hotspots for crime is an unusual experience for any Indian girl. I have traveled in buses in India with men gazing openly at me and other girls from top to bottom. Even if you are wearing a veil, their lusty eyes will still make guesses about your figure. Some overly clever men try to be friendly by pretending to be helpful, though their intentions are not hidden from any of the girls on the bus. Some make comments, some make sexual advances, and we even have instances of brutal rapes in moving buses. The best example to quote here is how a girl was raped in the capital city of India when she took the bus home during late hours. The horror of the incident penetrated deep into the minds of every Indian girl. Even those girls who think of themselves as modern and are empowered fear walking alone, even on the main roads, at night. But here in Bangkok, I never have to face men hunting for girls. The bus drivers are men who have morals too, and they make sure their passengers get safely home.

Yes, I have feared men in India. I have felt tense when I walked past a group of boys staring like preying cats. I have remembered Gods when I got out of work late, driving alone on empty roads. Yes, I have been chased by men on foot, on cycles, on cars, on bikes. I have friends who have been victims of sexual abuse by male servants. I have known women who have suffered at the hands of their drunkard husbands. I have heard stories about women being raped by their own brother and father-in-law. For a woman like me who has feared the presence of strange men, what I experienced in Thailand was nothing less than a dreamland. Yes, I fear murderers, I fear thieves, but I don't fear men as such in Thailand.

For my Indian friends back home, this is something unbelievable. When I tell them I travel alone, that I have never had a single man comment on my appearance or harass me during my entire stay in Bangkok, they envy me. And why shouldn't they? For an Indian expat woman who has felt the chill of fear walking alone on the road even during the day time in her own country, who is never able to ward off unwanted male attention, who, despite her conservative attire and mannerism, comes home with stories of molestation and sexual harassment, this late-evening travel in crowded buses is certainly not an ordinary experience. In Bangkok, I experience safety the way I never did in my own country. And coming home to see that your husband is not worried about you, despite knowing it's late and you are traveling on a bus with strangers, further illustrates my point. This is the confidence that husbands can never have when their wives are working late or traveling in local buses in India.

My own husband would have reacted differently had I been in India. In fact he would not let me take a bus at all. Most Indian husbands don't appreciate the idea of a wife coming home late. They know it's not safe out there after dark. If they have to stay out late, they make sure someone from home comes to pick them up from the office. My own husband would call me several times if I was coming home late, but here in Thailand, he is always at peace and never worried about my safety.

I can say this because I am an Indian. Because I know what it means to be a woman in a conservative country like India where girls are raped in buses, autos, offices, hospitals, on highways. I never thought that women could ever be safe outside until the day I came to Bangkok. In my one-and-half-year stay in Bangkok, I have felt more safe and confident than I ever felt in my twenty-five years of life in India. I could stay home alone, I could walk alone, I could wear the dresses I only saw actresses wearing in movies, and still, I don't have to carry pepper spray in my handbag.

Thai society is more or less driven by women. That's why you see women everywhere. If I go to the coffee shop, the attendants are girls who offer coffee with their usual 'sawadee' or Thai style of *wai*. If I ride in a taxi, the driver is a woman in formal dress. If I go to a bank, the manager is usually a girl. If I go to the work-permit office, the officer is a lady who truly understands my visa hardships. With all the girls around, I feel as if I am at home even when I am certainly not. I always feel safe, even in places where I would expect to be vulnerable just because I am a foreigner. Being a girl is never a reason for fear.

My parents and parents-in-law worried about my safety in Bangkok. They had heard notorious stories about Thailand from their friends who have been here as tourists or through Indian media that highlight the nightlife in Bangkok, giving little information about the real Thai society. For all these reasons they worried a lot about me. They even warned me not to step out at night. Sometimes they even scolded my husband for not acting like my personal security guard, the way husbands do in India. They knew that I don't have many friends, that there are no relatives to help me in case I have a problem; that I travel alone scared them the most. For one year, they kept calling and asking if I was having any problems at work or anywhere else. I could not explain to them why I was fine, despite being a foreigner woman. Only after my parents came here and saw with their own eyes did they understand why their daughter was safe traveling alone at 8 pm in local buses. It would certainly be a matter of concern for them if I was in India. They went back happy and satisfied that their daughter was in a good place and in good hands.

And even after they went back, I kept sharing with them the stories depicting the honesty of Thai people and how caring and concerned they are, particularly about women. One day coming back home after work, I fell asleep on the bus as I was too tired. When my stop came, I got down just in time, but realized only after I had reached home that I forgot my handbag inside the bus. It had all my money, some gold, my passport, and my mobile. For a moment I felt that I had lost everything. The thought of losing my passport was making me shiver. My legs started shaking. Suddenly I realized that I had my mobile inside my handbag and if I called it maybe somebody would respond. I called my mobile, and the conductor picked up the phone. I said, "This bag belongs to me. I forgot it on the bus." The bus driver said that he was going to come by the same bus stop in the next two hours so I should come there and collect my handbag. Though I was skeptical, I decided to go back to my bus stop and wait for the bus there.

While I was waiting, I imagined all sorts of negative things. Would the driver really return my bag, or was he lying? What if he asked for lots of money in return? I felt helpless. But the moment the bus came up to the stop and I saw the driver come out with my blue handbag, I gave a sigh of relief. I thought, *At least the handbag is there.* I even thought that I would give him some money for his effort and honesty. The conductor and driver both came down from the bus with passengers inside, returned my bag, and asked me to check the bag to make sure everything was there. I offered them money but they politely refused. I got my handbag... with everything inside. I thanked both the conductor and driver, who smiled and said, "*Mai pen rai,*" which in English means, "It's okay, no problem."

This is the beauty of Thailand.

Neha Mehta is a freelance writer. She has a master's degree in Mass Communication and Journalism and has worked with several newspapers and magazines. She has written articles for several medical portals like MedGuru and MedIndia. Presently she is living in Bangkok and is working as a lecturer at Assumption University of Bangkok. She is also associated with Bangkok-based magazine Masala, which caters to the Indian community in Thailand.

BREAD AND KNIVES

By Jennifer S. Deayton

FIRST it's two: a pair of neighborhood cops on patrol responds to the call. Then a junior detective and two more uniforms show up to make it five. Add two crime-scene technicians, another junior detective, and ultimately a senior detective in a well-made suit and, in less than an hour, the final tally comes to nine. Nine male police officers arrive at our Midlevels flat the morning after we're robbed. No one is hurt. Not much has been taken. But we're expatriates living in a nice neighborhood in Hong Kong. The show of force is both absurd and comforting.

It's the week of Thanksgiving, and I'm thirty-six weeks pregnant with our first child. Eight and a half months gone, and I am huge. Swollen and uncomfortable, tired and anxious. I feel the baby's elbow, or it could be a knee, lodged in my ribcage almost every night. I waddle more than I walk, and I get lightheaded if I don't have something to eat every two hours. I'm trying to work up to the very last minute, wrapping up all of the loose threads before my maternity leave, even though I'd rather be at home napping, reading, or watching *Prime Suspect*. I should be leaving for the office right now. It's Monday morning of my last week at work, but I've got the gangster squad in my living room and a husband with a morning meeting he can't miss. We want to get a police report in case we need to file an insurance claim, so I call my office about the delay, kiss my husband goodbye, and sit down with the senior detective.

I can't help but notice his hair, which is gelled and immaculate.

Does he lay out his clothes the night before? Or wake up extra early to put himself together so well? He is calm, friendly but professional. He moves between English and Cantonese with an ease and fluidity that puts my college French to shame. He opens his notepad and asks me to describe what I saw...

*

The cats don't greet me, as they usually do, when I wake. It's only 6 am, the sun not yet up, but already I can feel the heat of the day in my swollen hands and feet. The back of my neck is moist, as is the bed sheet half covering my legs. My husband, Paul, doesn't stir as I push myself up and out of bed. I feel tired already.

The summer refuses to break, even though it's almost December, and the relentless warmth is driving me crazy. Where is my cooling fall? My turning leaves? I pine for a North American autumn of pumpkins and homemade soup, sweatshirts and football games. In Hong Kong everyone is still wearing shorts and T-shirts, sunglasses and sandals. It's enough to make me curse the blue sky.

I pad to the bathroom—shoulders back, hips pressed forward, not quite ninety degrees upright—and I'm expecting one of our cats to weave between my legs and herd me into the kitchen for breakfast. But neither cat appears, and I don't hear a single meow coming from the darkened hallway. In the half-light from the bathroom window, I sit down on the toilet. The tiles are cool under my bare feet. I close my eyes and try to cradle my head in my hand, but at eight months I can't comfortably lean over the bulk of my body. I try to rest here awhile.

A mosquito has snuck in through the floor drain to investigate my ankles. I can hear it, but I can't feel it, so I shift my feet in a futile attempt to avoid a bite. I want to stay on the seat as long as I can, with the cool tiles below me, but my thighs are starting to tingle, to fall asleep from the constricted blood flow. So I stand up and shake out my legs. I wash my hands and splash water on my face. The towel next to the sink was clean yesterday, but today it's damp and already smells of mildew, an annoying scent that's transferred to my face as I dry myself. The only things I can do are wash again and pull out a clean towel. The heat, the damp, the open drain in the floor, sewage rushing through pipes outside the window. We're paying the equivalent of US$5000 per month in rent, and yet the air I breathe smells no fresher than what I imagine permeates a Kowloon tenement. Thick and squalid. The tropical haze of humidity, the relentless march of decay. And like the genteel ladies of a century ago, I need a handkerchief dipped in rosewater to press to my nostrils.

It's these moments—too late to return to deep sleep, too early to be busied by the day's needs—that I dread the most. I have time to consider complications and surprises. I fear for a stillness inside me and, God forbid, for all these weeks to end in sorrow. The baby books tell me I should feel movement every two minutes in the last trimester. Thirty times in one hour. I try not to be paranoid, to put these thoughts out of my head, but I can't help but pray and rub my hand over my belly at regular intervals.

Down the hall, I stop in the doorway of the baby's room and more smells—fresh paint fumes—greet me. We left the windows open overnight, but it will take another day to clear the air. Paul and I decided on buttercup yellow with an African animal theme. I admire the clean white crib and changing table, the sweet round rug on the floor. The new jungle-animal curtains hang listlessly in the breezeless dawn. It's all there waiting for our baby, for our new life.

I swore up and down that I'd never have children in Hong Kong, that I'd wait until we could live in a house with a backyard, the way I was brought up. After Paul and I got married, we discussed Hong Kong as a one-year option, long enough for me to complete my master's thesis, before we'd explore someplace new—London maybe. Four years later, we're still here and my body can't wait. We've moved out of our newlywed's shoebox to a colonial low-rise with high ceilings, a deep balcony, even a barbeque grill. We bought a secondhand car from a couple of teachers who were retiring to Cyprus. We got cats. It's what passes for roots in Hong Kong.

My husband's colleagues and my friends from work ask if we've hired a helper yet. The part-time cleaner we employ loves animals---doesn't love children—so yesterday I began interviewing domestic helpers. I don't know exactly how to interview someone who's going to be watching my precious baby eight to nine hours a day, but a friend has given me three handy questions to ask. Question 1: Can you show me your passport? If the woman is in deep with money-lenders, not uncommon in Hong Kong, she'll have handed over her passport as security. And if she can't repay the loan, you'll be the ones hearing from Shylock when he wants his cash. Question 2: What would you do in an emergency? If it's not life-threatening, you call your boss first and foremost. And Question 3: What do you like to do on Sundays (her day off)? Because if she's smart, she'll say she goes to church and not the bars of Wan Chai. Ultimately, my friend tells me, you trust your gut and get a reference.

From the nursery I cross toward the kitchen door. I don't see my wallet until I half-kick it across the floor. I look down and find it's lying open, credit cards and receipts scattered in a jumble nearby.

My hand goes to my belly. I can't think of a reason why my wallet would be on the floor. Last night, Paul had a late hockey game; we stayed out for dinner, then home, bed. The baby gives me a reassuring kick. I take a step forward.

There is a small storage room to walk through before you reach the kitchen, and I can just get round the corner without being seen. The walls in this odd bit of house are covered in white tiles and cabinets. A mantle of light over the stove in the kitchen creeps toward me. I try to stay out of its reach. *Some detective*, I think. My stomach will surprise the thief before I do. I press my cheek to the cool white tile and lean ever so slightly toward the kitchen.

No one's there. The baby kicks again and I can exhale.

I pick up my wallet and remember that I had no money in it. My ID, credit cards, ATM card are all accounted for.

The sun is rising, but the cats have not appeared. I walk across the living room and see that the television and stereo are still there. I go into the small guest room off the living room and find my purse dropped on the floor, messy but intact.

Paul's awake and in the shower now. I tell him what I think has happened. Once he's dressed he discovers that his laptop and mobile are gone from the dining table, along with an old Walkman, which was in a closet and didn't work anyway. We decide we'd better call the police. Paul's wallet is still in his hockey bag, which he'd brought into the bedroom last night. He holds it in his hand, like a little lifeline, as we stand in the middle of our bedroom, looking at each other but not wanting to say it aloud: that a stranger—strangers?—broke into our flat and wandered around while we were asleep. We hope the computer and phone were enough for the thief, that maybe he didn't open our bedroom door and have a look. We hope he didn't stay long.

Hong Kong, you see, is not Third-World-compound land, like Indonesia or the Philippines. We don't live behind walls and razor wire. We can go to almost any part of town or climb into any taxi, drunk on a Friday night, and know we'll get home safely. And if we're unlucky enough to get into a car accident, we don't need to drive on out of fear of extortion or vigilantes. We're safe to stop and call the police.

But now, the fact that someone has come into our house throws us. Makes us feel small and vulnerable. Makes us check our doors and windows for weeks to come. On the edge of parenthood, we're getting a quick lesson in what it means to worry.

*

The detective needs an inventory of the stolen items, so I tell him what we've lost. He says it was probably an illegal immigrant, a mainlander, looking for cash or anything to sell, looking for food. He asks me if anything's missing from the kitchen, anything from the refrigerator? Any knives? Any bread?

That's when I start to see him, the thief in my home. The detective explains how he probably climbed in through the open window in the baby's room. How it was a simple crime of opportunity. But I'm not really listening. I'm imagining this man in my kitchen, and I can see his face. His wind-reddened cheeks and dark eyes, so dark there's no difference between the iris and the cornea. His coarse brown hands and crooked teeth are stained with nicotine. His black hair is unkempt, unruly. The description by an old travel buddy, calling China 'a nation of bedheads', pops into my mind. I can see his clothes bag and fall around his under-fed, wiry frame.

He's a peasant, a farm boy, who's never known comfort or softness or luxury. Only thin mattresses to sleep on, cold weather and field work in the mud and the rain.

I've seen him before, so many like him, squatting outside the train stations of Shenzhen, Foshan, Dongguan. Blameless, shifting men come in from the countryside, borrowed suit jackets hanging limply off their narrow shoulders, wearing ill-fitting, dusty slip-on shoes. They're looking for work and wives in the towns that have sprung up amongst the cow pastures. Shell-shocked peasants, a constantly replenishing supply, flocking to the southern cities to polish computer parts and to shovel shit, to fall off building sites and to head *xiang qian*! Towards money. I've seen the stunned, dazed expressions on their faces, like time travelers dropped into a future that they can't comprehend.

*

The police inspect the flat; they dust for fingerprints and confer in muted voices outside the kitchen. Then the senior detective tells me it's unlikely they'll ever find the guy. He's probably back across the border by now.

Even so, the detective explains, my husband and I will have to come down to the Central Station to be fingerprinted for comparison and to sign the police report.

He motions to my stomach and smiles. "Please come down as soon as possible," he says.

"Of course," I say.

Later, after everyone leaves, and the cats finally appear from under our bed, I return to the baby's room. I need to get ready for work, but for a moment I stand at the open window. It's midmorning and I've been awake for hours. The day's heat clings to me, thick and unyielding. I look out the window. We're only two floors up, easy access for anyone desperate enough to shimmy up a drainpipe and climb inside.

Any knives? Any bread? For some reason the detective's questions stay with me for a long time. A window into impulses both threatening and sad. And I imagine our thief stuffing bread into his mouth in the dark kitchen, bread that's probably gone moldy, as it always does in Hong Kong if you leave it out for more than a day or two.

An officer has dusted for prints on the window frame, where the robber crawled in. The dust has left behind a greasy, black film, and I find tiny specks of it on the inside of my baby's bright new curtains. I'm trying not to succumb to tears, trying for that steely resolve that expat wives are supposed to have. If I were back in the States, I'd be three days away from my dad's pumpkin pie, the Cowboys game on television, and a long holiday weekend.

I'm just tired, I tell myself, as I stare out at the car park and the stacks of dull apartment buildings beyond our flat. I've had an easy pregnancy; there's no reason the birth should be any different.

Jennifer S. Deayton currently writes and edits for travel shows, which you can find on NatGeo and Discovery TLC. She also likes to get together with friends to make short films. At therockmom.wordpress. com, *she writes about music and parenting, and is a featured blogger on SassyMamaHK.com and ExpatBlog.com. In a former life, Jennifer worked as an editor and technical director for CNN International. She recently finished her first novel and is in the middle of the excruciating rewrite process.*

THE TRUTH ABOUT CRICKETS

By Pamela Beere Briggs

I awakened disoriented, finding myself curled up across the short width of my bed with my head pressed firmly against a window screen. In a half-dream state, my brain repeated the sentence I had been writing just before bedtime to my new pen pal in California: *We live on Tonoyama-cho (cho is the same as street) in a neighborhood called Shukugawa on the outskirts of the city of Kobe, Japan.* Then I remembered why my bed was not in its usual place. Out of growing desperation that came from being too hot to fall asleep, I had finally shoved my bed sideways to the closest window and squeezed my pillow onto the windowsill, where a whisper of a breeze finally soothed me to sleep. My head had left a dent in the screen like a shallow bowl. The garden was somewhere out there, covered in pure darkness, with no hint of the next day.

The crickets were still in the midst of song, confirming my suspicion that I hadn't been asleep for long. Although I had learned the previous week that it was the rubbing of their wings that created the sound, I still liked to imagine them divided into choir sections with mouths wide open. Too sleepy to move my body, I laid my head back on my pillowcase, damp with sweat, and listened to the alternating waves of sound fill the air. They sounded like a million squeaky wheels racing each other. As I scratched an itchy mosquito bite on my knee, I remembered another cricket fact I had shared with my younger sister.

"On the side of their knees, that's where crickets have ears," I told Meg, who had wrinkled up her nose and stuck out her tongue, believing I was making it up.

The pleasant sensation of sleep was beginning to wash over me when I heard another sound that immediately made my entire body tighten up. In the quiet of the night, a human voice cut through the thick walls. My entire being could detect the tone of anger. A crashing sound soon followed. Meg, who was sleeping in the twin bed next to mine, did not stir.

"Jesus Christ, Ellen," yelled my father. His voice, though muffled, was like a punch.

"You liar," my mother screamed.

I covered my ears tightly, willing the voices to disappear. After a few minutes, I checked to see that Meg was still asleep and released the pressure on my ears. I dared not breathe. To my immense relief, I heard only the crickets and a frog that had joined their chorus.

A few seconds passed. Then I heard a door open and close. I heard the sound of my father's footsteps descend the stairs. Finally, the clicking sound of the front door being closed tight mixed with my mother's muffled sobs.

I stared out into the garden at the tall maple tree, whose strong, dependable branches I loved to climb. I watched the sky lighten gradually. Some things happened so slowly, it made their changing almost invisible to the eye.

The scent of my mother's lotion awakened me, even before I heard her words. "Wake up, sweetie. It's late," she whispered so as not to awaken Meg. The sleeve of her silk bathrobe slid across my arm as she bent over to kiss me on the forehead.

I opened my eyes and stared into my mother's face. No sign of tears. Had I imagined the argument? Or had it all been a bad dream?

"Don't go back to sleep. I'm going downstairs to make breakfast. You can eat it in the car."

I dressed quickly and then grabbed my camera. I snapped a photo of myself in the bathroom mirror, dressed for school in my light-blue cotton jumper. I was recording everything about my life in Japan for my pen pal in California. As I walked past the open door of my parents' room, I backed up and stopped to see if there was any evidence of the fight I had heard. The bed had been made, magazines and books stacked neatly on the table by the window, and bedclothes put away. Then I saw proof that the sound had not been in my imagination. The mirror over the dresser now had a crack in the bottom corner.

"Are you ready?" my mother called from the hallway. She stopped me at the bottom of the stairs, holding a hairbrush and two rubber bands. "Wait one minute, miss."

As my mother parted and plaited my hair into two long, tight braids, a chaotic series of questions popped into my head. Who had broken the mirror? What had been thrown? Why was my father a liar? And why were they arguing so much lately?

Instead, I asked, "Where's Daddy? Isn't Shibata-san driving him to the office?"

"He took an early train."

Usually my father let me know when I would be riding alone. "He didn't tell me he had to leave early."

My mother paused in the middle of twirling the rubber band at the end of my braid. I could tell she was trying to figure out what to say, but she didn't end up answering any of my questions.

"You're taking your camera?" she asked me instead.

"I'm taking pictures to send to my pen pal," I answered curtly. Then I ran out the door and down the steps to the walkway. Glancing over my shoulder to make sure she hadn't chased after me, I felt a smug sense of satisfaction. By the time I had reached the bottom of the hill and street level, my anger had shifted to incredulity. I had learned the word *incredulous* only the day before and had found the perfect use for it already. As I stopped to catch my breath, I imagined my mother's perplexed reaction. Did she really think that I didn't notice when she chose to ignore my questions?

I walked toward a Toyota sedan, where I found Shibata-san's eyes closed, his head leaning back on the linen-covered headrest.

"*Ohayogozaimasu*, Shibata-san," I called into the window.

Shibata-san's eyes popped open and he gave me a big smile. "Good morning, Pamera-chan."

As he maneuvered the car into the road, I craned my neck to look out the rear window at our house. From a distance, its cracked stucco and chipped paint were invisible. In fact, it looked quite regal, like an old king sitting atop its hill. Prior to moving in a year earlier, my father had been told that it had been built by a German businessmen in the early 1930s. A hundred yards from our house stood my favorite house in the neighborhood, a Japanese home with expansive gardens. Although it was much older than our house, it had aged much more gracefully, surrounded by a classic Japanese stone-and-stucco wall and strategically placed wood-framed windows to provide peeks into the tranquil garden. From the car, I could see the tall peak of the house's black shingled roof.

The two houses overlooked a neighborhood of Western-style and Japanese houses. Shibata-san gingerly maneuvered its narrow streets, finally reaching the main road and the Shukugawa train station. My mouth watered as I saw the adjoining newspaper and magazine stand that sold stationery supplies and delicious chewy milk caramels. I had grabbed the handle of my lunch pail as I ran out the door, but I hadn't taken the time to pick up the small paper bag next to it, which would have contained my mother's standard late breakfast: a piece of toast and jar of yogurt.

Beyond the train station were the markets where Yumiko-san, our housekeeper, shopped for food. Sometimes I accompanied

"Yumi" on her trips to the vegetable, fish, and rice markets where I loved to watch the shop owners add up totals on their abacuses. My favorite stop was the rice market, where the old lady scooped rice into a tin, weighed it on a giant scale, then figured out the price on her abacus, sliding black beads up and down, quickly and accurately, calling out the total in a soft voice. As she poured the rice into a thick paper bag, it sounded like raindrops hitting a roof.

Shibata-san drove along an avenue, wide enough to be divided in the middle by tracks and station stops for an electric streetcar. Although early in the day, the air was already turning hot and muggy, and I watched two Japanese businessmen simultaneously wipe perspiration from their foreheads with folded white handkerchiefs, which they carefully refolded and then tucked back into their suit jacket pockets. I checked to make sure I had remembered to put my handkerchief in the pocket of my jumper.

Crossing the intersection, we passed a chauffeur-driven car. In the back seat, a foreign businessman was engrossed in his newspaper, just the way my father was some mornings. Stopped in a traffic jam, I retrieved my camera to take a photograph of a mother who was fanning the baby on her back with a folded newspaper.

Finally, we started to move again.

The car made a little groan as it went into a lower gear, and then struggled up the steep hill to the Stella Maris Girls School. Shibata-san braked outside the main gate, opened his door, and circled around to open my door.

As I passed under an arched entry, a statue of the Virgin Mary smiled down at me. Inside my classroom, Sister McGowan was covering the chalkboard with the multiplication tables for sevens and eights.

All the girls were still talking, in English, with a multitude of different accents: Indian, Dutch, British, Chinese, and Pakistani. I was one of two Americans, which everyone could tell by my brightly colored lunch pail. The boxy bottom compartment held my lunch, while the rounded top held a Thermos of milk. The whole thing was painted red to look like a miniature barn, with stalls for cows and horses on the bottom half. My father always bought us new lunch pails at the beginning of each school year at the Navy's PX, his favorite place to shop.

"One day we might go back to the States, and then you'll see how all of the children carry a lunch pail," he repeated each year as if I might have forgotten.

As soon as the bell rang, everyone stopped talking and found their seats, our attention on Sister McGowan, or at least the visible parts of Sister McGowan: her face and her hands. As she set the small brass bell down on her desk among a tidy stack of books and papers, I couldn't imagine that her white summer habit was any cooler than her black winter habit on such a muggy day. Nevertheless, she looked far more rested and cheerful than I felt.

"We're going on our first field trip next week," she announced to our claps and cheers.

"We will be visiting Nara, the capital of Japan from AD 710 to 784. Nara was the last stop along the Silk Road, which we will be studying this month."

By mid-morning the skies were heavy with dark clouds and Sister McGowan decided we would take our morning recess early.

Some of the girls scooped up jump ropes and rubber balls from the tall wooden cabinet at the back of the room. Anita, Anneka, and I ran to an empty corner of the yard and faced each other, our fists touching briefly before moving up and down.

"*Jankenpon!*"

Anneka and Anita's hands landed mid-air, index and middle fingers in the shape of scissors. My hand, wrapped into a tight fist, was in the shape a rock, which would break their scissors.

"You win," Anita and Anneka called out in unison while they stretched the jump rope straight. Swinging it back and forth as I began to jump, they recited one of our favorite jump rope rhymes. "Cinderella, dressed in yella, went upstairs to meet a fella. By mistake she kissed a snake. How many doctors did it take?"

My braids smacked me on my back as I leapt over the rope.

"One, two, three, four..."

*

Later that evening, Meg and I lay on the tatami floor in Yumi's room, enjoying the cross breeze and Yumi's company. As I watched Yumi iron my mother's paisley blouse, I recalled the day when the seamstress came to fit the blouse and its matching skirt. In the midst of the fitting, my father had arrived home from a business trip to Tokyo. He presented my mother with a small, beautifully wrapped box.

Was it the last time I had seen them happy?

Heeding the seamstress's warnings of the pins in the skirt and blouse, my mother had gracefully turned around like the twirling dancer in my jewelry box. She had oh-so-carefully unwrapped the wrapping paper and handed it to me, knowing that Yumi and I would want to turn it into an origami flower, bird, or fish.

A string of creamy white pearls emerged from the box. My mother glowed.

"They're beautiful," she said, and reached out to give my father a kiss.

My father had then turned toward Meg and me and asked, "Which hand?"

Meg pointed to his left arm and out came a baby doll, dressed in a lacy pink dress. She squealed with delight and jumped up to reach for the doll. She gave it a hug.

"She's so pretty! I love her!"

My father brought his other hand forward. It held a leather case, which he held out to me.

"A Brownie for you," he said.

"A brownie?" I asked, baffled.

He pulled a camera out of the case. "They're called Brownies," he said as he handed it to me.

I immediately placed my eye up to the viewfinder. I pressed the shutter. Everyone laughed as the flash went off.

"I'll go unpack," my father said. "By the way, there's already film in it!"

As the seamstress placed her pins, measuring tape, and marking pencil back in her sewing box, my mother began unbuttoning her blouse.

"*Ki o tsukete!*" the seamstress had admonished.

"Careful, Mommy," Meg echoed the seamstress's gentle voice.

In her slip, bra, and pearls, I had never seen my mother look so beautiful. Without thinking, I had placed the camera up to my eye and framed the shot.

Click, the camera went.

My mother gasped and then scolded, "You have to ask before taking pictures of people. Especially when they don't have their clothes on."

Meg laughed and pointed at her doll, whose dress she had removed.

My mother reached for a dress on the stool and slipped it over her head. When her head reappeared, she smiled coyly and wagged her finger at me, "That picture is for your eyes only. It does not go into the family album."

When I was in bed much later that night, I heard the front door open and then the distant voices of my parents as they walked up the staircase together. Before leaving for a party, my father and mother stopped by Yumi's room together to say goodbye. They were in a good mood, and I noticed that my mother was wearing her pearls.

"You drank too much," I heard my father say.

"I didn't," my mother giggled.

"Yes, you did."

I lay awake listening to the usual chorus of crickets. I thought about the male crickets, rubbing their wings together to attract the female crickets. Another fact I had learned about crickets: the females preferred the strongest chirpers.

*

I was awakened later by another sound I was getting to know too well. I reached for my alarm clock. What was there to argue about at three o'clock in the morning? I folded my pillow in half and placed it over my head, but it didn't help. I sat up and looked at Meg, who, of course, was still sound asleep. I climbed out of bed and tiptoed to the bedroom door.

The downstairs entry was dimly lit by the shaft of light that snuck through the glass panes above the front door. I made my way to the swinging kitchen door. Squeezing my pillow close, I paused to allow my eyes to adjust to the dark room. Drawn toward the shape of the stove and its dimly lit buttons, I remembered that if I pressed the button on the far end, a gentle light illuminated the top of the stove. I pressed the tiny green button and was rewarded with a warm glow.

Yumi walked into the kitchen, wearing one of my mother's old robes folded across her nightgown like a kimono.

"*Daijobu?*"

I nodded even though I wasn't fine. I had never wandered

downstairs in the middle of the night. Yumi offered to walk me back upstairs, but I shook my head.

She noticed my pillow. "*Kimashoo.*"

I gladly followed Yumi into her room. Laid out on top of the Japanese tatami floor was a futon bed. Yumi's compact buckwheat pillow rustled as she moved it to make room for my fluffy pillow. I fell sound asleep.

When I awakened in the morning, I was alone. I spent a few minutes staring up at the ceiling, studying an old water stain and listening to the sounds of morning activity. The door slid open, and Yumi entered.

"*Ohayagozomaisu.*" She smiled.

"Good morning, Yumi," I answered.

"I made special lunch for field trip," said Yumi. "Must hurry and get ready, ne?"

I jumped up, excited to be reminded of the trip to Nara. Yumi handed me my pillow.

"Thank you, Yumi," I said, not meaning the pillow.

*

On the bus ride to Nara, Sister McGowan led the class in Japanese, English, and French songs. Anneka, Anita, and I couldn't help giggling whenever she turned into this animated singing nun. "Do you suppose she thinks we can be like the von Trapp family?" Anita whispered in her melodious Indian accent.

"In the *Sound of Music*?" Anneka and I giggled in disbelief.

When the bus arrived at Nara Park, Sister McGowan went from being the singing nun to the colonel nun. She barked out a list of instructions, which included a reminder about using quiet voices in temples, meeting places, and bathroom locations, and during lunch.

She paired us up and instructed us not to separate. My partner was Anita.

We exited the bus with Sister McGowan leading the way, looking as if she had led her troops here hundreds of times before. Immediately, we noticed the scattered groups of deer. In every direction, deer rested on their haunches or walked around nimbly. Sister McGowan had explained in class that the deer were considered sacred animals. I noticed that sacred animals still went to the bathroom, as I focused half of my attention on avoiding clusters of brown pellets on the walking paths.

I stopped to pull my camera out of its case. I held the window of the viewfinder up to my eye and moved in a slow, circular movement, looking for the photograph I wanted to take.

A Japanese man, who looked as ancient as the surrounding temples, sat alone in one of the many porch-like structures set up to sell snacks and souvenirs. His calligraphy scrolls were displayed behind him.

"*Shashin tote?*" the man called out to me.

"*Hai.* I'm taking pictures."

"*Nihongo hanasemasuka?*" the man asked.

I spoke a little Japanese.

"*Skoshi,*" I answered shyly.

I watched as he dipped his brush into ink and began to paint new strokes on a piece of paper. He finished one character, and then dipped his brush into the ink. The tip of the brush once again touched paper to begin the second character, the squat, solid shapes contrasting with the delicate curves of the first.

Anita, who had walked on with the rest of the class, had dashed back to my side when she realized I was missing. "Everyone has gone ahead. They're going into the temple to see the Buddha."

"Wait one minute."

The man completed the last stroke. He leaned toward the paper to blow the ink dry. Then he lifted the long scroll and handed it to me. I carefully took hold of the narrow piece of paper and studied it. As I had not learned *kanji*, the most complicated Japanese alphabet, I did not know what the letters said. The first character looked like a girl with a ponytail in her hair, leaning forward to gaze east. The second character was a series of vertical and horizontal lines that sat on two squat legs, strong and steady.

"*Shashin.* Photograph."

"You speak English?" I asked.

"*Skoshi,*" he answered with a twinkle in his eye. "Little bit."

He turned his focus to the paper, "It is Japanese word for *photograph.*" He pointed to the first character and translated the meaning: *to copy.* He pointed to the second: *the truth.*

"For you," the man said in English. "Dry *skoshi* more minutes, then tie," he instructed as he handed me a string.

"I can carry your lunch," Anita offered.

I accepted the gift, carefully taking hold of each end so that the ink would not smear. Bowing deeply, I said, "*Domo arigato gozaimashita.*"

"*Ki o tsukete,*" the man said, just before reaching for his brush.

"I'll be careful," I promised.

Anita rushed onward, a striking sight with her long, thick black braid against the light blue of her uniform, her arms balanced by the weight of the two lunches, one multi-colored Indian batik bag, and one red lunch pail.

"Anita, wait one second," I pleaded as I stopped to roll up the scroll, which had dried. I held the string between my teeth. Anita set the lunches down and took the string. She wrapped the string around the scroll, securing it with a bow. We then scooped up our lunches and ran.

As we entered Todai-ji Temple, we were greeted by unexpected silence. Our classmates were staring up at an immense bronze statue of Buddha that was at least fifty times their size. The Buddha appeared to be watching them with a mild expression that inspired quiet. Anita and I looked up, equally transfixed. The scent of incense tickled my nose. I turned away, pressing my finger below my nose to attempt to suppress my sneeze. That is when I caught sight of Sister McGowan, who had silently come to stand a few feet behind me. I saw her wipe away a tear with her long sleeve, but was reassured to see that she did not look sad. In fact, she was smiling. She began to speak in a soft voice that made the girls move closer to her.

"One of Buddha's teachings is that all things change."

She reached her arms around the two girls standing closest, which included me.

"We don't want things to change and yet they do. Some things change quickly. Others change slowly."

I turned my gaze back to the Buddha.

"Buddha taught his followers to be generous and compassionate toward other people. In addition, he taught them some rules."

"What are the rules?" one of the girls called out.

Sister McGowan kept her eyes on the Buddha.

"Say nothing to harm others. Do nothing to harm any living creature. Choose a job that hurts no living thing. Try to become a good person. Learn to control your thoughts and emotions to quiet your mind."

"Like when we pray?" I heard Anneka's voice ask.

"Yes."

One of the girls had noticed that a large hole was carved out of one of the beams in the building. In a voice filled with awe, she read aloud a sign affixed to the beam, "This hole is the size of the Buddha's nostril. If you can crawl through it, you will enjoy eternal happiness."

The girls turned and congregated around the beam. The largest girl in the class skeptically studied the hole.

"I hope I can fit inside Buddha's nostril."

She dropped down to her hands and knees and stuck her head and body into one side of the hole and reappeared out the other. Laughing, all of the other girls lined up to do the same. Holding her index finger up to her lips, Sister McGowan tried to quiet us, while laughing herself, "Shh, children."

I stayed back as the rest of my class exited the temple building. I knew I had to be quick. I placed my lunch pail and scroll inside the replica of Buddha's nostril so that I could take a picture of the Great Buddha. I took my time to get a second shot, and then grabbed my lunch pail before running out of the temple.

The bus ride back to school was calmer than the morning journey. Tired from all of the walking, the girls carried on quiet conversations with seatmates or leaned their heads against bus windows or armrests.

The bus headed west toward Osaka, a bustling city southeast of Kobe, where our school was located. Leaning back in my seat with my eyes closed, I tried to distinguish the sounds of the city. Horns, voices, buses, and cars blended together.

Opening my eyes, I watched as we passed through crowds of people, office buildings, and neon signs. I saw a mother bend down to talk to her young son, while the baby on her back looked up in my direction. I hurriedly pulled my camera from its case and snapped a photograph.

The bus moved a few feet, and then stopped for more traffic. I stared at a woman in an exquisite kimono, decorated with yellow, orange, and white painted birds and flowers. She gracefully scooted across the sidewalk in *geta*, Japanese wooden shoes. Her hair, so carefully constructed into fancy crescent rolls, did not budge. She stopped to look into a shop window. I looked through the viewfinder of my camera and saw what I had not noticed with my bare eye. My photo would include, in the foreground, two teenaged girls in modern dress, waiting at a bus stop. In the background: the woman in the beautiful kimono. I smiled with pleasure at this discovery.

The bus lurched forward, this time moving without interruption for three blocks. It stopped again. I closed my eyes for a moment. Without the sights to distract me, I realized what the city sounded like. Crickets! I opened my eyes and glanced out the window.

The revolving door of a hotel caught my eye. I looked down at the tiny window on the top of the camera that showed me the number of pictures I had taken: eight. I still had four left. A group of three businessmen, dressed exactly alike, popped out of the revolving door onto the sidewalk. I snapped a picture of them, holding matching briefcases, and thought of the three French hens in the Christmas song.

A foreign couple exited and approached the street to summon a taxi. I was still holding the camera up to my eye. I watched as the man held up his arm for a taxi, obscuring his face for a moment. A taxi pulled to a stop at the curb, and the man guided the woman, whose long auburn hair was mostly covered by a red silk scarf, toward the open door of the backseat. They stood talking for a moment, the man's back to me. When they gave each other a hug, the woman leaned her head on the man's shoulder, resting her red leather purse on his back. The red of her scarf on his shoulder, next to the red purse resting on his back, were pretty. I snapped a photo.

The man turned his face to say something into the woman's ear. I tightened my hold on the camera, my index finger frozen on the shutter. I recognized that face. I knew this man. Yet, how could it be? Keeping my eye up to the viewfinder, I both wanted to and didn't want to see. What was my father doing with this woman?

The woman got into the taxi alone, and my father looked up for a moment in my direction. I gasped, thinking that he might see me.

I kept the camera up to my face, hiding, hoping that he would not see me. My father entered the next taxi, and I finally lowered my camera. Pressing my face against the glass, I tried to keep sight of the taxi, but it was hopeless.

From somewhere deep inside my chest, the cry I tried hard to push down rose higher and higher. I held my breath so that no sound could escape. The next thing I knew, Sister McGowan was sitting next to me, her face staring into my eyes, as she pressed a cold cloth against my forehead.

"You fainted. Take deep breaths and you'll be fine," Sister said. "We'll be back to school soon."

I closed my eyes and heard crickets. I couldn't get them out of my mind. I remembered another fact about crickets I had totally forgotten. Crickets had many eyes, yet their eyesight was very poor. Their hearing was much better. How I wished I had kept my eyes closed, just listening to the sounds of Osaka.

With sudden dread, I began to search around my seat. I had forgotten the scroll! I had left it in the nostril of Buddha. The loss of the scroll was almost too much to bear, for now it seemed it might hold an answer I knew I needed.

I tried to recall Buddha's rules. Frustratingly, I could only recall one of them: learn to control your thoughts and emotions to quiet your mind. That was impossible.

Shibata-san came to a stop at the bottom of the hill. Yumi was waiting at the gate as Sister McGowan had phoned ahead. She rushed up to the car and opened my door.

"Is Mommy home?"

"*Hai*, with baby Amy," Yumi answered.

When we reached the front door, Yumi bent down to untie my shoes. She led me into the kitchen, where a pot of tea waited on the countertop, along with a tray of rice crackers and a plate of peeled tangerine. She turned and wrapped her arms around me, hugging me close. She touched the back of her hand to my cheek, the way she did to check for fever and asked, "*Hatsui desu ka?*"

I shook my head no. I wished I were hot instead of cold. I wished a fever had made me faint.

Yumi poured a cup of tea and handed it to me. I took a sip, which tasted good but did nothing to soothe the ache in my chest. On the drive home, I had finally remembered Buddha's other rules. One continued to echo in my head: say nothing to harm others.

From upstairs, my mother's voice called down, "Yumi-san?"

"*Hai*," Yumi answered.

"It's okay. I'm okay," I said, even though it and I were far from okay.

Yumi pushed the swinging door open and disappeared. The kitchen was still and quiet. I leaned against the counter, sipping tea and thinking. I knew what I had to do. I had to keep the truth to myself, for sharing it would certainly harm others. I went to my school bag, slowly undid the two buckles, and retrieved my camera from the big inside pocket.

*

I went outside and leaned against the maple tree. I thought of the Great Buddha, whose expression had seemed to change subtly even though I knew it was impossible—it was a statue. Yet I wondered whether anyone else had noticed. Might the photo I had taken have captured his expression?

I looked up at the house where I lived, where everything was changing. I heard Yumi singing a Japanese song to Amy, which quickly soothed the baby's cries. I wondered if my mother and father were going out for the evening. If so, would my mother notice that anything was different?

I looked back down at my camera. It had seen too much. Was there a way to get rid of the one moment and keep the rest? I pressed the button on the back of camera, which released the latch. The back of the camera swung open, revealing the negative from the last few images I had photographed, including the final photograph of my father with the woman. Holding the door open, I raised the camera to the sky and waved it around. That would erase the last few images, but possibly save the earlier ones.

Sighing deeply, I sat on the ground and leaned against the tree trunk. I gently placed the camera on the ground in front of me and prepared to close the door and re-wind the film. Instead, I stared at the film and saw a tiny scroll. I had captured a truth, and it was too painful to see. Carefully, deliberately, I removed the shiny, light brown cartridge from my camera, and slowly began to unroll the film. Then, holding my arms taut, I held the long scroll to the sky.

Born in Japan, Pamela Beere Briggs spent her first decade in Kobe. She moved "home" to Napa, California in 1968. Realizing years later that "Napa" is "Japan" spelled backwards without the J describes her memory of leaving: turned around with a missing piece. She went on to become an award-winning documentary filmmaker and has written essays for a variety of publications. She is currently working on three World War II novels for middle-grade readers and blogs with her teen daughter at www.TwointheMiddle.com.

FINDING YUANFEN ON A CHINESE BUS

By Kaitlin Solimine

Place: Kunming Railway Station
Time: Morning, Chinese New Year, 2001

I F there's one place to avoid at all costs, it's a Chinese train
station at the start of the Lunar New Year. But I'm too young
and inexperienced to escape such blunders, and I stand in an
exorbitantly long and unruly ticket "line" (more closely resembling a
swarm of angry bees), a rising sun pouring unexpected heat onto my
head. I need a sleeper bunk on the next departure to Hong Kong,
where I'm meeting a friend.

I'm wearing a too-thick sweater. Sweat pooling beneath my
armpits, I curse the warmth of this late-winter day. In Lijiang, extra
layers were required to fight the chilled mountain air in from Tibet.
In Kunming, sun reigns over wind. I should be enjoying this, but
I'm too preoccupied with my own narrative of romantic tragedy:
last night, I left behind my on-again, off-again boyfriend Austrian
Martin (so known in our Beijing early-20s expat circles to differ-
entiate him from Polish Martin) in the mountainous backpacker
enclave of Lijiang. Martin and I suffered a relationship like a water
snake: as soon as we gripped it tightly, it slipped from our hands. The
slipping part is where we'd found ourselves in recent weeks.

This solo journey, as a 20-year-old woman, from China's backwater Southwest mountains to the glittering isle of Hong Kong

was to be my *coup de grâce*, a traveler's soliloquy to prove my independence. But at the same time, I'd hoped it could save me, and thereby Martin and me, from the endless insecurity that plagues early romance.

Finally, it's my turn to buy a ticket. I elbow past a man with garlic-tinged body odor who's cut in front of me. Planting my hands squarely on the booth's overhang, I shout above the sound of the busy station, "One ticket to Guangzhou!"

The ticket agent sitting in the florescent-lit booth wears the requisite attendant uniform, short hair cropped to her ears, dandruff speckling her shoulders. Grime rims her fingernails: she's the ultimate Chinese bureaucrat.

"Hard sleeper," I clarify, indicating my choice of service.

She scoffs at my request without looking up from her keyboard, her bulky computer a relic from China of the '80s, a bowl of oily vegetables at her side: breakfast.

"You'll have to wait at least four days for standing-room only," she says.

My Chinese, which I've studied since age fourteen, is near fluent. Unfortunately, this doesn't buy me camaraderie with the bureaucrat.

"There's always the bus," she offers, picking something green from between her teeth with grimy fingernails before shooing me away with a terse nod.

Step aside. Good-bye now. The universal Chinese gesture to imply there are a million (or more aptly, a billion) others waiting with the same request. Perhaps in your home country you are large, significant. Here you are trite, disposable, and fighting for a shrinking piece of a very small pie. It's a humbling experience I would recommend to any self-absorbed teenager.

Off the station's main square, I find a public pay phone—really just a vendor allowing patrons to use his red rotary phone for a fee. Sitting on a plastic stool, I pull an international calling card from my wallet to phone my mother in New Hampshire. I tell her I'll be on a bus for the next three days so I won't call again until I reach Hong Kong.

"Is the bus safe?" she asks.

The buses line a brick wall opposite the station. They're mostly in one piece, wheels dusty, undercarriages rusted.

"Yeah, I'll be safe," I tell her, but a knot inside me clenches tighter. The week before, I'd taken a bus from Chengdu to Lijiang that navigated what had to be some of the world's most perilous and narrow mountain roads; when the bus blew a tire, my friends and I hitchhiked to the nearest town. It took an entire day to travel 50 miles. I don't tell my mother of the incident.

Hanging up, I sense my mother's apprehension from ten thousand miles away, like a chilly wind blown in from the Himalayas. Two years before, at eighteen, I'd traveled alone throughout Manchuria as a researcher-writer for the travel guide Let's Go: China. The entire summer, my mother paced the hallways of our New England home each night, eagerly awaiting the daily phone calls I promised.

I sling my backpack over my shoulder, leave five yuan for the payphone operator, and walk to the buses with the steadfastness of a soldier recently deployed: in choosing a young life of solitary travel, I'd quickly learned the necessity of not thinking too long about those you've left behind, nor the precarious state of the bus you're about to board. Questions could only lead to more questions, which could only lead to you high-tailing it to the nearest luxury hotel and a commercial flight back to the States. Some things are best left unexamined.

The Guangzhou-bound vehicle, or so says the rusted placard on the dashboard, is empty, save for a driver lounging in the front seat, loafered feet on the steering wheel, hands folded behind his head, eyes closed.

I knock on the door and he startles awake, shaking his head

like a Polaroid camera—I'm an apparition taking form. Slowly, he understands what I want and cranks open the door.

"Is this the Guangzhou bus?" I ask, my smooth Chinese resettling him: now we are equals, sort of.

"Yes. You have a ticket?"

I ascend the crooked, dented stairs and hand him the ticket I bought minutes earlier from a man I swore was ripping me off even though the fare was only $8 for a 1600 kilometer, three-day journey. I'd lived in China long enough to know there's always the "locals" fare and the much-adjusted "foreigner" fare. It made me unreasonably suspicious and cynical, a terrible combination in a young woman.

"When do we leave?" I pile my overstuffed bag on the single bunk nearest the door, just behind the driver's compartment. I'm close enough to see the dandruff in his hair. Everyone in this station is in need of a good shower. Then again, I haven't showered since I left the guesthouse in Lijiang. I probably don't smell like roses either.

"We leave when the bus is full," the driver says with a shrug, reclining again. "But you won't want to sleep in that bunk—too drafty at night."

I look to the rest of the empty bus. The only other bunks are doubles I'd be forced to share with a stranger. I choose a cold night's sleep over sleeping next to a potential rapist or murderer. To calm myself, I think of Martin, his back turned to me as he had returned to the Lijiang guesthouse and I had left for the Kunming-bound buses the night before. We were so involved in the story of us that we'd forgotten to look up at the snow-capped Jade Dragon Snow Mountain towering over the small town like the gateway to a wispy, transcendent heaven. On the overnight bus, I hadn't glanced away from my book at the passing scenery—so preoccupied with

Plath's *The Bell Jar* and my own narrative of romantic sadness, I hadn't considered there may be something larger worth attending to. Perhaps this is both the beauty and tragedy of youth: each moment, each relationship, feels so utterly indispensable.

I'm exhausted as I lean into my bunk, awaiting the other passengers who are slow to join, and wishing I had something other than an already-read Plath in my bag, a packet of over-salted instant noodles, and a nearly empty stash of deodorant. Three days on a bus seems an interminable amount of time to be alone, but then again, I remind myself, I chose this journey.

*

When you live abroad at 20, everything feels ripe for the taking: every man, every city, every discotheque. Time flutters between days on a calendar; weeks turn into months, months to a year. For me, that year was 2000, the millennium recently dawned, the entire world waiting for an instantaneous burst of recognizable change like a wing elbowing a chrysalis. My second homeland, as it felt since I lived in Beijing in high school four years earlier, was China: a nation on the verge of something bigger, trapped in that nebulous moment between adolescence and adulthood. Everywhere, the city showed evidence of optimistic change: the new office towers in Chaoyang, the potential Olympic nod, the increasingly Gucci-clad citizenry. The city's geography shifted as much as the sands in the nearby Gobi: in 2000, the fourth ring road was barely complete, and by 2012, there were six rings in an ever-expanding urban landscape. What my friends and I once lovingly termed our "Beijing boogers" (the black coal soot clogging your nostrils) was being replaced by the more noxious, pervasive smell of industry—factory fumes and automotive exhaust. Near the city's quaint *hutongs*, the shadowed alleyways that made me feel both protected and liberated, construction cranes towered menacingly—in the next decade, over half of Beijing's famed architecture would meet the wrecking ball.

I was spending the year studying in Beijing University's International Relations department. Living on the leafy campus in the Soviet-style "Shaoyuan" dorms for foreign guests, there were scant plush or foreign-friendly accommodations: shared squat toilets reeked of bodily refuse; tattered underwear and dirty socks hung to dry on laundry lines strung between hallway walls. My roommate, Wang Xin, was a Chinese-Canadian on a post-college fellowship. She was tall, beautiful, and innately Chinese in her language and personality: she showed her love in scathing criticism ("Your face is too skinny!" meant that my diet was working).

Wang Xin aligned with the Chinese at the university, so with her I hung with the school's basketball team, the team's groupies. The other expat students mostly ignored their Chinese counterparts: the Europeans were one tribe, Africans another, Koreans and Japanese boisterous in their unexpected Northeast Asian union. Most Americans arrived via a study-abroad program that kept them to themselves in a separate part of campus. Because I'd enrolled on a scholarship through my university and had already lived in China before, I was, even there, an anomaly.

In autumn, Wang Xin and I flitted between Moon Bar outside the East Gate and the rustic cafe Sculpting in Time down a *hutong* alleyway outside the West Gate. Not long after my year at the university, both student hangouts were demolished to make way for multi-story office buildings. But for now, the city around us was head-high. We could bicycle down dirt roads surrounding the Summer Palace as if we were Manchu empresses, hand-plucking fresh peaches off farmers' carts pulled to the city by donkeys.

Within the cradled comfort of this carefree existence I fell in love the way you do at that age, as I had with China: at first sight. I had been sitting in my dorm with Wang Xin when I saw Aus... Martin outside our window, walking from class to the cafeteria. He was rugged, introspective, with a sheepish smile. Quickly, a ritual was born: every day I watched for him and his gaggle of European friends heading to lunch. There was something inaccessible about him, his standoffishness like a Great Wall I was determined to scale.

Finally, Martin and I found one another outside the squat toilets at Moon Bar. It was Halloween. I was Bam Bam. He was a German punk rocker. We were both drunk.

"Hi," I said, swaying, the alleyway so dark I could hardly see his face.

"Hi," he said, drawing closer. He tugged on my highly-positioned ponytail. I ran my fingers through his hair. A kiss was inevitable.

Soon, I learned everything there was about him: how one summer he walked the length of Ireland alone, camping in sheep pastures. The next, he hiked from his home in Austria to Italy's boot. By himself. Without a plan of action. He was impossible not to fall madly in love with, especially in a city like Beijing with its impending winter of dry, desert winds.

But I also learned Martin left an ex-girlfriend at home in Austria. Although they'd broken up, he still felt connected to her, strangely guilty at our budding romance. Whenever we grew too close, he'd shy away, becoming that impenetrable wall again, too distant for me to conquer.

In the meantime, five of us, Martin included, along with two Swedish girls and a Canadian guy, planned to head south to warmer climes for Chinese New Year. It was bad timing—Martin and I were growing distant just as we were to spend such intimate time exploring China by train and bus.

A few weeks before we left, I spent Christmas Eve alone at Tiananmen, whispering carols into the empty square and warming my hands with my breath. When I returned to the dorms, I could hear the European students at their Christmas party on Martin's floor: a cacophony of languages I couldn't speak, Martin's somewhere among them.

Three days later, I met a man I called "The Swede" at a bar on Sanlitun South Street's Jam Bar. I let him woo me, spending a few extra days with him in Beijing, telling my traveling friends, Martin included, I'd take the train alone to meet them in Chengdu the following week. Something about this detour felt natural, and I welcomed the attention of someone who didn't seem distracted by a romantic past in which I played no part.

When I got off the train at the Chengdu train station, Martin was there, the only foreign face smiling for me among the local horde awaiting arrivals. Four hours later, in our hostel, I finally told Martin about my dalliance with The Swede.

"How could you do that?" he asked, turning away from me to look out the window at the city streets bustling with mopeds, street vendors selling stir-fried noodles, puppies, anything with a price tag.

"I don't know how this is going to work when you're always falling back in love with *her*," I said, confident in my decision, but at the same time wanting him to prove me wrong. I was too young, too enamored to realize I was merely hurting him out of self-defense.

"I think you should bunk alone tonight," he said. "I don't want to talk about this anymore."

For the next few days, he ignored me at meals and we sent one another handwritten letters airing our frustrations via our traveling companions, who surely found the debacle amusing, if not immature.

Later that week, halfway through our climb of the famed Taoist Mountain Emeishan, we spent the night in a working Buddhist temple. The rooms were doubles, but we were five. Because Martin still wasn't talking to me, he slept with the Canadian. The Swedish girls bunked together.

I spent the night alone in a drafty temple room, unable to

sleep, fearful of the monkeys playing on the roof. I imagined one would climb through my window—they were curious, aggressive creatures and had, earlier that day, reached into one of the Swedish girls' pockets for a pack of peanuts. Fortunately, there were no monkey visits; after sunrise, the temple bells roused us like a soft rain, reminding us there was still a good portion of the mountain to climb.

Over a breakfast of cold vegetables and soggy noodles, feeling somewhat cleansed from the night in the monastery, I wanted to apologize to Martin, but what could I say? The entire year I'd been trying on masks, discovering who I could be with and without different men—although who I was with Martin was clearly my favorite, I wasn't sure this was who I wanted to be for the rest of my life. Wasn't I too young to decide?

After breakfast, a monk escorted us from the temple up the steep path, holding his robes in one hand and a shotgun in the other.

"To scare away the monkeys," he assured us.

On the iciest section of the climb, the robed, bald-headed monk reached for my hand as we ascended. He didn't let go for several minutes. For the span of that grasp, I fell in love again, but Martin didn't seem to mind, or maybe he noticed, as did I, that my footing was growing sturdier with each step.

*

Place: *Kunming Long Distance Bus Terminal*
Time: *Five hours later*

Slowly, the bus fills. Despite the driver's protests, I sit staunchly on the front bed (really a cotton pad above a wooden slab) while others make do with the shared accommodations elsewhere, the top bunks least desirable due to their inaccessibility.

When the bus is nearly full, a woman in a tight black suit decorated with glittering green-and-white rhinestones boards. Her stiletto heels mark her pace down the aisle where passengers who've already removed their shoes pull their knees to their chests to allow her to pass.

"It stinks in here! *Ai-ya!*" the woman declares, pinching her nose.

"Do you think you're a foreigner or something?" someone shouts from the back, implying such complaints are unbefitting of a Chinese woman. The well-dressed lady rolls her eyes, paces the bus. She can't find a satisfactory home. Finally, she dramatically climbs over a man in the bunk behind me and makes her bed near the window.

W. Somerset Maugham, upon traveling to China in the 1920s, wrote in *On a Chinese Screen*, "…Now, the Chinese live all their lives in the proximity of very nasty smells. They do not notice them. Their nostrils are blunted to the odors that assail the Europeans and so they can move on an equal footing with the tiller of the soil, the coolie, and the artisan. I venture to think that the cesspool is more necessary to democracy than parliamentary institutions."

He's correct: there's nothing more egalitarian than sharing a long-distance bus with the unshowered. I hear the well-dressed lady huffing and mumbling to herself about her discomfort. I want to tell her I'm with her, but then again, I'm the foreigner here. Immediately, I'm intrigued by this woman and make a mental note to befriend her at the first rest stop.

That night, over a dinner of soggy Southern-fried noodles, I sit beside her at a rickety wooden table at a rest stop. She tells me she's visiting a friend in Guangzhou for the holiday. Her second husband is a businessman in a suburb of Kunming; she's a homemaker who has a teenage son from her first marriage. She, like all of us, has been wearing the same outfit for the trip's duration, but I notice she changed the fake diamond pin on her breast, rearranged her hair for the meal. These must be the small ways she makes herself feel beautiful. Meanwhile, I'm dressed like an American backpacker: jeans, hiking boots, sweatshirt. I haven't washed my face or worn makeup in days, and although this feels strangely liberating, there's also something admirable in my new friend's commitment to femininity, an unlikely humanness on a journey so utterly anonymous and dehumanizing.

My friend is chatty and girlish despite her middle age. She doesn't think it's strange I'm a young foreign woman traveling alone on this long-distance bus. Instead, she views the happy coincidence we're riding together as something more: "*Wo men you yuanfen,*" she explains as we finish our first meal together. *We've got fate on our side.*

After dinner, while the bus driver blares the horn and curses at donkeys blocking the road, she climbs into my bunk to chat. She wants to hear everything about my life in the States, particularly my love life. I tell her about Martin, The Swede, how alone I feel despite having two men who seemingly care about me.

"Maybe I should be alone. That's what I deserve," I admit, defeated. I have no idea what I want, and traveling solo on Chinese buses all my life seems as good an idea as any.

She's having none of my pity party. "Don't talk like that. You're so young and lucky! Besides, you don't need to get married yet."

I say yes, that's true, but even though I'm "young and lucky" I want to believe every relationship I enter bears the possibility of forever, of the *yuanfen* my new friend believes brought us together on this bus. Otherwise, what's the point? But she doesn't live with such introspection. She rides out every day, every marriage, while she can.

"My first husband thought I'd gained too much weight," she says, "So I said to him, 'You have a child and see how much weight you gain.'" I pass her a moist wipe to wash her face as we ready for sleep. Her cheeks glisten in the moonlight like a baby's freshly cleaned bottom.

I say, "You were smart to leave him."

She quickly corrects me: he was the one to leave. Another woman. Well, several women actually. Someone at the office. Another: a masseuse. She laughs—*the cliché of it!*—acting like none of this emotionally roils her, but I wonder how much her quick retorts, her glittery pins, and her well-made hair are a cover for some deeper messiness she's grown much better than I at wearing on the inside.

I tell her I've gained ten pounds this year. The oil in my beloved *yuxiang* eggplant. The alcohol. I've picked up smoking, but only at bars, because of the Europeans. I'm good at misplacing blame.

"Oh, don't drink like that," she says, assuming the role of a chastising mother. "It's not womanly and it makes you gain weight. And the smoking is bad for your skin. Next time, tell the chef to use less oil."

I nod. She's womanly. She'd know.

The second night at midnight I get a gift from the gods of womanhood: my period. Apparently my body wants to prove its reproductive capabilities despite the fact I look like a caveman. My only blanket is a towel I've brought along, so with the bath towel draped over my bottom half, the dark Chinese countryside streaming by, I reach beneath my pants and surreptitiously shove an American-brand tampon where it's needed. Everyone around me is asleep. The bus shudders over potholes, careens around thin mountain roads.

My new friend is asleep in the bunk behind me, her hand flung over her head like a Chinese Scarlett O'Hara, an eye pillow sliding off her eyes with each bump. I want to tell her about my feminine feat, for her manicured beauty to brighten with a smile, her hands to pat me on the shoulder and congratulate me with a "Well done, girl." But maybe this, like many other experiences I will come to bear, is best kept to myself. Maybe it's less womanly to make everything so public.

I watch her sleeping, unable to doze while my mind spins tales:

I wonder where Martin is now, if perhaps he's found some new woman with whom to bunk that night, perhaps one of the attractive blonde Swedes. I have no idea where I am—China's back roads don't announce provincial borders so I can't tell if we've left Yunnan for Guangxi or Guizhou. I can barely see the skeletal outlines of mountains, the pitched moonlit slant of village roofs. No one on the bus knows my American name—my Chinese friend only knows me by my Chinese name: Su Li-Ming. I could run away at a rest stop but who would follow? This untethered existence is alternately terrifying and exhilarating; it makes me uniquely lonely in a way I've never experienced.

I recall that Gao Xingjian, one of my favorite Chinese authors, once wrote,

A tree or a bird may seem to be lonely, but this is an attribute bestowed by the person making the observation... The feeling of loneliness produced is thus a form of aesthetics, in that while observing one's external environment, one is at the same time examining the self that is located within it, and to a certain extent this is an affirmation of one's personal worth.

But I don't feel worthy tonight. I can't sleep. Beyond the window, my reflection plastered over everything, I watch the world—suddenly, briefly caught in the scanning flash of the bus's headlights is a town placard: **PU PU**, Population 300. I laugh to myself, incapable of explaining this hilarious linguistic hiccup to anyone who'd understand, and I realize that laughter, like loneliness, makes us human. It indicates our pleasure or our need for validation. With no one to share my laughter, the joke loses potency, but also makes me feel enough outside myself to witness the necessity of being here, alone. It's only a glimmer, a brief sheen of a face I hope to become.

The next day, I change my tampon during a rest stop in a farmer's field, just out of sight of hunched, elderly farmers raking the earth. My new friend instructs me to leave my toilet paper in a ditch, along with the used tampon. Another bathroom that afternoon is an open tiled room with drains along the sides, no partitions for privacy, just all of us women squatting, chatting, and picking at our teeth while waiting for our refuse to slide away.

The women on the bus have already built a sturdy camaraderie. We eat together at rest stops, find the most suitable places to relieve ourselves when needed (the buses have no bathrooms). I wonder how women where I come from are anything other than this. Here, we are friends due to circumstance and boredom, but I learn everything there is to know about the well-dressed woman and she of me: she is remarried to a nice (if a bit portly) businessman, who buys her jewelry and lets her travel alone whenever she wants; her parents live in a village outside Kunming; her father has Alzheimer's, her mother, lung cancer; her son plays too many videogames, and she worries about his studies. I tell her about my childhood in New Hampshire, how desperately I dreamed of foreign travel, how I'd attempted to dig a hole to China one afternoon when I was ten. Like most women, she wants to hear the details of my romantic life, how many partners I've had, which man treated me the best. After I've divulged, she tells me to forget about Martin, The Swede, any man.

"Women like us need to stick together," she says on the warmest morning so far, our last day of the journey. We walk out of the shared public toilet, her arm snaked in mine, ready to face the world together. But part of me wonders if this woman overestimates me, if she's placing her own face atop mine, incapable of seeing the reality of the world outside herself for the jaded view from behind the mask.

*

The rest of the year, Martin and I attempt a relationship, but it never quite works—we're on two separate tracks while around us our expat friends are still drunk, still lost, still perpetual travelers readying for their next adventure despite the fact they linger in Beijing for durations never anticipated.

As a last-ditch effort, Martin and I spend a week together over the May Day holiday in Xi'an visiting the Terra Cotta Warriors. Martin, ever the creative traveler, suggests we rent bicycles and find our way from the city to the soldiers by bike, unlike all the tourists on the crowded air-conditioned tourist buses. On the way home, we get lost, our thighs burning, foreheads scorched. It's too dark to continue on, so we stumble into a suburban inn that asks for our marriage license. We laugh at the request, slightly buzzed from the sun and a rest stop where we downed two beers, and convince the front desk manager we forgot our license in Beijing. That night, I dream we are actually married, but even marriage itself is not a life but a ritual filled with dancing, drinking, and the promise of never letting go. I tell Martin about my dream when I wake up. He kisses the words away as I'm brushing my teeth, but the next day we're back in Beijing where the idea of becoming who we were in Xi'an feels buried beneath stone walls. Martin's still not ready to let go of his past, and I'm not ready to commit to my future.

A week later, I join a band and am seduced (like many a lead vocalist) by my drummer. He's Chinese, from Fujian. His hair is shoulder-length and he once had a crush on his male drumming instructor. I tell my boyfriend he's bisexual, but he seems to like me just fine and this makes me like him more. Or maybe I just like the idea of him, the idea of us walking through the night markets of Wangfujing as an American woman and a Chinese man, as something other than what I was with Martin. Even in the early days of this relationship, I can tell it won't last, not because I fear commitment, but because I still don't know who I'm meant to be.

Before Martin returns to Austria that summer, I tell him about the drummer. He's angry again, but in a defeated way. We walk circles around The Nameless Lake at our campus's heart, trying to figure out what made us so incompatible.

"I don't understand," Martin says. We're at that deflated part of our story where we know no matter what we do, we'll never find our way back to the beauty of the beginning.

"Me neither," I say, without knowing we're too young to understand our failed romance had nothing to do with who we were, but everything to do with who we were afraid of becoming. Our stories had to be told separately, our journeys, for now, solo.

A few years later I return to that lake with the American man who will become my husband. It's the only place that feels somewhat the same in a city already unrecognizable to me—Moon Bar is now a six-lane highway, Sculpting in Time replaced by a high-rise office building. I've lost my physical markers in the city where I first learned how to love.

*

Place: Guangzhou-Hong Kong High-Speed Train, Somewhere in Guangdong
Time: Mid-afternoon, February, 2001

On the high-speed train from Guangzhou to Hong Kong, an attendant passes out free moist wipes and I collect as many as I can, having exhausted my supply on the long bus ride. I am covered with exhaust, the filth of a 45-hour journey by sleeper bus. I quickly open the packages and rub my body raw. Soon I smell like an American sterilized toilet.

When I arrive, Hong Kong is just like it looks in photographs: sparkling-clean and ritzy compared to where I've been. The city glistens above the bay, bright reds and golds flashing on the skyscrapers in celebration of the Chinese New Year. Children set off firecrackers between buildings. Taxis idle at stoplights. Young women click in high heels down crowded streets, Louis Vuitton handbags swinging, cat eyes hidden behind dark Chanel glasses.

I think of my new Chinese girlfriend walking the streets of Guangzhou, shopping at the back-alley malls she'd proclaimed to love, eating the Southern-fried noodles she says she only partakes of on vacations (this, her secret to keeping a good figure—only indulge once a year). Eventually, she'll return to her home in that Kunming suburban high-rise. She'll be someone's wife, just like eventually I will as well, but for now she is blissfully free to live her life as a woman of the world, riding on buses and befriending young foreigners to whom she can dispel free relationship advice and feel like a girl again, as if the world is hers—ours—to conquer.

Before my friend arrives from Scotland, I take a long, hot shower at our hostel, the infamous Chungking Mansions. I contemplate calling Martin, but he doesn't have a cell phone and I have no idea which itinerary he and the others decided to take—would they stay in Lijiang or depart for Dali, or further yet, the treacherous trails of Tiger Leaping Gorge?

I spend an hour picking my pimples, exfoliating my cheeks with a coarse washcloth, plucking my unruly eyebrows. My friend will be arriving at the airport, where I am to meet him, any minute now, but I almost wish he weren't coming, that I could explore this island alone, unfettered by the demands of someone else, able to climb whichever forested hill, wander into whichever gaudy temple, drink in whichever noisy pub I choose.

I apply a layer of concealer over the bags beneath my eyes, comb dense mascara into my eyelashes, brush glittery blue eye shadow on my lids. I check my reflection one last time, as if to confirm its existence, before striding out the door and into the crowded streets where I am anonymous, myself, once more.

Raised in New England, Kaitlin Solimine has considered China a second home since 1996. She's been a Harvard-Yenching scholar, Fulbright Fellow, and Donald E. Axinn Scholar in Fiction at the Bread Loaf Writers' Conference. She wrote and edited Let's Go: China (St. Martin's Press) and her first novel, Empire of Glass, won the 2012 Dzanc Books/Disquiet International Literary Program award. Her writing has appeared in Guernica Magazine, National Geographic, Kartika Review, China Daily, and more. She is a co-founder of the curatorial website, Hippo Reads, and currently resides in Singapore.

GODS RUSHING IN

By Jenna Lynn Cody

YOU could hear the drums before you even pulled into town.

For the second time in six years, I stepped off the bus in Donggang for the opening day of the triennial King Boat Festival. A makeshift night market strung with halogen lights and blinking LEDs had been slapped together around Donglong Gong, the town's main temple. An ornate golden gate fronted Donglong Gong, showing how much money flowed through this fishing town in southern Taiwan.

King Boat is held in celebration of Wen Hong, also known as Wufudadi, the Thousand Years Grandfather, Dai Tian Xun Shou, or Wang Ye (Chinese immortals tend to have a lot of names), a god known for driving away pestilence and disease. He's the main deity worshipped in Donglong Temple. Legend has it that he attained godly status after he—a 7th century man named Wen Hong—was killed when his ship sank on an ocean patrol.

Every three years, his spirit is called in from the sea, implored to come inland by the myriad cries of a thousand other gods, and is paraded and feted around Donggang and its ancillary villages for the next week. Wang Ye is supposed to drive out sickness and disease during this time, as well as bring good fortune.

We had attended King Boat for the first time three years ago, and had decided to return to see the opening ceremony one more time.

Delegations from temples around Taiwan, carrying idols on carved palanquins, held up traffic. Many of these sedan chairs were dotted with LEDs, and some blasted their own music: traditional temple music, local pop hits from the '70s in the Taiwanese language, or occasional Western hits. One went by thumping "Empire State of Mind." Another proudly filled the streets with "Gangnam Style." The gods, apparently, have very eclectic taste in music. Drummers followed and firecrackers snapped underfoot. The three of us elbowed through the crowds to drop off our bags.

Tonight, my husband Brendan, our friend Joseph, and I would see the King Boat itself, sheltered in the temple complex, and make wishes on the little wooden plaques that would hang on a fence around the perimeter of the boat for the next week. We would then feast on the freshest seafood at a row of restaurants in the harbor's famous market.

Tomorrow, we would head to the beach and watch as gods, spirits, and immortals rushed in from the ocean to a gruesome display of blood, incense, and pierced skin. They would possess the bodies of hundreds of trained spirit mediums. We'd look them in the eyes. We'd see what they could do with spiked clubs and balls, swords, pins, and burning incense. Tomorrow, there would be blood.

I wasn't quite sure why I'd come back. I'd ostensibly seen everything there was to see three years before. In fact, I wasn't quite sure why I was still in Taiwan. I had spent a semester in Madurai, India and loved it—from climbing a rock escarpment over neon-green rice paddies to a Jain monument at the summit to running into a *puja* to the goddess who watched over the local market, as well as the everyday joy of living with a host family. I swore I'd move back. I've visited many times since, but never returned for good. I'd lived in China for a year after college as a travel-happy, pseudo-ambitious young graduate. I had countless adventures—including being on a bus that drove up a flight of stairs—and announced I wanted to move back in order to continue studying Chinese. I never did.

Taiwan was different. I had just put in my application for permanent residency, wishing to stay but not fully understanding why.

I approached the King Boat. It was bedecked with lanterns, ornately painted in traditional Chinese patterns of dragons and clouds, and surrounded by a wall of wishes. For a small fee, you could buy a wooden plaque about the size of a smartphone. On it, you would write your name and address, followed by your wish. Most people wished for personal fortune: *I want two children, a son and a daughter, and a promotion at work. I want to study in Australia. Please help me find a good and handsome husband. I want a perfect score on my college entrance exam! I want my in-laws to move out. I want to get a job in Singapore. I want my girlfriend to say yes when I propose to her. I want a bigger apartment, and I want my boss to notice my hard work.* Predictable but moving wishes. Everyone's common struggle on little pieces of wood, destined to reach the sky in a cloud of smoke.

You can put more than one wish on one plaque, so I made two. One was for my permanent residency application to go through without any more problems, of which there had already been many. The other was simple but political: I made a wish for Taiwan – for its recognition and sovereignty.

Why did I care so much? This wasn't my homeland. I had no ancestral or cultural connection here. I could have wished for a continued happy marriage, or for a career break, or more money. Everyone else had. In America, my country of birth, I probably would have. It wouldn't have even crossed my mind to wish anything "for America." Although I was an expat, I wasn't wishing as one. Taiwan's unique history has brought Chinese, Japanese, and aboriginal influences to its shores. This mix has created a unique culture, but sadly one that attracts little international interest. A culture that, due to the nature of Chinese folk belief—indigenous and multifaceted, grounded more in tradition and ceremony than concerns about the spiritual health of its followers—is quite accepting of the vagaries of individual belief. As a skeptic who has clashed with and felt judged by people in the United States who question my personal beliefs, this was an important facet of life in Taiwan for me. I would make a wish to Wen Hong precisely because it didn't matter whether I believed in his power in order to make that wish. That may sound odd from a Western perspective, but in Taiwan it is perfectly normal. The ability to hold these two ideas in your head—doing the rite, yet believing as you please—is considered a measure of the most basic intelligence.

And so, I circled the boat three times and tied my wish to the fence with red cord.

One week later, the King Boat would be loaded with ghost money, wishing plaques, and other offerings, and brought to the beach, where it would be engulfed at dawn in a spectacular bonfire that would burn for up to three days. Wen Hong would be sent back out to sea laden with gifts and money and take all of Donggang's illness and bad luck with him.

We barely slept that night – the processions wound their way through the darkest hours; firecrackers abided no time restrictions. Puffs of music floated past the window of our bathroom-tiled hotel room near the harbor until dawn. We woke into a muggy heat, took ineffective showers, and sought a breakfast shop before heading to the beach.

"I can't wait to get a traditional Taiwanese breakfast!" Brendan said.

"What, you mean a sandwich with some corn in it?"

"Exactly!"

A true "traditional" breakfast in Taiwan would be rice congee with cabbage, egg, and preserved tofu, but white-bread sandwiches with improbable fillings, chased down with soy milk, were now a far more typical way to break one's fast in Taiwan.

We could still hear the drums. They had now left the temple area and beaten their way down to the beach. More temple delegations arrived from the corners of Taiwan bearing idols of Matsu, goddess of the sea, the Baosheng Emperor, god of herbal and Chinese medicine, Wenchang Dijun, god of literature, and more. We followed the noise and light over the bridge and onto the sand.

Troupes of Eight Generals began to appear – men and boys in elaborate face paint who participate in temple processionals around Taiwan. Each painting style was different depending on the general being portrayed. The Eight Generals act as the protectors of gods and people, and may not talk or smile when in their roles. At certain points in a processional—generally in front of important temples— they do martial demonstrations accompanied by ominous trumpets and deep drums. The weapons (pitchforks, tridents, swords, and spears made with real metal), the concentration, the unique makeup, and the powerful gazes of the performers make the Eight Generals seem terrifying despite their role as protectors. Although they originated in a temple in Fujian, China, they are now associated exclusively with Taiwan.

I snapped photos. Such festivals were all but gone in most of China, and difficult to track down in India. I felt closer to the common practices of local folk culture in Taiwan than I had in any other country, in part because they were closer to me. We had traversed most of Taiwan to see this procession, but when you live here, one may very well pass right by your front door. I often run into the Eight Generals, tall gods (people wearing tall bamboo casings topped with ten-foot-high costumes depicting various immortal beings), dragon dancers, and lion dancers on my regular ramblings around Taipei. I've been stuck on a bus trapped behind a tall god, forced to move out of the way for a group of lion dancers, and been made to dance around unexpected fireworks.

The beach had turned into an encampment under the rising haze. Entire temple delegations parked themselves on small dunes, sticking incense into the sand. There was no water, no toilets. Some troupes of Eight Generals (there were many, and not all numbered eight) were idling about, holding their fans to their faces to chat quietly, answer phones or smoke, all things prohibited when in costume. The fans hid their sacrilegious pleasures from the eyes of the gods. Palanquins with their own generators to keep the lights flashing and music pumping were carried dangerously close to the sea. Some were dragged into the water, held aloft by enthusiastic— and I imagine not very risk-averse—devotees.

We wandered a bit. We sat in wet sand. We drank down our water supply. I clipped off a few more photos. We asked when it was all going to begin. "Soon," everyone said. "It'll happen soon."

"Any idea just when?"

"Three, maybe."

"It'll start right after lunch."

"Four, I think. Later."

"Now, I think. Just wait."

"I don't know."

Finally, someone answered us straight: "It'll start when the gods say it'll start."

I noticed one woman, fortyish, apple-shaped with a wide-face, standing alone and staring at the ocean.

Gods don't wait for human thirst, so we didn't trek back to the market for fear that it would begin without us. A second slapdash congregation of food vendors had popped up at the entrance to the beach.

You could hear the drums, and now some of them had entwined their previously disjointed cacophony and beat out a steady, entrancing rhythm.

It was then that I noticed the man next to me was shaking.

His hand rose and fell. It looked as if he was doing musical kung fu, conducting a martial-arts orchestra. He lifted his head toward the glowering sun. His lips shook and his knees wobbled, but he did not fall.

I heard a moan, quite distinct, from the bubbling of the waves at my back. It wasn't coming from the shaking man, though. It was coming from the water. The woman I'd seen before was now standing knee deep. Someone had tied a red sash around her waist, and she was moving her arms in circles as she cried.

The man had a red sash now, as well. His movements grew more elaborate and he was holding a bundle of burning incense. He uttered a long, deliberate "OooooooOOOoooh" and slowly put the incense, burning end first, into his mouth.

It was starting.

An old man I had seen three years before ran up to my left. He was compact and grey-haired, with teddy-bear features. He dangled a spiked ball from a cord and shouted at the sea, talking to the waves.

Two men—one older, with grey hair and heavy-lidded eyes; one younger, with smooth, tan skin and a buzz cut—stood near each other. They were gazing serenely across the mayhem erupting down the shoreline. Both had pins the thickness of drinking straws in their cheeks. One turned; he also had flags of the kind often found on the back of Chinese folk gods piercing his back, his skin folded to hold them in place. A man near them was beating his back bloody with a spiked club wound with red thread. A woman in a long white robe was grunting and doing tai chi-like moves with her hands. A man holding an aluminum sword cut his own shoulder blade in one fluid motion. Another, holding an idol, got a wild look in his eyes and began to dance slowly, one leg in the air, knees bent, hopping and twisting. He danced with the man with the sword, the idol hoisted into the air and waved about as though its thick wooden weight were nothing.

A man sat in the surf, his yellow silk robe covered in artfully arranged colorful patches swirling in the foam. He wore an oddly peaked yellow hat embroidered with the sign of the Buddha and drank deeply from a medicine-gourd-shaped bottle. Then he laughed, spraying spittle and liquor high into the air. He was possessed with the spirit of Ji Gong, an eccentric, wandering 10th century Chinese monk.

These were *jitong*, called *dang-ki* in Taiwanese, who were falling into trances and, so the story goes, allowing their bodies to be taken over by the spirits of gods and immortals. They started shaking, they fell, they screamed incomprehensible words, they sang and moaned, they ran into the ocean, and they mutilated themselves as the drums beat louder. They are a common sight at temple festivals in southern Taiwan, and those versed in the local folk religion will often listen closely to what they say for clues about the future and the deity's will.

There were hundreds of them: the whole arc of the beach was overrun with people who were not people, but bleeding, screaming gods. Each one wore a bright red sash. They had attendants, people who sprayed antiseptic and pressed ghost money into wounds, who kept them from drowning in the ocean, who kept onlookers like me from getting too close, and who found them whatever tools they asked for.

Why now, why here, and why so many? Because they, by allowing themselves to act as the earthly vessels of these motley spirits, called in Wen Hong.

All for the Thousand Years Grandfather, you could hear the drums.

What struck me was that not everyone on the beach believed. Certainly the *dang-ki* believe. What is claimed to be spiritual possession requires some degree of faith to work, especially if that possession entails shrieking, singing, and self-mutilation. It's also claimed that, when possessed, the *dang-ki* don't feel any pain and their wounds heal quickly. Those directly involved with the temples must believe as well. Others, though—onlookers, photographers, locals who come out to see the show, visitors like us—generally don't.

I am an avowed atheist. I feel comfortable in Taiwan because nobody cares whether you believe or not. Often, even if you are Taiwanese, as long as you do the rites, nobody minds whether you actually peg your faith on them. In the West this idea is often met with contempt. Why would you perform a ritual you didn't believe in? I found it freeing: you could meet your family and cultural obligations, but there was still space for you, as an individual, to believe as you liked. It was eye-opening to observe such an outpouring of tradition and belief and feel completely welcome, with nobody breathing down my back about my own faith. While I do believe the *dang-ki* are entranced (I view it as more of a garden-variety hypnotism with the weight of belief behind it) nobody cared that I saw no gods in their eyes. I was still welcome. A local who had come to see the gods rushing in, whether he believed in the gods' existence or not, would be treated no differently.

I appreciated the history of most of these gods. They were, more often than not, based on real people. The human origin of so many folk gods means that, at the very least, they have some foothold in verifiable history. Gods are often created when those who pray to a deceased person of note enjoy enduring good luck. More people come to pray, and that newly minted god grows in popularity. Such gods are being created even now: in the Taiwanese city of Hsinchu, there is a temple to Chiang Kai-shek who is worshipped in much the same way, often by those who hold him in living memory.

I can easily imagine a King Boat Festival in 500 years that includes a *dang-ki* possessed by the spirit of, say, Sun Yat-sen. The gods dancing on the beach in our time, however, are of an older vintage.

A woman threw a red spiked ball wound with red cord and caked with blood into the air and caught it on her back. She was wearing an embroidered yellow smock and blowing raspberries in a distinct rhythm. Another had a similar spiked ball stuck into the skin on the crown of his head, tied in place with one of the ubiquitous red sashes.

A man sank into the sand in a ballerina's split, grabbed some incense and held it aloft. He stared straight at me, and I wondered what he could see. Me? Nothing? Ghosts? Whatever a god sees?

The woman removed the spiked ball from her back; an attendant took it. She danced in jerky motions up to two more women, also wearing smocks. One had devil horn-like ears fashioned out of ghost money stuck in a headband. All three waded waist-deep into the sea, unconcerned with the tumult of the surf. They began to sing and moan in a weird melody, at once harmonic and dissonant. I waded a little further out, lifting my camera above the waves, happy that I'd worn my quick-dry hiking pants but aware that my shirt was also soaked. I took a few pictures, even a short video.

I could hear the drums, and feel the waves. Firecrackers erupted into tufts of smoke, clouds of incense wafted out to sea. The women moaned and sang, and I tried to keep my balance. The unrelenting sun beat down, waves of heat following the rhythm of the drums. I had long since run out of water.

One woman held incense, another brandished a sword. The third held nothing in her open hands, her arms outstretched, begging the sea to grant her incomprehensible, raspberry-blown wishes.

I don't know when I stopped taking photos. I was barely aware of my camera in my hands, and yet it remained dry. It was hot and bright. I was thirsty. I was engulfed by heat, smoke and noise. There was no end to it: *dang-ki* raged and pleaded at the ocean all around me, saltwater in their wounds. It's a good thing that they feel no pain.

The women started moaning in crescendo, following the steady swell of the waves. They came more roughly now; the tide was coming in. I could hear the women but the sun was so bright that it was difficult to see. My back was to the ocean.

"Aaaaaaaahhhh!" they cried, on the crest of a wave. "AAAAhhhhhh!"

I felt lightheaded.

"AAAAAHHHHH!"

At their third cry, there was a gust of wind as a large wave pummeled my back, and I was forced closer to shore. I could hear the drums. Everything went white. I could smell smoke. I couldn't see.

"Jenna, are you okay?" Joseph's voice pierced the din, and my vision came back. I was still holding my camera, and it was still dry. The women had ridden in to shore on the wave.

I was very dizzy, hot, and quite disoriented.

"I'm okay, but what the hell was that?" I asked in Joseph's general direction. I don't think he heard me.

I stood in the wet sand, holding my forehead and surveying the crowd as my dizziness abated. The women had congregated around their idol, and their temple delegation seemed pleased. Joseph wandered off, and a chair appeared under me. I sat for a few moments. A bottle of water was handed to me and I took a swig.

A few people around me were very solicitous; I noticed one was holding one of those spray bottles of antiseptic used on the *dang-ki*.

My rational brain knew this: it was hot, and the drums, smoke, and chanting had gotten the better of me. Now, others were making sure I was okay. I wondered if I'd just acquired a few *dang-ki* attendants of my own, and how long I'd been in that trance. It couldn't have been more than thirty seconds, maybe a minute, counting the time when I stopped taking photos. Not more than ten seconds of blindness.

It didn't matter that I don't believe in spirit mediums and possession. It didn't matter that I was a woman, or even that I was a foreigner. Those around me interpreted what they saw as possession; I viewed it as earthly entrancement—after all, what is more earthly than having your head scrambled by heat, sun, sand, and smoke? There was room on that beach for both interpretations.

I was fine, though, and after a few minutes the attendants dispersed. When my dizziness abated fully, I wandered off to take more photos.

There were both male and female *dang-ki*, although other aspects of King Boat are the provenance of men. Only men may build the boat and carry ghost money and offerings to it on the beach. Depending on which family oversees the festival, some years women are not allowed to join in the communal firewalking (yes, I have firewalked. No, it's not as scary as it sounds, but then for communal firewalking they don't make the coals very hot).

On Earth as it is in heaven: there are aspects to traditional festivals that women may not participate in, even in 2013, but nobody questions a god's right to call upon a woman to act as the conduit of its spirit. If the gods do not discriminate, it is not for men to say that women cannot act.

This is the final insight that King Boat afforded me: the three *dang-ki* in the surf with me were women, and despite the gender discrimination that local and expat women rail against across Asia, they were treated no differently than the men.

I considered this in the days and weeks following the festival. Although things are not perfect, I have been able to live in Taiwan, as a woman, without experiencing severe gender discrimination. I felt the weight of sexism in India and China, and although I could not articulate it then, an inability to accept that level of sexism in daily life is one of the reasons why I did not stay in those countries. In both countries, I was admonished at times for my feminist outlook. In Taiwan, certain ideas regarding how women should act and look persist, but there is more space in the culture for women who can't or won't meet those expectations. Of course, these expectations are somewhat fluid in all three countries and Taiwan is far from being a feminist utopia: I am aware of the fact that the personal decisions of Taiwanese women often face their families' friendly fire, and that as an expat I am exempt from this. Compared to the rest of Asia, however, I have felt more accepted here as a woman and a feminist.

All those adjectives-turned-pejoratives one hears the United States—*feminist, liberal, atheist*—are just descriptors here. Labels you can wear or not. Others may disagree with you, but won't use your own labels against you.

On a quiet corner of the beach, a man and a woman were dancing. They were both possessed; they were both wearing red sashes and each held a fistful of incense. They were moving their arms in a coordinated motion. Both had scars, now clotting, running down their backs. The man held his incense out over the woman's head, and she pulled hers back. Then he retracted his arm and she stretched hers forward, holding her incense over his head.

A swath of fireworks exploded—thousands, all at once. The drums began banging together, joined by gongs and cymbals.

A thousand balloons were suddenly released from a spot on the southern end of the beach as people clapped. Those still possessed began to come out of their trances, all at once, and reverted to being humans. Red sashes were shed. The Thousand Years Grandfather had arrived.

Jenna Lynn Cody grew up in upstate New York, but has lived abroad for most of her adult life. After a semester in India and a year in China, she attempted to settle down in the USA. Unable to sit still, however, she took off again for Taipei, Taiwan, where she has lived for the past seven years with her husband, Brendan. She works as a corporate trainer and blogs at <u>Lao Ren Cha</u>.

OUR LITTLE PIECE OF VIETNAM

By Sharon Brown

SUMMER in Vietnam is hot. Not just hot, but a stifling, perspiration-soaked, still-hot-after-four-daily-showers heat that pervades every moment spent outside of an air-conditioned space. Yet you wouldn't know this by looking at Vietnamese women. Unlike places where climate dictates what people wear, in Vietnam, dress has little to do with temperature. Despite the heat, Vietnamese women often cover themselves from head-to-toe in business casual work clothes, or long silk "Vietnamese pajamas," large sunglasses, face masks, elbow-length gloves, and stockings: every inch of them shielded from the sun. Respecting this form of dress, a combination of cultural formality and a desire for white, unblemished skin, was part of life as an expatriate in Vietnam. But at nine months pregnant, dressing to go out in the heat became one of the few discomforts of an otherwise easy pregnancy.

Aside from the heat, being pregnant in Vietnam was enjoyable. During my previous visits, I had been repeatedly asked whether I was married ("Why not?"), whether I had children ("Why not?"), and when I planned to accomplish both of these desirable goals ("Soon!"). Now that I was on my way, my growing belly made me quite popular. Neighbors, street vendors, women in the markets, all acknowledged my pregnancy with friendly comments and smiles. The most common question was, "*Con gai? Con trai?* (Girl? Boy?)"

My response, "*Con gai*," was always met with approving nods. I'm sure if I understood more Vietnamese, this question would not have been the last. Unfortunately, or perhaps fortunately, I was spared further conversation due to my inability to communicate beyond, "Girl? Boy?"

For two years, my husband and I had been living in Ho Chi Minh City where he was working as a teacher at an international school. We had moved to Asia to further explore the diverse cultures and destinations we had come to know only briefly on a previous trip. Once in Vietnam, we immersed ourselves in the southern culture with an apartment in a traditional urban neighborhood, Vietnamese language lessons, frequent visits to local restaurants and food stalls, and even learning how to navigate a motorbike in Ho Chi Minh City traffic. Being health-conscious, we especially loved the holistic Eastern approach to health, emphasizing balance, prevention, individual responsibility, and of course, regular massages.

When we learned I was pregnant in August of 2009, we were excited to experience this new phase of life in a country we'd grown to love. After our initial celebrations, we began to discuss healthcare options. I watched the documentary "The Business of Being Born" and read books promoting natural-birth options. I learned about the domino effect of unnecessary interventions that can occur in hospital settings, where artificial induction could lead to caesarian section and where medical intervention sometimes works against the body's natural ability to birth a child. Since I was terrified of needles and all manner of operating equipment, an epidural and cesarean were things I hoped to avoid at all costs. Yet, while I wanted a natural-birth experience for our baby, I wasn't looking forward to the painful part of natural childbirth. I had read that things typically discouraged in strict medical settings—movement, water, natural birthing positions—could help to ease some of the pain. I wanted my birth experience to be as natural, and yet still as painless, as possible.

When I began searching for an environment and practitioner who would accommodate a natural-birth plan, my husband was supportive, but ultimately, he just wanted to be there.

I began with what I knew. "I could fly home to deliver. There are lots of birthing centers in Florida."

"That's a long way to go to have a baby. Isn't there anything around here?"

"Singapore has water birth and hypno-birthing classes. Women go there from all over Southeast Asia to deliver." I envisioned delivering in a day spa, gazing out the window at the gleaming towers of downtown Singapore.

"That would be cool, but it sounds expensive. Do they accept Vietnamese insurance?"

"Hmmm, probably not. Let's see… Thailand has an international hospital that promotes natural birth. I've heard the nurses will even fly here to accompany you on the plane." My mouth began to water at the thought of three meals of Thai food a day.

"Thailand would be sweet, but what if the baby comes early? How would I get there in time for the birth? What about a hospital here?"

"A hospital here?" After a year of Vietnamese lessons, I could confidently order two beers at the corner store and tell my neighbors I was going to the market, but I was pretty sure I wouldn't learn enough to ask for a birthing ball by May. Was there even a Vietnamese word for *birthing ball*?

With my husband's encouragement, I learned of a nearby international hospital and began contacting other women who had delivered there. Over multiple glasses of *ca phe sua da*, sweet Vietnamese iced coffee, I interviewed other new expat mothers. Each woman I talked with had a different story, but each had a happy ending. Many of the women also wanted control over the birth of their child and were satisfied with their experience. They encouraged me to follow through with our decision to deliver in Vietnam. The hospital was staffed with French and Vietnamese professionals; everyone spoke some combination of English, French and Vietnamese; and they adhered to the highest of international medical standards. Only the story of a nurse standing on the table, physically pushing on the mother's abdomen gave me pause, but ultimately we decided to stay for practical and financial reasons. It would not meet many of my hopes for a natural birthing environment, but it would be safe and professional, and hopefully, we would have some control over the experience.

We made our initial appointments at the international hospital and began taking childbirth preparation classes from a British midwife with other expatriate couples expecting in the spring. Aside from one woman who was flying home to deliver, the others were all delivering at the local international hospital and all had the same doctor, Dr. Thomas, a Frenchman practicing temporarily in Vietnam. Neither my husband nor I had heard of Dr. Thomas; we had met with a Vietnamese doctor at the hospital. She was professional and experienced, if not overly warm, but so far we were satisfied with her care. Yet after our first class, we began to doubt our choice.

Most of the women in the class had questions and concerns similar to my own, and the midwife's answer to them all was, "If you are with Dr. Thomas, you will be fine."

"What if I don't want medication?"

"If you are with Dr. Thomas, you will be fine."

"Will they strap me down? What if I want to walk around?"

"If you are with Dr. Thomas, you will be fine."

"What if I don't want to be induced unless medically necessary?"

"If you are with Dr. Thomas, you will be fine."

And then me: "What if I am not with Dr. Thomas?"

"If you are with … oh, well. I would talk to Dr. Thomas and see if he can take you on."

Later that day, my husband and I made an appointment to see Dr. Thomas. I knew I would not have a truly natural birth experience in the hospital, but I did hope to have some control over what happened. I wanted to be free to walk around during labor, to avoid artificial induction, to deliver without medication, and to nurse and bond with our baby immediately after birth. I also hoped to avoid lying on my back with my feet up in stirrups, but that, I was told, was the only option for a hospital birth in Vietnam, even with Dr. Thomas.

Dr. Thomas saw us the following week. He was friendly, warm, and welcoming. My shoulders, tense since the previous week's class, finally relaxed. Maybe there was hope for our natural birth after all. Yet after listening to our concerns, Dr. Thomas immediately told us there was no need for us to switch doctors. He informed us, contrary to what the midwife had said, his practices were no different from those of the other doctors. He tried to assure us that we would be fine with the doctor we had selected and made no request for us to return. As public displays of emotion were taboo in Vietnam, I held back my tears until we arrived home.

At my next doctor's appointment, I presented our doctor with a birth plan, in both English and Vietnamese. I asked if I could explain it to her and she listened patiently while I described the birthing experience I hoped to have. When I was finished, she nodded and said, "Yes. I have seen these. Foreign women bring them in all the time. I will see what I can do, but ultimately, we have to do what we have to do at the time the baby is coming." I respectfully restated my case, silently hoping our baby would be born on our doctor's day off.

Next to the actual delivery, many of my reoccurring fears revolved around the logistics of getting to the hospital when I went into labor. Our apartment in central Ho Chi Minh City was in a traditional urban Vietnamese neighborhood. Small winding alleys lined with narrow, multi-level homes opened onto a wider residential street. This central street, lined with small family-owned restaurants and businesses, led out to a busy thoroughfare. To get to the main road, we had to walk down our narrow alley, around a few corners, down other narrow alleys to the central street, then down the central street to the main road. Once there, we still had to select our mode of transportation.

Roads in Vietnamese cities are typically filled with motorbikes, small 100 cc scooters that swarm the streets at all times of day, taking over sidewalks during rush hour to keep the flow moving. Taxis and other cars are relegated to one lane in order to allow the motorbikes safer passage in the other lanes. Unlike the motorbike riders who seem to disregard all rules of the road, taxi drivers rarely breach this one-lane rule, making taxi rides much longer than the same distance on a motorbike. While I thought it would be more comfortable riding to the hospital, in labor, in a taxi, there was a risk that we might not make it in time. I wasn't sure which would be worse: laboring on a speeding motorbike or delivering in a taxi. Ultimately, I decided to put the decision off until I went into labor.

One decision that could not be put off was when to fly home for the summer. As much as we loved Vietnam, we had decided that we should at least be closer to, if not quite in the same country as, friends and family back home once we had a baby, so my husband had accepted a teaching position in Central America for the following year. He had to report by the end of July, which gave us only a short window of time in which to visit family and friends at home in the summer. In order to be granted permission to leave the country with our baby, we had to secure multiple documents—a Vietnamese birth certificate, a Certificate of Birth Abroad, an exit visa, and a passport—in a process we had been told would take three to five weeks. We wanted to select a day to fly which would leave us enough time in Vietnam to secure all of the necessary paperwork and enough time to visit family and friends in multiple states back home before leaving again. As our daughter was due on Monday, May 10th, we figured that flying home on Tuesday, June 15th would give us the time we needed on either end, but with very little room for error.

By Monday, May 17th, I was starting to get nervous. Now, in addition to my typical first-time-mother fears of childbirth and my worries about delivering in the back of a Vietnamese cab, I began to worry that we would miss our flight home. When I showed up for our appointment at the US Consulate, the consular-staff member looked around expectantly when I presented my paperwork, only to look confused when I pointed to my still-pregnant form. While I was relieved when the consular staff graciously assured me they could expedite our paperwork whenever the baby decided to come, I was still plagued with nagging fears of artificial induction and an operating room, so my husband and I stepped up our own induction efforts.

Sitting in the small street-side dining room of our favorite Indian restaurant, we requested "Indian" spicy food for dinner, despite the heat outside. We sought out the bumpiest routes home on our motorbike. We even stepped up the pace on our evening walks around the track, trying to ignore curious stares as sweat pooled in our shoes. Despite our efforts, by my appointment with the doctor on Wednesday, May 19th, the baby had still not budged.

Our doctor suggested we schedule an induction for that Friday, May 21st. She cautioned against waiting too long after the due date to deliver, saying it could pose risks to the baby's health. Anxious and frightened, yet not wanting to harm my child, I agreed and left for home, still secretly hoping the baby would come on her own. Later, knowing how strongly I felt about laboring naturally, my husband suggested we put off the induction until Monday the 24th since the baby was not technically two weeks late until that day. With his support, I called the doctor's office and rescheduled the induction for Monday. At 42 weeks pregnant, I turned our brisk mile walk into a full speed run around the track. By 7:00 Saturday morning, our weeks of waiting and worrying were over. We called our families to tell them the baby was coming.

After a mad dash around the apartment to collect our things, we were ready to go. Not wanting to get trapped in rush hour traffic, we decided to risk the trip by motorbike. The twenty-minute trip led us down busy city streets packed with motorbikes, past beautiful French colonial hotels, over bridges, past river ports with enormous cargo ships, and into Ho Chi Minh City's modern suburbs. We blended easily into the seamless flow of vehicles, no one giving even a second glance to the Western woman in labor on the back of a motorbike amid the heavy flow of traffic, except, maybe, when I pulled out our video camera to document the ride for the amusement of our child in years to come.

We arrived at the hospital around 7:30 am and went straight to the maternity ward on the fifth floor. When we entered the ward, we found five nurses standing around the nurses' station and no other patients in sight. The nurses looked at us quizzically without saying anything, so I began to explain that I thought I was in labor and that my contractions were two minutes apart. The nurses all looked at us and then at each other. Finally a nurse looked down at a file on the counter and said, "Ms. Sharon Brown?"

When I said yes, she replied, "That patient is not here yet."

Confused, I explained, "I am Sharon Brown."

The nurse looked at the file again and said, "You're not supposed to be here until Monday."

"Yes," I explained, "but that is for a scheduled induction. I think I'm in labor now."

She looked at me again, consulted the file on the counter and said, "You were supposed to be here on Friday."

"Yes," I agreed, my voice rising a bit in panic, "that was the original appointment, but we changed it to Monday. But I am here now and I think I am in labor." The nurses' brows furrowed. As I looked around nervously, a customer service plaque on the wall caught my eye, "Number 1: Excellent patient communication!"

As I looked back at the nurses' station, one nurse motioned for us to follow her. Grateful, we followed her out of the maternity ward, to the elevator and down to the second floor to Labor and Delivery. Once I realized my mistake, I understood the nurses' confusion, as women do not usually go up to the maternity ward until after they deliver their babies.

Once on the Labor and Delivery floor, we were led into a double room. I was hooked up to a machine that monitored my contractions, along with the baby's heartbeat and movements. The machine immediately began recording a heartbeat and movement, but, to our surprise, no contractions. After another thirty minutes, with my husband diligently timing them on his stopwatch, my contractions returned, but not at the rate that had brought us in that morning. The nurse came in and told us that we could go home. "No baby today. You have baby tomorrow," she predicted.

As I was walking out of the room, I felt a strong contraction that made me pause in the hallway. Another one came on down in the lobby. By the time the next one came on, as we walked out to the parking lot, I told my husband that it might not be a good idea to go home. I reminded him that my mother had short labors. He nodded, but suggested it might be better for me to labor at home where I was free to move around unhindered and get something to eat and drink. I agreed, not wanting to face induction merely because we had been in the hospital too long without progress. So we headed home, making a quick stop at the international grocery store for a box of pancake mix—after all, I was still pregnant and craving banana pancakes.

Because my contractions were now much stronger, the ride home on our motorbike was less enjoyable. Once we arrived home, I was positive that the hospital, even if just the lobby, was where I should be. Thirty minutes later, after a hastily prepared batch of banana pancakes, we were back on the motorbike, recording, "Baby's Ride to the Hospital, Take Two."

Once we arrived, the next two hours at the hospital passed in a painful blur of shameless screaming on my part, mostly about the fact that I couldn't do whatever they were asking me to do: a) breathe, b) don't push, c) push, d) don't scream, in a room full of Vietnamese woman repeating, "Don't cry, don't cry, don't cry," and "You try, you try, you try." From their panicked reaction to my outbursts, I assumed that their typical deliveries took place with happily sedated mothers birthing in peaceful silence. In the end, with my husband's reassuring hand on my arm and a small Vietnamese nurse standing on my bed pushing down on my abdomen, I delivered a healthy baby girl.

Although our daughter was born without medication, I did not consider my birth experience natural. Except for the absence of artificial induction and pain medication, I was subject to continuous fetal monitoring, made to remain lying in bed during active labor, given an episiotomy against my wishes and had my daughter removed by vacuum. She was taken immediately for examination and returned only briefly for a short five-minute bonding period, before being whisked off to the Neonatal Intensive Care Unit (NICU) for monitoring due to the meconium in her lungs. The experience left me frustrated, disappointed, and exhausted, but it culminated in the birth of a healthy baby girl, and for that I was grateful. The Vietnamese emphasis on deference to authority and adherence to a rigid hospital rule structure did not allow me the birth experience I had hoped for, but their competence and professionalism delivered my daughter safely into, if not my arms, at least the arms of the doctor. While I mourned a little for the "magical" natural birth experience reported by others, I was ready to forget it all and move on to the business of caring for my daughter, but even that wouldn't come easily in Vietnam.

For the first weeks of a baby's life, new mothers are expected to focus all of their energy on their own recovery. Infant care and all other tasks of daily life are taken over by close friends and family members, allowing the mother to rest. This expectation begins in the hospital, where mothers rest in their rooms, while a host of capable nurses take crying babies and return them, expertly swaddled, in a peaceful sleep.

Because I was determined to nurse our daughter from the beginning, I was hesitant to let her spend any time in the nursery. I had been warned that Vietnam was a very formula-friendly environment where nurses would give bottles to babies even when expressly asked not to do so, not out of any form of disrespect, but simply because that was the way things were done. During the four nights I was in the hospital, I spent hours pacing the halls with a crying baby, acting out a familiar scene from many American movies and television shows. I felt it was my duty. I paced the back halls, taking care to avoid the nurses' station where I was inevitably met with requests to take the baby or confused smiles. Ultimately, each night around 4 am, after a few near misses with doorways and some stumbling attempts to catch the baby before dropping her on the floor, I gave in and handed her over. Each morning, my red-faced, screaming child would be transformed into an angelic bundle presented to me in a neonatal cart by a smiling nurse. I knew infant formula was a part of the spell that was cast over my child, but in my early-morning sleep-deprived state, gratitude won out over any concern I had about future nursing struggles.

As is the case for many expatriate couples, both my family and my husband's family were twenty-four hours away on the other side of the world when our daughter was born. Once home, we would have no doting grandmothers to take the baby and allow us to sleep, no generous siblings to bring dinner. We did, however, have our friends, a second family that we had made over the years, who came to visit, bring treats, and hold the baby. For our families at home, we kept up a regular stream of newborn photographs and videos, and a promise to bring our daughter home to visit them during our upcoming summer break. Many of my daydreams included the moment I would place my daughter in my mother's arms. But for that to happen, we needed to get home.

In addition to the seclusion of their mothers, newborn babies in Vietnam typically remain inside for their first one to three months of life. Our daughter, unfortunately, did not have the luxury of time on her side. After just four days in the hospital, my daughter and I were out on the streets, taxiing to various governmental offices for paperwork to secure her Vietnamese birth certificate and exit visa, which we would need to apply for her certificate of birth abroad and passport to leave the country. Because of this breach of custom, we received a lot of attention from the grandmothers in our alley. Each time we left our apartment, they stopped us to look at my daughter and dispense some sort of advice. I couldn't understand much of what they said, but there were two obvious themes among them: the baby was too young to be out, and she was underdressed!

Given that Vietnamese women cover themselves from head to toe in ninety-degree heat, it should not have surprised me that this would be the case for babies as well. I had become comfortable wearing the characteristic face mask and the more formal coverage required by local custom, but as a new mother, I was hesitant to risk overheating my baby. Each time we were stopped, we would be given instructions via sign language. In addition to her regular clothes, we were told, the baby should be dressed in a hat, socks, and gloves: the hat to protect her head, the socks to keep her warm, and the gloves to keep her from scratching her face. For the first few days, I responded with an understanding nod and a gesture to my bag. Out of respect, I indicated that I had all of the necessary articles of clothing, even though my daughter wasn't wearing them at the time. After two days of admonishments from little old Vietnamese women, I caved.

For our morning outing on the third day of bureaucratic paper-gathering, I dressed my week-old daughter in a onesie, matching socks, a hat, and little pink gloves. As we walked down the alleyway, inquisitive glances turned into approving smiles. As I neared the end of the alley feeling quite pleased with myself, I was stopped by a young Vietnamese man who addressed me in unaccented English.

"Hello. Is that your daughter?"

"Yes."

"How old is she?"

"One month," I replied, feeling bad about my lie, but hoping to avoid a lecture on another grievous breach of local custom.

"Why do you have her all bundled up? It is way too hot for all of those clothes!"

"Are you serious!?" I exclaimed. "You are obviously not from around here! Where are you from?"

"Canada," he replied, smiling.

Once in the cab, I removed all of my daughter's extra clothing and learned to live with disapproval for the next three weeks.

Finally, three weeks after the birth of our daughter, we had collected all of the necessary paperwork, packed our bags, and were headed back to the United States. Because we had to report to our next post in late July, we did not have any plans to return to Vietnam in the near future. We were sad to leave, but happy to be taking a big part of Vietnam with us: two years of memories and the unchangeable fact that our daughter was born there.

We hope one day Vietnam will not just be a place on her birth certificate, but a very real place she will come to know. A place where the present and the past live side by side, where the foreign mixes with the familiar. A country of narrow winding alleys and rainbow-colored houses, of country dirt roads and emerald green rice fields, of sleepy delta towns and bustling cities. Of hot "winters" and sweltering summers; of curious stares and friendly smiles. Of steaming hot pho and sweet iced coffee; of fresh grilled squid and savory shrimp pancakes. Of a deep love of country and a proud heritage; of a long, colorful history and a fast-moving present. A place where we made a life, friends, and memories in a culture that was once so foreign, and where one day, our daughter might return to make memories of her own.

Sharon Brown is a freelance writer and editor. She published her first essay on life abroad in Forced to Fly II and is currently working on a book about expat life in Vietnam. Sharon has lived and traveled throughout Asia and Central America. She currently resides in the DC metro area in the US with her husband and two small children. More stories can be found on her blog at Tales and Inspirations.

LOVE AND POLKA DOTS

By Suzanne Kamata

I'M wondering how I can get out of a promise I made to my twelve-year-old daughter, Lilia.

A few weeks ago, I invited her to go with me to Osaka, two and a half hours away by bus, to take in an art exhibition. The latest creations of the internationally renowned Japanese artist Yayoi Kusama—she of the polka dots, the pumpkins, *the polka-dotted pumpkins*—would be on display at the National Museum of Art in Osaka until the end of March. At first, I'd been planning to go alone, maybe while the twins were at school, or while they were stashed at their aunt's house, but it occurred to me that Lilia was old enough to enjoy and appreciate Kusama's art. Plus, if we went together, I wouldn't have to worry about getting back in time to pick her up from school, or asking my husband or my sister-in-law to change their plans and look after her. My son would be okay left alone for a few hours, but my daughter is multiply disabled.

Of course, when I proposed this outing, Lilia was eager to go. Art! A bus trip to Osaka! Polka dots! What's not to like? So we made plans. But as Lilia enters spring break and the exhibit draws to a close, I find myself dreading the trip. I doubt my daughter's capacity to keep herself entertained on the long bus ride to Osaka, and again on the trip home. If I go by myself, I could read, daydream, doze, but with Lilia along, I might have to chat—in sign language—for most of the trip. It would hardly be relaxing.

Also, I've been fatigued. A visit to my gynecologist the week before indicated that I am a tad anemic—nothing serious, just a prelude to the Big Change—but simply going up the stairs in our house leaves me winded recently. Usually, going to a big city involves a lot of walking, and we'd be wandering around the museum. I'd probably have to push Lilia's wheelchair up inclines. I might even have to carry her. At the thought of physical exertion, I just want to cancel everything and stay home. But Lilia reminds me.

"We're going to look at paintings tomorrow!" she signs.

"Um, yeah," I say, casting about for some excuse.

On top of all of my other concerns, we aren't really prepared. I was planning to show her a documentary I'd bought about Kusama's life and work, and then discuss it with her. I've read the artist's auto-biography, *Infinity Net*, so I know that she made macaroni sculptures because she was afraid of food, and phallic sculptures because she was afraid of sex. I know that due to mental illness, she has lived in a psychiatric hospital in Tokyo for the past thirty years or so, that she credits her art with keeping her alive. If she did not paint, she says, she would kill herself. In other words, I've done a bit of research about the artist and I have some context, but Lilia doesn't, not yet. Maybe we aren't ready for this.

Maybe she would be just as happy with a quick trip to the nearby Otsuka Museum, established by the eponymous pharmaceutical company whose signature products include the sports drink Pocari Sweat. The company seems to employ every other person in Tokushima Prefecture, including my brother-in-law, a couple of expatriate friends, parents of my children's classmates, and adult students whom I've taught during my twenty-five years in Japan. The museum houses tile reproductions of many of the world's great paintings. We could pretend to look at the *Mona Lisa*! Picasso's *Guernica*! Monet's *Water Lilies*! According to a magazine article that my husband read, this place was voted by Japanese visitors to be the most satisfying museum in the country.

Then again, it was me who wanted to see the Kusama exhibit in the first place. If I don't take advantage of this opportunity, I'll regret it later. And how can I allow myself to be defeated by a little fatigue? Friends and family older than me are running marathons, for Pete's sake.

On top of that, my daughter hasn't been out of the house in three days. I remind myself that Kusama, who works with simple motifs, could be potentially inspiring to Lilia, an aspiring artist herself. Although some paintings and drawings make Lilia twist her cheek with her thumb and forefinger—the Japanese sign for "difficult"—she could actually imitate the dots, the line drawings, the macaroni glued onto mannequins. Also, like my daughter, Kusama paints in spite of various challenges.

I want Lilia to understand the considerable hurdles the artist has had to overcome to become a world class artist. As a child, Kusama experienced hallucinations. She heard the voices of flowers and animals. She grew up in a wealthy but dysfunctional family, and her mother forbade her from painting. She did it anyway. She even found a way to go to New York City, where she made a name for herself.

*

Lately I've had to literally drag my daughter out of bed in the mornings. Although Lilia can't walk or hear without her cochlear implant, she is physically capable of throwing back the covers, getting out of bed, going to the toilet, washing her face, and changing her clothes all by herself. Even so, she has been lazy of late, making me wish for a winch and a crane. Now that it's spring break, I don't really blame her. But on the morning of our expedition, she is at her DIY best. She rises even before I do and composes a funky outfit – a black shirt with white polka dots layered over a white T-shirt with sparkles and a big pink heart, striped turtleneck, black-and-white-striped tights, and blue-and-yellow-striped socks. Perfect, I think, for a viewing of the art of Yayoi Kusama. She prepares her Hello Kitty rucksack and a handbag, making sure that she has her pink wallet, paper and pen, and books to read. She's ready to go before I am.

I didn't buy bus tickets in advance, but I manage to get front-row seats, the most accessible seats on the bus, both there and back. Thanks to the Japanese welfare system, Lilia's fare is half price. We will also be able to get into the museum for free: Lilia, as a person with special needs; me, as her companion.

We have a few minutes before the bus arrives, so we pop into a nearby convenience store to buy sandwiches for lunch and snacks to eat on the bus. We'll splurge on cake in the museum café later. I've already stuffed a bag of raisins to help with my anemia into my purse, but I buy some iron supplements and an Otsuka-manufactured prune Soy Joy bar containing extra iron for myself, and a chocolate Calorie Mate bar for the girl.

When the bus arrives, Lilia manages to hoist herself up the steps and into her seat with almost no assistance. I show the bus driver how to collapse the wheelchair, and he stows it in the belly of the bus.

There are not a lot of passengers now at mid-morning, and the traffic flows freely. It's a gorgeous day—sunny, albeit a bit chilly. Out the window we can see the lush verdure of the hills of Naruto. We pass the resort hotels along the beach, and then we're crossing the bridge that spans the Straits of Naruto where enormous whirlpools form when the tides change. I know that Lilia doesn't remember this, but a few years ago we took a glass-bottomed boat out into the midst of the whirlpools, and Lilia had been amazed at the sight of a multitude of jellyfish swarming underneath.

Now, she occupies herself with her book, her drawing. I read for a while, then feeling guilty, I propose a round of *shiritori*, a Japanese word game. I let her go first. She writes *momo* (*peach*). I have to follow with a word beginning with the final syllable. I scribble *mokuteki* (*goal*) underneath. She thinks for a moment, then writes *kiiro* (*yellow*). We take turns another ten or so times before Lilia gets tired of playing. Next, I try to get her to review the English words I've taught her so far. The teachers at the deaf school dissuaded me from using English with her in her early years, saying it was hard enough for a hearing-impaired child to learn one spoken language, but recently she's shown an interest in my language. I draw some pictures and simple words—*dog, eye, cat*—and encourage her to match them, but after a few minutes, she turns away. She isn't interested in studying right now. She just wants to be left alone.

We cross over to Awaji Island, with its many onion fields, and then come upon the Akashi Bridge that connects to Honshu, the largest island in the archipelago. The glittering city of Kobe sprawls along the coast, easing into Osaka, our destination.

Once we reach Osaka Station, we approach a cab. I worry that the driver will balk at the wheelchair, but he is kind. "Take your time," he urges, as I motion Lilia into the back seat. So far, so good. Within minutes, we're pulling up to the museum, and then we're in the lobby, preparing to look at "The Eternity of Eternal Eternity."

One might think that Kusama's oeuvre would be inappropriate for children. After all, at one time she was best known for her phallic sculptures, gay porn films, and for encouraging nudity in public settings as a form of protest against war. However, most of her paintings and sculptures are, in fact, child-friendly. The artist herself, who wears a bright red wig and polka dot dresses, retains an innocence in spite of her illness—or perhaps because of it. Much of her work is playful and whimsical. Also, children are more inclined than most adults to be attuned to an irrational fear of macaroni. In any case, my daughter is far from being the youngest visitor to the exhibit. Mothers and children in strollers fill the lobby and share the elevator with us as we descend into the underground museum.

The first gallery features a series rendered in black magic marker on white canvas entitled *Love Forever*. I hear a little boy say, "*Kowai!*" ("*That's scary!*") I'm not sure if he's referring to the proliferation of centipede-like figures in *Morning Waves* or perhaps the repetition of eyes in *The Crowd*, but he gets it; he feels Kusama's phobia, the intention that led to the work.

The next room is white with giant tulips dotted with large red circles, an experiential work entitled *With All My Love for the Tulips, I Pray Forever*. Lilia is delighted with the surreal space, the colors, the giant tulips, while I feel as if I'm in a Tim Burton film. We take several pictures, then move on to *My Eternal Soul*, in which many of the figures that appear in the black-and-white series re-appear in vivid pinks, oranges, yellows, and blues. For a Westerner like me, these colors and images seem joyful and exuberant, but in Japan, where mothers hesitate to dress their children in bright clothes, and married women tend to don somber greys and navies, such hues are unsettling.

Lilia likes the colors. She pauses before the bright paintings, then reads the somewhat baffling titles. *Fluttering Flags*, which applies to red flag-like images, is fairly straightforward. However the vibrant mood of a pink canvas covered with lushly-lashed eyes, a spoon, a purse, a shoe, and women's profiles contrasts with its title: *Death Is Inevitable*.

Among my favorite paintings are the self-portraits toward the end of the exhibit. As a foreigner in Japan, I can relate to *In a Foreign Country of Blue-Eyed People*, which recalls Kusama's years in New York in the 1960s as a rare Japanese artist among Americans. Red dots cover the face, suggesting disease: dis-ease?

Lilia is partial to *Gleaming Lights of the Souls*, another expe-riential piece in which we are invited to enter a small room with mirror-covered walls. Within the walls, dots of light change colors, giving us the feeling of being among stars or planets in outer space.

Finally, we watch a short film documenting Kusama's life and work. There are no subtitles, but Lilia can see the artist at work, the assistant who eases her in and out of her chair, and who helps her to prepare her canvases.

"See?" I want to tell her. "We all need a hand from time to time." But I don't want to disturb her concentration, so I'm silent and still, letting her take in whatever she can by herself, and then we move on to the gift shop. I buy a catalog of the exhibit for us to look at later at our leisure before we head to the café for cake.

On the way home, I feel pleasantly exhausted, but hopeful. The trip was not as arduous as I'd anticipated. I'm also encouraged by Kusama herself, by the fact that she's found a way to make a living—and to stay alive—through art, in spite of everything. I'm not pushing my daughter towards a career in the fine arts. As a writer, I know how tough it can be. I don't necessarily expect Lilia to become famous, or even to earn money through her drawings or paintings, but I feel sure that having art in her life will bring her joy and satisfaction. It will enrich her life and give her a means of expression.

I'm hoping that with today's expedition, I've pried the world open just a little bit wider for my daughter—and for myself. I start planning future trips in my head. The two of us can go to the Fashion Museum in Kobe, and the island of Naoshima. To the United States. To Paris!

Back home, on the island of Shikoku, my daughter is eager to tell her father and brother about the polka-dotted tulips, the mirrors and lights, and the chocolate cake. When she's explained enough, she signs, "Paper, please."

I give her a stack of white sheets, and she begins to draw.

Suzanne Kamata is the author of the novels Losing Kei *(Leapfrog Press, 2008) and* Gadget Girl: The Art of Being Invisible *(GemmaMedia, 2013), as well as the editor of three anthologies, including* Call Me Okaasan: Adventures in Multicultural Mothering *(Wyatt-Mackenzie Publishing, 2011). She is currently working on a mother/daughter travel memoir, for which she was awarded a grant by the Sustainable Arts Foundation. She lives in Shikoku, Japan, with her family.*

HAPPY ANNIVERSARY

By Stephanie Han

THE reason you became an expatriate in Hong Kong was not the glamour of travel, the lure of an exotic life abroad, adventures in meeting new people, or getting back to your Asian roots. Sure, you're Asian, but on your mother's side you are four generations removed from Korea via Hawaii. You already did the Korean Heritage Discover My Ancestors sojourn. No, the reason you are now an expatriate in Hong Kong is down to the man you married, who years later brought you and your son to Sun Lung Wai Village, Mui Wo, Lantau, Hong Kong. This is how it began:

You're walking down the street in Lan Kwai Fong. It's the night before the Handover—UK to China, 1997. You are near the California Restaurant, and you see The Man Who Brings You To Mui Wo eating a sandwich. This sandwich does not look like the sandwiches that you have seen in Seoul for the past year, which have been sad, sorry affairs consisting of two pieces of squishy white bread oozing green peas slathered in yellow mustard. This is a falafel pita sandwich. The guy holding it is blond, tall, wears two earrings (left/right) and a close-fitting, short-sleeve white sweater with a bold navy-and-green stripe across the chest. He looks like he's from Los Angeles. You're on your way home to California and you've stopped in Hong Kong for four days. You booked your return ticket like this over a year ago to see Hong Kong before it went back to China.

Why do you want to go to China, your mother asks. She doesn't know why you booked your ticket like this. She finds it annoying.

You're supposed to go to Seoul and come back from Seoul and we are Korean, and why would anyone really want to go to Hong Kong anyway, as the only reason one goes to Asia is to go to Korea.

You hopped off the plane from Seoul and did a lot of sweating. It's hotter here than in Seoul. You can't believe how hot it is, how humid, how uncomfortable. You look like a sweaty wreck most of the time, your hair scrunched up in a ponytail, the dirt caking in the crack of your forearms, behind your knees. You've been touring and toting the Lonely Planet guidebook in your daypack, heading back to a friend of a friend's apartment to crash at night. The friend, an ex-boyfriend, is now engaged, so his fiancée has stated that you are not allowed to stay in their home. On the scale of significant boyfriends, he was quite low, so you take no offense at this and chalk it up to her Old World or Old Country behavior. You swear you can hear a stringed instrument, some kind of gourd-and-wood number, moaning a screechy dissonant chord in the background whenever he mentions her. Not a big deal. He felt slightly guilty about this, so he asked his friend to put you up for a few days. His friend with the sprawling four-bedroom apartment with a view of a vast body of water has got to be one of the most annoying people you have ever encountered. He definitely reads books on how to make friends. No matter, you're out of the house most of the day, come back when the guy is sleeping, stay in one of his empty bedrooms. It's Handover weekend so it's not like there are any hotel rooms available anyway, you think.

With an Asian face, you spend a lot of time eavesdropping in Hong Kong, mostly on Westerners, English-speaking ones, because that's the only language you understand. Correction: you have also been listening to French conversations. In Hong Kong, you haven't heard any conversations in Korean, the language you have spent the past year studying.

The guy in the white sweater seems friendly, but not in an obtuse or pushy sort of way, and you ask for want of anything better to ask: *So, is there anything going on here tonight?* Mostly you stare at his sandwich. It looks very good. If you actually knew him in the slightest, you would probably ask for a bite, but you refrain from doing so. It's an offhand comment, but ushers forth a serious reflective response. Later he makes fun of you and says about your question: *Oh, gee, 150 years of colonial rule are ending!*

You are pleasantly surprised. The main reason is this: for the past two days, whenever you've had the chance to eavesdrop on English conversations about the Handover, mostly what has dribbled forth from the mouths of the English speakers are wild racist rants about The Chinese. *The Chinese do this. The Chinese do that. The Chinese.* It is beyond unpleasant. All you can think is this: *No wonder they want you guys out!* Wow. Colonialism. Intense. Empire. You think of TV miniseries with nineteenth-century costumes, people clothed in wool and velvet in the tropics. If possible, the Brits could possibly be worse than the Americans ranting about Koreans in Seoul. In Hong Kong, there seems to be little shame about such rants. On the subway, people say "Chink" in casual conversation! In Korea, it would be fair to say, you never heard an English speaking person say the word "Gook" or "Chink" in public. Privately, perhaps they used it, but never in front of you. Speaking in public like this strikes you as outrageous. This is not to say that you haven't had an amusing conversation over a beer with someone English since you've been touring in Hong Kong, but you have found them, on the whole, to be fairly, shall we say, *outdated.*

Despite all of this, you are up for adventure, and the sandwich suggests to you, probably because you are hungry, that this person may be somewhat tolerable. You find The Sandwich Guy thoughtful, if not intellectual and serious; strange really to be having this sort of conversation on a street in a bar area. You are intrigued. Instead of the rant about The Chinese, he discusses colonialism, fears that people have about democratic rights, concerns of the local population, along with obvious references to national pride, and rightful return of land. You're impressed. Yep. This one conversation manages to make you think differently about the other conversations you have eavesdropped on. Either this guy is a thoughtful exception, or he's not an exception and you just heard the wrong bunch of idiots in all public areas of Hong Kong over the previous thirty-six hours.

He's on his way to a rave. You end up at the same place much later at night. He gives you his number and card, and invites you to a picnic in the New Territories at someone's ancestral village where they grow lychee. You're allergic to lychee, but you accept the invitation. He was a traveler, he explains, so he offers to let you stay at his apartment, one traveler to another.

The person you are staying with is driving you crazy and has been offending you so much that you have bothered to record all of his insults in your journal every morning when you leave the apartment, but cannot be bothered to find another place to stay as it's Handover so everything is booked up. You realize the guy has a crush on you! This is why he insults you every time he sees you! You wonder if this is because he is an engineer and/or if he simply has bad social skills. You prefer nuance. Illusion. Obfuscation, even! You're a poet. There is an art to conversation. Geez. This is supposed to be a holiday. Friend of a friend is ruining it! You agree to meet The Nice English Sandwich Guy in the MTR station with your bag the next day. You're moving digs.

But it's the night that you agree to meet up after he gets off from work that you realize The Nice English Sandwich Guy is Someone Different. It's hot and humid, and it has begun to rain. You're sitting on a barstool in a Lan Kwai Fong bar, waiting for

Someone Different, and he walks in the door. He shakes the rain off his head. He's wearing a cream raw silk shirt with a mandarin collar. He smiles when he sees you. There's a light. You think maybe you are falling in love. Pretty fast. He looks beautiful. At the very least, this is a terribly exciting adventure-filled holiday. You will definitely recommend Hong Kong as a tourist destination to your friends. He takes you on what you think is a romantic stroll by the old Legislative building. It's hot. The lights are yellow and orange. There's a blur of people. Your first date is, in fact, a protest march. It's scenic. But it's a protest. In the voices over the megaphones you sense the worries, the concerns, the anger, the general confusion. It does not take an understanding of the language to hear this cry. In the years that follow, when you manage to walk alongside the Hong Kong people when they demonstrate, protest, and raise their voices, you will come to greatly admire this quality about them: their willingness to get up and be heard.

You go back home to California. Someone Different plans to relocate to Tokyo. Hong Kong was never his destination of choice. He arrived here as a compromise. These are the early days of email. CompuServe with its number addresses, and AOL with the hip monikers. You are both writers. You email, once, twice, three times, maybe four times a day. He writes beautiful emails. An epistolary romance. You ask Email Man to come for a visit to the US, where his brother lives, and where he has never visited. He agrees. Back in Los Angeles, you are house-sitting your friend's place. You have no job. You have a little savings. You have a car. Your friend's shoot gets canceled. Yikes. You have no place to live and you have a houseguest coming from Hong Kong. Your friend tells you: He's English. All Europeans love the Grand Canyon. Take Email Man on a road trip. Your friend is half-French. You figure she must be culturally sensitive. It's a plan. You pick Email Man up at the airport and tell him that you're heading out to the desert the next day. You later learn that Email Man lives for spontaneity. You have plenty of that, and not much else. Email Man does not seem to mind.

You tell a friend who's engaged to a guy who owns an auto body shop that you need an oil change before you head out to the desert with this guy coming from Hong Kong that you met for exactly three days while backpacking on your way home from Seoul. Concerned Friend tells you to swing by the shop. This guy could be some crazy axe-murdering freak, and you're driving out to the desert with him. Your body could never be recovered. This has never occurred to you. You think to yourself that Email Man doesn't seem like an axe murderer. He was charming and intelligent. But aren't those qualities found in serial killers? But he didn't email like a serial killer at all! Okay, okay, you agree to swing by the auto body shop in the early morning.

You introduce The Man Who Loves Spontaneity to your Concerned Friend and her Auto Body Fiancé. She tells you to come to the window, whispers he's fine, and giggles. Have a great road trip, she says. You thank Concerned Friend. You pile into the car and you, with the driver's license, drive out to the Arizona desert. Grand Canyon. Sedona. The Mojave. You drive back down to LA, then up again to San Francisco. Golden Gate. Chinatown. The Japanese Tea Garden. You have a great holiday. At the end of the six weeks, you have to face the reality of two nationalities and US immigration. You propose a trial marriage. He's kneeling. You say this: Here's how it's gonna be...

A few days later, you're driving to Norwalk, California, a burned-out industrial wasteland peppered by strip malls. The Man Who Loves Spontaneity has hair bleached white (fun in the desert hotel) and you're wearing a pink sweater your Half-French Friend tried but failed to sell at a yard sale, and a flower print cotton miniskirt from

Ross Discount Clothing that cost exactly one dollar. You have a few hours to kill before your appointment. You go into the 99-cent store while he moves the car. You're nervous. You pick out forty-three dollars worth of 99-cent store goods. It's for your new apartment. Tin foil. Plastic dish rack. A small rubbish bin. He buys it, along with plastic pens with fake US one-dollar bills floating in them. Why is he buying these? Souvenirs for friends in Hong Kong. You eat a bad Mexican meal. You have a manicure in the Vietnamese nail salon. You tell them you're about to get married. They ask if your parents know. You say no and the woman gives you an accidental big bloody gash on your cuticle. It's not intentional, but you have your doubts…

You and Your Future Husband stand under a white plastic trellis. You've brought two rings. A gold one from your parents. Another gold one from a Turkish rug salesman. A rug-salesman freebie after your father spent thousands of US dollars at a single rug store. That's what happens when your mother looks for mauve-colored carpets. The ring's worth about five bucks, tops. The judge smiles at both of you. You don't look at each other. The reason is that Your Future Husband told you not to—he's afraid he'll laugh. And it's a time for solemnity. Before she performs the ceremony, she tells you if you want the marriage certificate, which you want and need, you'll have to wait in line right after the ceremony, or it will take six weeks to mail. You marry. The rings are put on the wrong fingers. You kiss. You queue in line. You walk out of the courthouse: you are married.

Fifteen years on you're still married and have run the extreme in terms of the vows you repeated in Norwalk—for better or for worse, for richer and poorer, sickness and health—the whole thing. Yeah, you still love him. You must. You became an expatriate, joining him on what has become your family's stateless, peripatetic journey and have found that the narrative of nation does indeed pose interesting philosophical questions. You think about your fluidity of identity, or lack of it, when you try to make sense of culture and belonging, and how your Korean-American-British son with the Hawaiian name tells you he is Chinese.

Being an expatriate has made you face some hard cold truths about yourself. Like how you always thought of yourself as an animal-lover until the day you saw a coiled cobra at the front door and all you could scream was "Kill it!" not "That's a beautiful endangered species!"

You're surprised about the knowledge you've acquired and what you've witnessed: water buffalos poo in soft diarrhea-ish piles and cows poo in clumps.

The words *stereotypical gender roles* have no place in expatriate or local parenting. When an acquaintance bites another woman on the ankle, it's best to end that friendship before you experience bodily harm and no, it's not an Ilocano thing, despite what everyone in the village says. Blonde women who kill cows with SUVs become social outcasts.

You think about the meaning of country and identity, about how nation is supposedly a story, and you decide that your Hong Kong story is more or less like a French film. Not the kind that reach the move theatres, but the kind you see in museums. Fuzzy and stark. Surreal beginnings and endings. Beautiful colors. Images bleeding frame by frame. Repeat. Maybe not. Yeah, your expatriate life in Mui Wo reminds you of the rarely screened footage described in film theory journals read by a dozen people in Italian. You've forgotten most of your French and you only know a few words in Italian.

When you tell your husband about how you think of your life, he says, concerned, maybe we should celebrate more of your national holidays. He adds that he's not that into turkey, and Native American genocide probably should be discussed more when celebrating Thanksgiving. You don't celebrate July 4th, but he would wholeheartedly support this celebration, as he supports all political acts of rebellion against any empire anywhere at any time. Someone once called you an empress. You try not to think about that too much when he discusses empires.

You think to yourself that you are typically Hong Kong, but really, you are expatriates, and while you often wonder about how long or where you will end up, this is home, in all of its predictable unpredictability, dissonance and harmony, smog and rain and stinking heat. When someone asks you or your husband how you met each other, both of you tell the tale and then warn the person that marrying in a matter of weeks is not necessarily a good idea, but that yes, it works out, but you never know where you will end up. You warn them that geography is a serious concern when thinking of multiple ethnicities, nationalities, and cultural origins, and that it's best to remember that nations are a relatively new construct in the spectrum of human development and that there are some people who test this idea of nation, in all of its possibilities, limits, and configurations, and these people are often, but not always, expatriates.

Stephanie Han (MA, MFA) is City University of Hong Kong's first PhD student in English literature. She received two grants from the Los Angeles Department of Cultural Affairs and has published poetry and prose in Kyoto Journal, Louisville Review, The South China Morning Post *(fiction award),* Nimrod International Literary Journal *(fiction award),* Women's Studies Quarterly, Cha Online, KoreAm Journal, Disorient, Ampersand Review *and other journals. Her writing has been anthologized in* PEN-West's Emerging Voices Anthology Strange Cargo, *the Asian American Women Artists Anthology* Cheers to Muses *and will be included in anthologies* The Tao of Parenthood *and* The Queen of Statue Square. *Her literary criticism has appeared in* Contemporary Women's Writing, The

Explicator, *and is forthcoming in a 2014 volume by Beijing Foreign Studies University Press. She recently completed a poetry collection entitled "Expatriate".* <u>*www.stephaniehan.com*</u>

JEWISH IN CHINA

By Eva Cohen

Introduction

"OHH, youtai ren, so smart, so good at business!" *Youtai ren* is the Mandarin word for Jewish. When I inform someone of my cultural background in mainland China, they often light up with a smile and become excited to share what they have heard about the Jewish people. Sometimes, they take it further and draw a comparison between Jews and Chinese, saying, "Jews and Chinese have very much in common: very smart, have tradition."

Being a single female traveling around China, often to remote places where I am the only foreigner, the locals are already impressed by my "bravery." My Judaism creates an unexpected but entirely warm connection between myself and a people previously foreign to me.

Chapter 1: First Steps

I first arrived in China two days before Passover in 2011. I was to teach English at a tourism and hospitality college on the outskirts of Nanjing. I tried looking online to see if anything would be held in the city for the holiday. I only found information for holiday services in Shanghai, but I also came across the website of a Chinese professor who runs a Jewish studies program at Nanjing University.

Unaware of business practices in China, I didn't want to take a chance as a new employee by asking to take time off for the holiday right when I was supposed to start my position. Although the professor, named Xu Xin, did get back to me right away with a very kind email saying he may hold something small for Passover, I said thank you and decided I would need to miss that year's Seders (services).

Since I was not staying in the big city, I had immediately hopped on a Hangzhou-bound bus alone for orientation. The comments from strangers and treatment that would continue for the rest of my stay in Asia began: staring, pulling at my curls and asking if they are real, parents pointing and telling their children "*laowai!*", everyone trying to take pictures (but most frequently middle-aged men). If a person spoke any English, they would comment on how white my body is (for a Caucasian I'm still quite white and if not for pigment in my hair might be mistaken for albino) and thus how beautiful I am. And then I was told how brave I am.

Brave. I had never considered myself to be particularly brave before that comment began to be applied to me *en masse* in China. As a journalist who had traveled to the Middle East, and with aspirations to cover human-interest pieces on poverty and corruption in Africa, I had never thought venturing to China as a teacher would mean I am brave. But in hindsight, my choice to teach in a "middle of nowhere" school with no resources for me as a foreigner—and often being the first female foreigner some students had met—I see now that, compared to the majority of the world who never venture outside of their immediate community, I do appear brave.

I was proud to be an inspiration to my students, and any other person who gave that adjective to me. One student told me that she had only ever done what everyone else told her to do, but that by meeting me, she had begun to envision herself traveling around the world, and becoming a strong woman like me. How I felt when she said this was so... meaningful. To think about it still overwhelms me for a moment.

Throughout my life in Canada, and afterward in the UK for my masters, I had frequently encountered anti-Semitism. Wearing my Star of David necklace on campus on occasion elicited negative comments. Sometimes a conversation would be very pleasant until another student would find out my culture and then go into attack-mode about Israel or the history of my people. When this would happen, I'd often disengage because arguing and defending myself all the time exhausted me. I felt that while I am white and fit in on the outside, the reason others picked fights with me was hidden on the inside, which can feel worse than open discrimination. When people talk about visible ethnic minorities, I feel those differences are sometimes "skin-deep"; a person from another race will see a Chinese person and either like them or not, because they can see the differences, and if they don't care about skin color, then they will engage with them.

I had so much to learn about China and just assumed things would be the same, so I did not speak with my students about Judaism. I began to realize toward the end of my teaching stint that it could have been a great opportunity to share something my students had never encountered before. They may have only heard about Jews in the context of the "so smart, so good at business" stereotype. Today, when I meet people from mainland China and they wonder why I am not eating something—due to my kosher practices—I gladly explain that I am *youtai ren*. This teaching position provided a great starting point for me to learn about a new kind of bravery: to proudly teach people about a culture completely new to them.

Chapter 2: Nanjing Jewish Center

I write for several community newspapers in Canada, including the *Jewish Independent* in Vancouver. After my initial inquiry about

Passover services to the professor at the Jewish Studies department at Nanjing University, I pitched the idea to the Vancouver paper to write about it for them, and it was accepted.

It was a sunny Friday afternoon when I traveled an hour by subway from my college into the city to the large Nanjing University campus. For the first time in a couple of weeks, I saw other foreigners while I traversed the streets looking for the right building. When I arrived, it couldn't have been clearer that I was at the right place: plaques naming Jewish donors to the department lined the halls, Star of David designs graced the walls, and the door to a museum with a torah and other Jewish artifacts on display was ajar. In this far-away place where I had hardly seen any other foreigners, to see cultural symbols of my own was so unexpected.

A student greeted me and brought me to an office to wait for the professor. Inside, her fellow students were studying. All of the students were Chinese, but not only did they speak perfect English, but also Hebrew, and a couple of them spoke Yiddish as well. Their dissertations were on topics that rabbinical students learn in formal colleges in the US and Israel about important Jewish sages. These students were very happy to meet a Jewish female, and while they were shy and polite, as many Chinese students are, a couple of them were eager to share information about the department and tell me about the trips they had made to Israel. Professor Xu Xin stresses that a PhD student must first visit Israel before graduating, but several students had been there more than once, and others had studied for a year on exchange. I have been to Israel five times, and the students were keen to hear about why a Jewish girl had now decided to come to China. My easy answer: adventure, something new.

Once Xu was ready for me, I followed him into an office with walls covered in pictures of rabbis. Friendly and energetic, he looked like a youthful forty-year-old, but I learned he was born in 1949 and had been at Nanjing University for over forty years. That would make him an even more youthful-seeming sixty-something. He was excited I had contacted him and eager to share about his work, and to introduce to me his students and the topics of their research.

Xu Xin began his career teaching American literature, and through this topic he started to come across multiple authors of Jewish background. With these findings, Xu began lecturing about Jewish contributions on the international stage without having met anyone who identifies as Jewish. This happened for the first time in 1985. A Jew from Chicago came to Nanjing to teach, and the two men formed a bond which saw Xu going to the US to live with the man's family for a year and learn about Judaism.

Since then, he has studied Yiddish and Jewish texts in Cincinnati and New York and at Harvard University, traveled multiple times to Israel, received honorary doctorates, and lectured internationally, all while continuing to grow the Jewish Studies department at Nanjing University. It now has 15,000 English texts donated primarily from the US and England. The bond Xu formed with the Jewish community, dating back to before I was born, set the stage for me to walk into his department in 2011 and feel at home in the middle of China.

Before I left the center, one of his female students said to me, "*Shabbat Shalom!*" as the elevator doors opened. Ah yes, it was Friday afternoon, and while back on my campus at the college it was hard to remember, these Chinese students thoroughly respected my background and the value of taking a day of rest.

My article was published in the Vancouver newspaper. I valued the discussion I had with Xu Xin for the story, but I also appreciated his knowledge of the Jewish communities in China on a personal level. He shared with me about the Shanghai community, which prompted me to figure out how to get there for an upcoming Shabbat.

Chapter 3: Shanghai Visits

I still did not speak Chinese, but I had met enough students who were able to help me construct the sentences I would need to buy a train ticket. Shanghai is quite close to Nanjing via the bullet train, but to me living in the quiet, isolated countryside, it felt a lot further.

The journey was more than worthwhile. I booked a hotel near one of the synagogues, and upon showing up, I found that the community who attends the services are all French. Being from Canada, I have remnants of French in the back of my mind, so I was able to feel fairly comfortable there. There were several young exchange students attending the services, including Abby, a beautiful girl originally from Morocco who had moved to Paris for university.

She and I formed a friendship, which allowed me to learn about the Jewish communities in Morocco, France, and China. Her French background and awareness of the overall history of the French in Shanghai was also very educational for me. After the first week we met, I returned for a couple more Shabbats before her time in China was over, and we would explore the French Concession after synagogue services on Saturdays.

The French Concession is a breath of fresh air. The streets are lined with huge leafy green trees, called London planes, imported from France. There are cute fashion shops, artsy cafes, and French bakeries inside the European-style buildings. The scene is out of a 1900s-era novel, and one could mistake their visit with a stroll along the French Riviera. There are still many people on the road, but it feels quieter and more serene than other parts of Shanghai.

With Abby I got my first manicure, and we sat and spoke about what it was like to search for a Jewish community and services in

China. She told me what I heard frequently from Jews I met: that in coming to China they found themselves feeling closer to their Jewish roots than they ever had before.

Abby told me she had spoken with several of the other French expatriates in Shanghai and that many of them hadn't visited a synagogue in their own country for a very long time, but in China, they had sought out the Jewish center and become regulars.

Living in a place where everyone can see you are not from there seems to make people look inward at themselves and their own culture, and come to appreciate things they had previously taken for granted. The synagogues for expatriates in China are very warm and welcoming, and for those who have a difficult time adjusting to life there, it provides a place of respite. Since I had already traveled to many places on my own and sought out the Jewish communities wherever I could, I felt I had always carried an appreciation for my ethnic community, and that did not change for me in China.

Traveling back and forth between Nanjing and Beijing on weekends for Shabbat introduced me to the important history of the Shanghai Jews who found refuge in China from the Holocaust. At its peak, Shanghai was home to forty thousand Jews, and this was not the first time Chinese people had reached out to Jewish populations in need. Harbin in the north of China was at one time home to twenty thousand Jewish people fleeing Czarist Russia. In Shanghai there is a Jewish museum; a Jewish cemetery still stands in Harbin, as well as a museum and the old synagogue building, which has since been transformed into a backpacker hostel. Jews also have a long history in Hong Kong, with Indian Jews forming the basis of a strong community at the turn of the twentieth century.

To me, visiting all these places makes me feel a sense of pride. Thousands of others before me had encountered adversity, and instead of giving in to it, they built cultural outposts and flourished. The majority of these populations have emigrated elsewhere, but their resolve to make the best temporary home in China as possible makes me feel akin to them, beyond the obvious religious ties.

Chapter 4: A Unique Encounter

One of the weekends I spent in Shanghai, I was checking out of a hotel. The front desk staff did not speak very much English, and they were withholding part of my deposit for some reason. I was having difficulty communicating with them about what was going on when a tall young Chinese guy standing behind me asked in English if he could help. I still lived in such a limited reality in Nanjing, and although I had come to Shanghai, my dealings with locals there had been minimal. It seemed astounding to me that a local would have such good English skills. I accepted his help and he got my deposit back for me. I said thank you, and as I was grabbing my bag, he asked if I would like to go to lunch at the Western-style restaurant across the street. I had several hours until my train back to Nanjing, so I agreed.

Bespectacled and wearing a polo, Wang towered over me. He was probably 6'1", and not as thin as many Chinese men I saw in Shanghai. His easygoing way of approaching me and the very subtle Chinese accent made it apparent quite quickly that he had some experience dealing with foreigners. This was actually the first time I had seen that in anyone in China, aside from when I visited Xu Xin at the university. Wang was a year older than me and worked in consulting for the oil industry where most of his clients were non-Chinese. He had also spent some time outside of China tutoring Mandarin. This was before I looked up the synagogue or knew much about Shanghai, so his "Western" expressions and straightforward way of speaking were very refreshing for me.

Over lunch, the conversation turned to how the school I was teaching at had not given me the whole amount of my salary, and that my Canadian bank card was not working at ATMs, which left me with hardly any cash since most places will not accept Visa credit cards. Upon hearing this, Wang insisted on paying for the meal and ordering extra dishes. This was quite appreciated because I had become ill from the food choices at the school in Nanjing, and had begun to lose weight very rapidly. When food cost five RMB at school, the equivalent of seventy-five Canadian cents, a meal worth one hundred RMB seemed incredibly pricey to me.

Wang's job in the oil industry was related to my father's work as a hydrogeologist in Alberta. We spoke about where I'm from and my father's work, and the conversation turned to my cultural background. This excited Wang because it gave him even more respect for my father's work. He imagined my father must have a great work ethic, and he began to speak to me about how much Jews and Chinese have in common. He told me he had read an article by a Chinese scholar that said the Chinese people, because of the Nanjing massacre by the Japanese, and other assaults on their territory and beliefs by previous foreign groups, understand the pain of the Holocaust. He said this understanding creates a strong and unique affinity between the two groups. He proudly described the Shanghai Jewish refugees, and China's history of reaching out to the Jewish people in their times of need.

The conversation turned back to lighter matters, and I told him how I was a bit upset about my iPod mini being stolen a couple days before. I had opened my side bag to reach for something, and a guy put his hand in the unzipped pocket, grabbed my iPod and a fistful of cash, and disappeared into the crowd. It had been a birthday gift from my father right before I left for China, so it was especially upsetting.

"Close your eyes for ten seconds," said Wang.

I gave him a quizzical look, and then shut my eyes and counted to ten.

When I opened my eyes, in front of me on the table sat an iPod.
"Oh, no, I can't take that!" I said.

"It's okay, it's an old one with not much memory and I have a
new one and don't use it anymore anyway," he said.

The gift ended up being a lot more than just the iPod, because
on it were audio tapes and songs in Chinese, which enhanced my
learning experience.

After lunch, he was being so nice, so I agreed to accompany
him to his nearby office. I had mentioned I wanted to see Jing'an
Temple, and it turned out his office was in a tower right across the
street overlooking the golden structure.

He gave me money in case there was an entry fee to visit, and I
went out to take some photos before returning to the office tower.
After his help at the hotel, the lunch, and the iPod, I didn't resist as
much when he offered to give me some small cash to get into the
temple. I resolved to pay him back at some future time by finding
him again somehow. He insisted on helping me because he said he
knew how dishonest some Chinese businesses could be, especially
those that bring in foreign teachers, and he seemed to feel a sort of
responsibility if other Chinese people were leaving me in a less than
ideal situation. He felt he should help.

I wasn't attracted to him, and I didn't get a sense that he was
being more than friendly because he did not invade my personal
space or make me feel uncomfortable. But, it was nice to converse,
not only in English, but about things I might speak about with my
friends back home, like current events, or future travel plans.

We continued on to a pub for dinner. I started to feel bad he had
spent the day with me, but he said he didn't have anything else to do,
and that it was really his pleasure to show me the "real" Shanghai.
By this he meant places that someone my age, but who is Chinese,
might go to day-to-day.

We entered a Western-style establishment with hockey playing on the screens—my good ol' Canadian pastime—and this was an especially pleasant experience for me. Wang was set on making sure I got back to Nanjing in one piece, so he came with me and paid for the cab to the train station. Before walking me to the train platform, he told me to wait on the sidewalk for a moment. A couple of minutes later, he came back with two thousand RMB (three hundred USD) and asked if that was enough. I had learned by this point that I should not say no to him. It seemed he was a young guy with a lot of money he wanted to spend on a nice girl, so I bashfully accepted the money. It would indeed help me out over the next several days while my employers continued to make excuses as to why I was not paid on time. At his office, he had added me on LinkedIn and Facebook, and I said I would come back to Shanghai again once I got paid. Until the very end, I obviously wondered if he would be expecting anything of me. As a solo female traveler I am careful and pay attention to my safety, but the entire time, he remained polite and respectful, and didn't attempt to be anything more than friendly with me.

I usually share the iPod-and-money part of this story with people because it was so shocking. While it was nice to get the help and strange to accept so much money from a stranger, the sentiments Wang expressed and the feelings of similarity between his culture and my own are really what have stuck with me.

Some people believe that during the biblical days of King David, the "Ten Lost Tribes" traveled eastwards, and there are people in China who may be the descendants of these Jewish tribes. While there is no historical proof for this connection, the idea is quite interesting to me. It could suggest a much deeper relationship between the two cultures than their shared experiences of suffering.

In the city of Kaifeng there are actual Chinese Jews, whom

professor Xu Xin has published books and research papers on, most notably *The Jews of Kaifeng, China: History, Culture, and Religion.* These people look Chinese and mostly speak Chinese, but can trace Jewish roots back a few generations and have passed down remnants of Hebrew prayers. This presence of Chinese who identify as Jewish, and the folklore about how perhaps many other Chinese are descendants of Israel, has created a different lens through which I see the people.

I cannot say everyone who has helped me on my travels in China did so due to my cultural background, because many just saw me as a *laowai*, but traveling as a minority with a skin color that people are already not used to seeing in many parts of the country caused me to be even more grateful that these people did not care about religion and just wanted to help me. Moments where, for example, an old woman who does not speak a word of English takes me by the arm when I look lost and points in the direction of a subway station, fill me with gratitude; these moments push me to keep going in my China travels, despite moments of stress or agitation. To have my unique background that isn't immediately visible to those who meet me spurs me to learn as much as I can about the cultures I encounter.

Chapter 5: My Friend Rachel

After my teaching contract ended, I backpacked for three weeks around China before returning to Canada for the summer. It began with a visit to the small town of a girl I met at the Nanjing college. I had been having trouble getting out of the subway station gate. I had not bought a token for enough stops, but not knowing this, I was considering jumping over the barrier.

"Can I help you?" said a female voice to my left.

The girl told me to stand with her and, scanning her own token, had me walk through at the same time as her. Once through the gate, I said thank you and began walking toward the steps down to the street. She was heading in the same direction and came up beside me.

"Can I walk with you?"

Her English name was Rachel, and upon my telling her that my middle name is Rachel, named after a great grandmother in Russia, she felt as if we were meant to meet. I told her right away that Rachel is a Jewish name from the Bible, and the name of a very strong woman. We chatted until the road parted toward her college across the way. We exchanged phone numbers and began meeting once or twice a week for her to teach me some Mandarin. She helped me to choose my Chinese name, which I hadn't wanted to pick randomly, as I am too aware of people from other cultures who pick bizarre English names.

She explained that a Chinese family name is best when it is one character, and that she liked characters that are not incredibly common. My last name, Cohen, means priest in Hebrew and translates into *mushi* in Chinese, so we took the *mu* character. For my personal name, I had wanted something cool like *Firefly*, but it was too many characters and had sounds that when I was first learning Chinese sounded very harsh to my ears. I decided *shui* for water sounded nice to the ear. Rachel came back after the first lesson where I mentioned my desire to find a name, saying, "I thought about it, and I think you should have the word *ya*, which means *elegant*, because I think you are very elegant." And thus, Mu Shuiya and my Chinese identity had a concrete base: a name.

I learned after meeting Rachel that I was the first foreigner she had ever spoken to, and yet her vocabulary was quite good and her accent not strong at all. I think it was very brave of her to come up to me like she did, with so much confidence, having never dealt before with someone who looks like me. She told me she had learned

English through watching American movies, and she loved the same actors as me, such as Robert Downey Jr. She gave me Chinese music to listen to (Jay Chou and MayDay from Taiwan), and helped me to learn about modern culture in China.

When we set off to her town in northern Jiangsu Province, she described Binhai as if it were a small backwater place. I realized though, with slight amusement, that her perception of what constitutes a small town is entirely different from my own. I come from a city of one million people and consider it to be large, as it is one of the major cities in Canada. In comparison, Rachel's city of one million people feels miniature to her compared to the bustling population of eight million in Nanjing.

Her family was too embarrassed to have me stay at their small apartment, so I booked a cheap but nice hotel room and Rachel stayed with me. The first evening I learned about Chinese opera by watching a TV programme that she translated for me. The following day, we explored the town until it was time to go to dinner with her family. She had not been home in several months, so her grandparents came as well, and the dinner was held at a restaurant. As happens every time I meet new people in Asia, they were very impressed that I know how to use chopsticks. I used the sentences Rachel had taught me to communicate.

The restaurant owner came up toward the end of the meal with free plates of watermelon, saying he had never had a foreigner at his establishment before, so it was something special. All I could say was "xie xie" (*thank you*) and appreciate that Rachel's family was happy about the gift as well.

At this gathering there was more meat at the table than usual, and while I had been taught to say "*Wŏ shì chīsù de,*" meaning "I am vegetarian," many people ask why, including Rachel's parents. I explained that because I am Jewish I have certain restrictions over what I eat.

The questionable food and the dangers of eating at restaurants using reused "gutter oil" or serving unsafe meats had caused me to return to my kosher upbringing and order vegetarian options whenever possible. This request is difficult for Chinese people to understand, and often in a restaurant when I would say "*meiyou rou*" (*without meat*), they would take off the beef but leave the pig, as they couldn't fathom someone wouldn't eat pig.

However, in more intimate settings, such as with Rachel's family, where I had someone to explain for me that I do not eat meat, I was not given any trouble about it. Once her mom found out there was a particular dish I liked from the restaurant, when we went to her home the next day, she made the same dish especially for me. When I exclaimed about it, she beamed at me. Since this experience, I have sat at many more Chinese tables, and have encountered numerous warm smiles. While I don't eat from every dish, the women serving love to see me eat, and refill my plate and pass things to me more frequently than any other country where I have been a guest.

After a couple of days in Binhai, I said goodbye to Rachel and got on a 14-hour train northbound to Beijing. I have not seen Rachel since, but I think of her often. We exchanged a couple of emails after I left, and in the last one her words really touched me. She wrote: "I have to visit Vancouver sometime in the future, though it may cost a couple of years, but that's a deal. We definitely have the same beginning of the story, like a movie happening in a city might have; it took place in the subway. Great, isn't it?"

Rachel is a Chinese reflection of many things her people have said of me: smart, kind, brave. I feel my life has reached a new level of fulfillment by traveling to the other side of the world to meet someone I could so well relate to, despite growing up surrounded by such different cultural norms, traditions, expectations, and beliefs. I do truly hope that one day she can see Vancouver and the part of the world I am from.

I often think of the words she wrote to me and I have to agree: when did my life become like a movie? How did it become that I thrive off of being the only Jew, the only female foreigner, or only foreigner of any kind that people have met, and probably ever will meet in the future? This is such a great opportunity for me, and I grasp it with all the tenacity I can.

Eva Cohen is a Canadian-American journalist from Edmonton, Canada, who is currently based in New York. Her bylines have appeared in publications including the Financial Times, Forbes, Vancouver Sun, Jerusalem Post, Foreign Policy's "Passport" blog, Seattle Globalist and a number of community papers. In stories Eva has published from China, she highlighted women's issues, including sports in China for local women, accessibility of lesbian centers in Beijing, and a special piece on exceptional businesswomen in Beijing for International Women's Day 2012. She received her B.A. in History at Carleton University in Ontario, Canada, and M.A. in International Journalism from the University of Leeds, England.

KAMPONG HOUSE

By Barbara Craven

THE small airplane fell twenty feet and the Malay boy sitting behind me threw up in an airsick bag. He was nine years old and the nephew of my friend, Khalilah, a supervisor in a computer factory on Penang Island. The three of us were flying over the interior of Malaysia in a frail twelve-seat plane that lurched and bucked while casting its shadow on an endless jungle cut by rivers of raging muddy water. I wondered if the wind would slam us into the tarmac when we tried to land over on the coast. It must be worse there, I mused, with gusts coming off the South China Sea.

I wondered what I was doing there on that plane. Like I would so many times in the days ahead, I wondered what I was doing in Malaysia at all, and why I planned to live in a country that I had to leave every three months to renew my tourist visa.

I'd succeeded for the last hour in blocking out the memories of what had happened back home. I had nothing left in Seattle now. No house, no job, no son to speak of. It was 1991. I was forty years old. Not only had I lost custody of my teenage son to a father living far away, but I understood deep down he had meant what he said: that he would bury me in every way he could, punishment for having divorced him. He refused to send the boy for required visits, or to put him on the phone. He had a certain charisma, and the judge would not act on my complaints. There hadn't been any point in staying. I just wanted to get away—far, far away.

An American man had convinced me of the advantages of living in Malaysia: many citizens spoke enough English to get by, it was economical compared to Singapore, hospitable, interesting. He lived there with his educated Malay wife, Muslim according to law, and could introduce me to the country. They invited me to stay with them for a few weeks. I traveled around Southeast Asia for a couple of months before taking them up on it.

I'd been in Malaysia for three months when Khalilah invited me to visit her brother and his wife on the East Coast, the traditional part of the country, mostly Malay. I'd leaped at the opportunity.

In the airplane, she sat across from the boy, and I had to turn in my seat to ask if Josef was okay.

"Yes," she replied. "He gets carsick, too."

She had her hair hidden under a bright yellow scarf, the only hint of her Muslim heritage. She looked quintessentially Malay with her black eyebrows and dark brown eyes, not as soulful as some, but certainly as haunting. The rest of her skinny brown body was covered with jeans and a T-shirt. I'd met her in a noisy cafe off the winding alleys of George Town, where she was hosting lunch for a few of her employees from an American computer company, and she invited me over from the next table. At the time, her graciousness surprised me. I would learn later that this is the way of the Malays.

I peered at the sea of vivid, bobbing scarves in front of me on the airplane—bright reds, purples, and greens—and a woman two rows up caught my attention. She stood out because nothing concealed her long black hair, and therefore, she was more like me than anyone else on that plane. I wore a loose lavender blouse and long, floppy cotton pants, vibrant purple so I wouldn't look bland next to all the colorful clothing the local women donned every day.

All the rest of the female passengers wore the traditional Malay dress, the *baju karung*, a sleek ankle-length skirt and matching blouse, along with a scarf that entirely concealed the hair. My heart pumped a little faster as I scanned the plane. These Malays were so culturally different from myself that I hadn't a clue how I would bridge the gap. I glanced at Khalilah. She stood between a deep loneliness and myself.

The plane suddenly dropped again, and I felt like a person stepping over the edge of a cliff. I glanced around in panic. A collective, high-pitched "Oh!" came from the passengers. "I didn't expect *this*," someone said in English, but everyone else spoke in Malay. I did not understand their words, only their frightened tones.

"That was a bad one," Khalilah acknowledged, almost laughing.

She was beginning to get on my nerves with her cheerfulness in the face of imminent disaster. Just then the plane suddenly plummeted another twenty feet, leaving all our bellies in the air. This time I was looking at her when it happened, and I saw the flash of fear in her eyes.

An hour later we dropped steadily through thick clouds. From nowhere, in a cut in the steamy jungle, the runway appeared below us. And then, we arrived on the east coast of Malaysia, an Islamic country. It was 4:00 pm, on a Friday in February 1991. A world away, US bombs exploded over Baghdad.

We crawled out of the plane, then trudged through steam rising from the rain-soaked landing strip towards a white building slightly bigger than a gas station. A sign across the top read *Terengganu*. Just that: the name of the town.

I followed the other passengers carrying their luggage and plastic sacks of jackfruit and lychee, and made feeble attempts to catch up to Khalilah, who seemed to be racing now that we were so close to her brother's home.

I got a whiff of sea air. It seemed to come suddenly and from nowhere, and its beckoning tang made me high. The rain had jacked the humidity up to 100%. I felt dizzy from the heat even though

I'd been in Southeast Asia for months already. I ignored the sweat running down my face. We clambered into the car and rode out of the airport.

Khalilah and the driver talked in lilting tones in the front seat as we drove along, and I sank into a pleasant state close to hypnosis. Nothing broke the stillness of the *kampong* houses and lush vegetation lining the road.

"It's there," Khalilah said, turning around to talk to the boy and me, and then cocking her head down the road. "Abdul's house." Her brother's house.

Made of raw brown wood, the house nestled with open windows behind a flimsy metal gate along with neighboring houses. It was a *kampong* house, a house in a compound, the traditional style of neighborhoods left over from the days when the jungle was the enemy. I'd heard Malays consistently extolling these traditional houses, and I'd tried to understand what about them deserved such praise. But eventually, I'd realized that their penchant for these homes rests solely on nostalgia; comfort has nothing to do with it. Our driver eased the car in front of the locked gate, and within moments we piled out. Khalilah called to her sister-in-law inside.

While we waited for the door to open, my thoughts strayed to the difference between the house before me now and the one I currently lived in with a Chinese family on Penang Island. Even from outside the *kampong* house, I knew that the ants could crawl in through slits between the wood, and that the mosquitoes would just fly right in through the open windows. In the house on Penang, the ants had limited entryways due to its cement construction, and screens on the windows and doors prevented all but the most persistent mosquitoes from gaining access. I knew as I stood there looking at it that the *kampong* house would test my endurance.

And what about Khalilah's relatives? Because of the Gulf War, would they regard me as their enemy? Did they know they would be hosting an American? On Penang, when I'd announced my plans to venture to Terengganu, the young father of the Chinese household, Lee, had raised his eyebrows and replied, "You better not go. I've been hearing things in the cafes. Things the Malays have been saying. Stay here with us where you are safe." He was referring not just to the home we lived in but to the housing development, mostly Chinese, on the north side of Penang Island, not far from Ferringhi Beach where Lee made an excellent living selling knockoff watches to foreigners. "Don't tell anyone you are American," Lee had continued. "Tell them you're... Swiss."

This seemed ludicrous. Why would a fanatical Muslim care which Western nationality I belonged to? Actually, I'd entertained the thought of disguising myself if worse came to worst. I could pass for a Malay if I dressed like one, I'd thought. I was darkly tanned, and I am short and have black eyebrows.

I had stared at Lee with great skepticism. While he was thinking of how to respond to my look, CNN on the TV flashed a photo of an American pilot whom the Iraqis had beaten up.

"See?" said Lee. "See what they do?"

I shrugged at Lee about the slim possibility that horrible tortures might await me if I wasn't careful. After all, if things were as bad here as he was making out, my American friend would let me know. Living on the other side of the island in the Malay section, surely he had a finger on the Muslim pulse.

"I'm going to the East Coast," I had said, turning my back on Lee and his wife, and marched up the stairs to my room.

In Terengganu, we climbed the *kampong* house's porch stairs, and swung into the bedroom where Khalilah changed into a sarong. "Are you going to teach me how to tie one of those?" I asked.

"After I pray," she said, as though we'd discussed this before, although we hadn't. "Here, I have an extra." She tossed me a brown batik sarong, then unrolled a dazzling red prayer rug that had been in her carry-on bag. In one quick movement, she spread it on the floor, knelt facing Mecca, and immersed herself in prayer, completely tuning me out.

I felt uncomfortable standing there and staring at her, although, plainly, she didn't mind. I decided to lie down on the bed and read, maybe doze a little. Within a minute, a red ant had bitten me. I found myself trying hard not to swear while Khalilah prayed on.

In about ten minutes, she got up and stuffed the prayer rug into her bag. "I thought you were going to put on the sarong?" she asked.

"You have to show me how to tie it."

She made it look a lot easier than it was, then she had a good laugh at my bumbling efforts, but ultimately I succeeded, and, strangely, I felt relieved. Somehow, now that I was dressed like women I had seen in the markets and on the streets, it was as though I was a part of Southeast Asia.

Just then, a man's voice called in Malay from the other room. Khalilah's face became animated and she trilled back to him.

"It's my brother, home from work!" she announced. He had a job teaching music, including rock and roll, at the small local university. I figured he couldn't be too conservative. Still, this was the heart of Iraqi-sympathizer territory. Some years later, the newspaper would report that the East Coast of Malaysia had become one of Osama bin Laden's hangouts. Might Abdul harbor some deep-seated antagonism towards me that even Khalilah was unaware of? I wondered.

Now, with the sarong tied around my waist, I followed Khalilah into the living room. Abdul was a bit of a shock. He wore a black goatee and mustache, and, with his long, serious face, he looked like he'd just stepped out of a Middle Eastern desert. Khalilah introduced us, and Abdul made small talk in very good English. I decided to find out where he stood right away. No use beating around the bush for the next week.

"Thank you for inviting me," I said. "I was a little surprised."

"Why?" he asked, frowning.

"Well, some Malays aren't too happy with Americans right now."

He reeled backwards as though I'd hit him. When he recovered he said, "You're welcome here."

I was so pleased I couldn't say anything for a while.

By then, his wife had spread a cloth on the floor and placed orange wedges in a bowl on top of it. "Come," Abdul said. "Let's eat and talk."

Clearly, neither his wife nor Khalilah were invited to this event. His interest was in talking to me.

Khalilah retreated to the kitchen with her sister-in-law. Abdul and I got along famously. Music, and his stay in the capital, Kuala Lumpur, had catapulted him into worldly ways. He wanted to know about California. I told him it was a horrible place. He would like Seattle much better.

Like most Malaysians, he frowned at that. "Too cold," he said.

Half an hour later, Khalilah eased herself onto the floor next to me. By then, Abdul and I had eaten all the oranges. "Take these peels out to the kitchen," he said to her.

She gave one of her little laughs, looked him straight in the eye, and said, "Why should I? I didn't eat them."

I don't think I've ever seen a more shocked look on a man's face. Clearly, he was accustomed to ordering her around. They stared at each other for a long, long time. Then she jutted out her chin at him. That made his eyes widen even more, and his jaw dropped. He was angry, but more than that, he simply couldn't believe this was happening.

I thought we would sit there like that all night. Neither brother nor sister would budge. I was certain that she wouldn't have staged this rebellion without someone like me at her side. I felt somewhat responsible for the awkward silence.

"Uh," I said. "*I* ate the oranges and I don't really feel like a guest, not when I'm staying a whole week. I'll clear." No one objected to that. They were still caught up in their staring match. The tension eased as the orange peels disappeared, but I don't think things were ever quite the same between those two again.

A week later, I stood outside the gate on Penang, peering through the bars at the house. I saw Lee's wife step from the garden to the driveway, heading my way and calling my name in excited tones. "I have my key," I shouted, not wanting to trouble her.

"Never mind," she replied, "I get gate for you."

I sighed, so happy to be back. I watched her amble towards me, and realized I had missed her. We greeted each other with pats and smiles and how-are-yous, and eventually made our way to the door where I kicked off my shoes and stepped inside.

Their boy and girl, both under ten, squealed, jumped up from their seated positions in front of the TV, and shouted my name over and over. I wasn't sure I liked all the attention, yet it felt good to be greeted so enthusiastically. Lee, at the polished dining room table, lowered his newspaper so he could raise an eyebrow at me.

I threw my arms to the side. "I'm all in one piece," I said in reply, and to rub it in, "It was fantastic! I had a great time!" He went back to the newspaper. This would be my home, and they my family for the next two years of my stay in Malaysia.

Khalilah and I met frequently at restaurants while I lived on Penang. When she mentioned her brother and the East Coast, I knew who and what she was talking about. My stay over there, inside the house and out, had given me some insight into the tradi-tional culture that I could never have had otherwise. Awakened to the timeless ways that permeate the Malaysian soul, I carry that visit with me always.

Barbara Craven lived for three years in Malaysia on a tourist visa. She has published over one hundred articles and short stories in the United States, Australia, Malaysia, Singapore, and Hong Kong. Her publishers include airline magazines, newspapers, lifestyle magazines, and literary journals. "Kampong House" is the true account on which the first chapter of her unpublished novel, One More Border to Cross, *is based. She resides in Olympia, WA, United States.*

GIVING IN TO MONGOLIA

By Michelle Borok

WHEN you learn to ride a horse, the first things you want to know are how to make your horse go and how to make it stop. The beginner achieves this through force. It's a pendulum of pushing and pulling, constant kicking, squeezing, maybe the tap of a whip, pulling, leaning back, trying desperately to get an eleven-hundred-pound animal to do what you say. As the rider improves, she learns that force doesn't always work. Control inevitably belongs to the horse.

Giving and release are the keys to a partnership between rider and animal.

When you "give," you lighten your hold on the horse. You trust it to find its balance, speed, and footing without running away with you, and maybe more importantly, without veering off course. Along the way, you develop the skill to keep yourself in balance, and to move with the horse in a way that doesn't make its own natural movement difficult. Giving is a release of the tense control that makes you feel safe on a horse's back. For most people, it's one of the most difficult lessons to learn: a gradual comfort with letting go.

I learned this lesson at thirty-four, on my first trip to Mongolia.

I had been nearly five years out of an eight-year relationship. I had started riding horses again, one of the many things I returned to when I found myself on my own. I first rode horses at fourteen, and briefly in college, but gave it up for nearly a decade as the priorities of a partnered life outweighed my solo interests. Returning to the things I once loved played a vital role in redefining my individual identity. I felt that so much had been lost in our relationship merger.

I was coming to a crossroads at a job that I loved but which left little time for anything outside of its gravitational pull. For seven years I had worked for a small publishing, art, and retail company. It was a ground-up operation that required dedication, long hours, and creative energy, and had started to define my social as well as professional life. I curated art shows (for several years, thirty-six a year), worked with young artists, oversaw the operations of our stores and galleries in three cities, wrote and edited for our magazine and website, and worked closely with the owner of the company to see our way through the recession. I didn't make a lot of money doing what I loved, but I kept doing it. I cashed in on the recognition and social perks to keep the fears of financial insecurity at bay. I spent twenty-four hours a day thinking about work or the people I worked with. Work always came first. I was passionate about what I did, but I also knew that there was more to who I was. Being consumed by my career was starting to feel unhealthy.

Something within—something registering larger than all the other shifts on my metaphysical Richter scale—was begging for a change. My search for self needed to move beyond daydreams and late-night confessionals with best friends. I had to go somewhere.

I chose Mongolia as my solo vacation destination because of the horses, but it also seemed like the right place to let go. All of my riding experiences had been in the ring and focused on lessons or competition. I wanted the freedom of open steppes.

I expected a break from the workaday grind and plenty of adventure. I got those. What I didn't bargain for was a complete life reboot. In my twenty days there, I remembered what it was to be master of my own agenda. I had no one to take care of, make decisions for, or oversee. I just got to be in charge of me, and I rediscovered how happy I could be with only myself for company. I walked city streets with people who looked like my own Korean and Portuguese reflection, a Eurasian blend of stocky builds and almond eyes. I forgot how to doubt myself out of taking chances, and I fell in love with this new-to-me brave woman I met along the way. After ten days on my own, my best friend (looking to fill the last pages of her passport) joined me.

We drove out to the countryside with our translator, Heegii, to Terelj National Park in a Russian jeep driven by Agii, a man with golden eyes, a gentle voice, broad shoulders, and close-cropped salt-and-pepper hair. He graciously made many stops along the road to Terelj so we could take pictures with camels, gawk at herds of horses gathered on the hillsides, and walk through the above-ground tombs of a Kazakh cemetery. Agii smiled shyly as I giggled. I was girlishly thrilled to be in the passenger seat beside him. He was seemingly amused by the way we took everything in.

Heegii did his best to tell us more about what we were seeing. Agii always stayed with the jeep, watching us as we picked our way around the tombs, nervously ignorant of local cemetery customs. We'd climb back in the jeep, giddy about each passing kilometer across the steppes bringing us closer to our adventure.

It was spring, and the land and its livestock were still recovering from a very harsh winter. The landscape a monochromatic rolling sea of yellow-and-brown grass under a gigantic blue sky. Only up close could you see bits of green coming up through the undergrowth and pushing out through the bark of spindly tree branches. The livestock we passed were shedding their winter coats in uneven clumps, and their ribcages pressed out they combed the grassy hillsides looking for something to eat. Every living thing we saw was eager for the

Mongolian summer, a season I had only seen in guidebooks and on postcards at the souvenir shops. Summer grasses are vibrantly green, tall, and lush. Despite the yellows and browns around us, there was something electric about being in the countryside on the cusp of the season. We felt as if we were in on a secret, seeing the behind-the-scenes version of what nearly half a million tourists a year come to see. The tourist camps we passed were mostly empty as their season still had another month before it opened. We felt as if we had Mongolia all to ourselves.

Terelj is the most immediate rangeland outside of the densely packed, polluted capital, Ulaanbaatar. Soviet-era cement-block apartment buildings stand in stark contrast to the modernity that foreign investment in mining has brought to the country. Journalists write the same stories and share the same photos of Mongolians in traditional dress walking past the Louis Vuitton store at the edge of the city's central square. It's hard to say which is the "real" Mongolia, the capital occupied by sixty percent of the country's population, or the nomadic countryside and its traditions—the national pride of its citizens. I was captivated by both.

Agii left us with Heegii at the *ger* (traditional home) camp of a nomadic herding family. Our guide was Zurigoo, a twenty-something herdsman whose family supplemented their income by hosting tourists looking for an authentic nomadic experience. They were used to people coming in and out of their home. Despite knowing that I was just one of many to pass through, the family's genuine warmth and hospitality made me feel instantly at home. The matriarch, Munkhtulgaa, fed us constantly, inquired about our lives at home, tried her hand at matchmaking, and tucked us in at night.

The trek took us around the valley where Munkhtulgaa's family lived. We rode for six to eight hours a day, stopping to make a modest lunch in forest clearings or beside small streams. We napped in the grass after lunch, watching herds of horses amble by, sniffing the air as they passed us. We spent most nights sleeping under the stars, our horses staked for the night twenty feet from our tent, but we also stayed with other relatives when the temperatures were too cold.

When we returned from our trek, we celebrated our birthdays with a big bonfire beside the stream that ran near Munkhtulgaa's camp. That night, as we slept, she covered me with her son's deel (the traditional clothing of herders) in the middle of the night when the ger stove's fire had died out. Mongolian hospitality is what has kept the nomadic culture alive for centuries, and it's what makes many people want to stay. At the end of the trek, I made a promise to return.

I went back to Los Angeles with my batteries fully recharged, but with very little interest in re-engaging with the demands of my life in the city. Nothing seemed worth getting angry or stressed out about. Everything seemed trivial. In dead stops on the jam-packed freeway I'd find myself staring up at the sky and hating how small it seemed compared to the limitless skies above Mongolia. Everything around me made me think back to my trip. It was becoming a problem.

I bought the horse I had been leasing before I left for Mongolia, knowing that he would provide a connection to what I had experienced there. Horse ownership was the perfect excuse for my shifting priorities, something that not everyone around me was comfortable with. He became the reason why I couldn't make it out to bars and parties ("sorry, have to get up early to feed the horse"), why I passed up dinners ("sorry, penny pinching to keep the horse housed and fed"), and why I finally stopped working sixty-plus-hour work weeks (no apologies needed). He was more than a cover for the changes, though; he truly was my connection to what I felt was slipping away with each day that passed.

There was a fullness and peace I felt in Mongolia, and every minute back home made those feelings feel further and further away. I was terrified. I had fallen so completely in love with the woman I was there, and I didn't want to think about slipping back into routines and the insecurities that maintained them.

I had to make good on my promise to the Mongolians I had met, but more importantly, I needed to go back to see if I could recover what had been lost. I needed to know if what I was still feeling about Mongolia was just an extended version of post-vacation blues, or if there was something bigger happening. I made plans to go back in the spring. I made arrangements with the translator I had traveled with, and counted down the days until I was back in Mongolia.

I had booked a short trip purely for follow-up analysis. Five days total. The morning after my arrival, the translator I had the year before showed up at my hotel with the same incredibly handsome driver who had taken us to Terelj, Agii. The translator, Heegii, knew I liked the driver and had hired him again as a surprise. Just as I had before, I sat in the passenger seat blushing and making translated small talk. Agii spoke only a few shy words of English. This time I pried. I was feeling braver than I had last time and I wanted to know how a man this incredibly good-looking spent his time. I wanted to know all about this guy, so I asked blunt personal questions, and after he answered them, he asked the same questions of me. All of this conversation was filtered through Heegii, and despite how shy I could tell Agii was, he became more confident as our drive and conversation carried on. He helped me pick out food and supplies to bring to the nomadic family in Terelj. We were clumsily flirting as best we could.

Eventually we got to the family I had stayed with before. They were happy to see me—surprised, but happy. After they had filled a recycled Fanta bottle with fresh cow's milk for Agii to take home (they liked him as much as I did), Agii and Heegii left for

Ulaanbaatar. I settled in for three days of trying to help with as much work around the camp as I could. I was sad to see Agii go. It was a long goodbye, which is taboo in Mongolia, but there was still a lot we both wanted to know about each other.

I had an incredible time with the family. Armed with a dictionary and a couple of phrasebooks, I lived like a second daughter to Munkhtulgaa, helping to clear dung from the sheep and goat pens in the mornings, sweeping the *ger* after breakfast, fetching water from a hole I had to kick open in the frozen river, collecting fallen branches for the fire from the nearby forest's edge, washing dishes after each meal, and helping to take care of my "sister's" one-year-old baby, so that she could tend the sheep and prepare meals for her husband. Everything felt so natural and familiar. I imagined myself living this life, but I knew I probably couldn't hack it. I also constantly daydreamed about Agii, wondering if he had done this kind of work. I imagined he had since he seemed so comfortable when he had been there. That just made him all the more appealing.

On the second day, Heegii called to see how things were going, and to pass on a message from Agii. Agii wanted to know when I would be flying back to the US after he was scheduled to pick me up from Terelj. He wanted to spend more time with me. I left Terelj one day early so that I could spend my last day and a half with Agii in Ulaanbaatar. It was the best decision of my life.

I had already fallen in love with Mongolia. I had gone back to make sure it wasn't just a crush, and now there was Agii, and it felt a lot like love as well. I had spent the first half of my thirties believing I wasn't capable of love, and now I'd done it twice in a row. For me the key to falling in love was learning to love myself. Mongolia opened the door for me, and it brought me Agii just to show how generous it truly was.

For the second time, I left Mongolia in tears, devastated to be leaving a place that felt more like home than any place I'd ever known. It was clear to me now that it was home to my heart, and that I needed to seriously consider what that meant.

I got back home re-energized but troubled. I knew now that what I had felt on my first trip was real, and that with all the changes I had made in my life, there was very little justification for ignoring the strength of that call. How could I be happy settling for any less? What would I be willing to sacrifice?

Agii and I had been in regular contact since we had said goodbye at Chinggis Khaan International Airport. He called me one morning, just a few days after I made it back home. I cried tears of joy when I realized that he felt the same way I did. We ended up speaking by phone or Skype at least once a week for the next ten months. We made tentative plans to be together again.

I spent the next ten months trying to purge myself of a life in Los Angeles that I had become very fond of. I sold and gave away the things I had surrounded myself with, the things that filled my home and that I had always believed defined me. What I came to realize, as I revisited memories of acquiring these things, was that they were monuments to my past. I didn't need them to stand in for me anymore. I was happy with who I was presently, without needing collections to legitimize myself. Every experience had made its contribution, but not every experience needed artifacts to preserve their memory.

The horse I had sacrificed so much to make mine, who had given me so much more than I could ever give to him, and who had become the most meaningful part of my life, was probably the hardest to let go. I was in denial about not being able to take him with me. After much hand-wringing and tears, the perfect buyer came along. He now lives the life he was destined to live, if he wasn't meant to live it with me.

The life I'd known was leaving me in bits and pieces. I cried, I reminisced, and I had lapses of regret, but above it all I felt myself getting closer to feeling whole. As I cleared away the clutter of who I had always believed I was, I was able to get a better look at who I had become and I saw how much room I had made to keep growing.

My plans with Agii became more and more concrete as my house emptied and my debts were cleared. We talked about how we spent our days apart, but we talked more about a future together. Our Skype sessions were aided by Heegii. Speaking through a third party took getting used to, but we were able to build on what we had started in Mongolia.

Eventually, February arrived, and it was time for me to go. I'd purchased my plane ticket, and said my goodbyes. I was eager to get "home" again. I packed everything I had left into nine giant suitcases and went on my way to start a new life in Mongolia.

After a day of being stuck at Russia's Sheremetyevo airport, I finally made it back to Ulaanbaatar. I hadn't showered in three days, and I was hung over from half a bottle of duty-free whiskey I had shared with another delayed passenger, but I came alive again when our plane touched down. Agii had waited patiently, and was there beyond the doors of the customs checkpoint, as nervous and ecstatic as I was.

We drove to Darkhan to start our life together. His family was waiting for us when we got to our one-bedroom apartment on the first floor of a Soviet-era complex. I was received as a new bride in a traditional reception, and his family was eager to meet this stranger who had come such a long way to be with their Agii. It was the warmest, most loving start I could have imagined. Milk was poured on the threshold, ensuring a clean, fresh start to our life together. Each family member, eldest to youngest, embraced me with an inhale of each cheek, and the matriarchs rushed me to the bedroom to dress me in a new cashmere sweater, camel-wool vest, and the white-and-red beaded headdress of a bride. I was shy and exhausted, but followed along.

We were married in May. My parents and two dear friends came out for the wedding and to see where I was living.

I gave birth to our daughter at the local hospital in December. While my own mother wasn't able to be there, every single woman in Agii's family was there to support, teach, and care for me.

Not a single thing about my life today is what I would have imagined before I first stepped foot in Mongolia. I learned to let go, give up the reins, and trust in myself and the world around me. I wrapped my head around the idea that dreams can be your present. Friends have said that I've inspired them to take more risks, and to do a better job of listening to their hearts. I wish that they could let go completely, but I also know what it takes to get there. I tell them there's no rush. Whatever's on the other side of trust will wait.

Michelle Borok is an American living in Darkhan, Mongolia with her husband and daughter. She moved to Mongolia from Los Angeles in 2012. When she's not editing The UB Post, or teaching English, she's spending time in the countryside with her Mongolian family. She writes about her life in Mongolia at Wonton Cruelty and also contributes to Giant Robot, Roads & Kingdoms, and other arts and culture websites.

AN AWKWARD PHONE CALL

BY CHRISTINE TAN

I 'M in bed at 12:20 pm, a perfectly fine hour to be in bed when your husband is away on assignment and you spent a sleepless Shanghai night watching the entire third season of *Downton Abbey* and crying over a baby's birth and a mother's death and good storytelling. A harsh buzzing from the nightstand informs me that my cell phone is alive with the desire of Someone Seeking Christine. The unknown number flashes, a random string of digits that mean nothing to me though my somewhat Asperger's mind tries, in that split second before I answer, to discern some meaningful pattern in the digits.

"Hello? *Wei?*" I say, prepared to end the call if it's a telemarketer with some great deal I might contemplate falling for if only I were fluent in Mandarin Chinese.

"Is this Chen Hui Ling."

If there is an inflection in his voice that makes this statement a question, it is lost on me. I am too surprised by this lightly accented, firm male voice speaking my Chinese name, a piece of personal information no one uses except Ma and Pa. He repeats my Chinese name, and what can you say to a strange voice that asks if that private Chinese name is yours, the three components rolling off his tongue like he possesses it, like he relishes that knowledge, that he is almost absolutely sure that you are she and he has found you?

"Ah, yes. That's… that's me?"

"Good," he says. I wait for him to speak some more but all I hear is background noise and anxiety. Fast, heavy breathing. Fingernails tapping against a desk. Somewhere, someone sneezes, a brazen sneeze that ricochets through the twenty-eight floors of my building. I imagine a phlegmy old man in apartment 1901, wearing a white singlet, perched on a stool in front of his TV, a poodle panting beside him. But the man on the other end of the line—him, I can't picture at all.

"Hello? Are you there?" I say this softly, tentatively. I sense that his confidence is gone, as if he had prepped himself for only one moment, and now that it's over—I've answered the phone, and it is me indeed—he's not quite sure how to proceed.

"Do you remember me?" he finally asks, and there's a desperation that makes him repeat the question. "Do you remember me?"

Am I supposed to remember you? I wonder. *What have you done, what have we done, that would oblige me to remember this voice calling from a number that hasn't been important enough for me to save?* I'm silent, and he says it again: "Remember me?"

"I'm sorry, I don't."

"I am David." He murmurs something in Mandarin: *I thought you would remember me.* My mind starts to drift the way it does, musing about how this Chinese man with an English name is seeking a foreigner out with her Chinese name. He forces a laugh but can't mask a sigh, and I suddenly understand that there must be romantic intent here, something to do with love and hope and dates and possibilities for holding hands or sex or marriage—that is the only reason for this call and his nervous laugh.

I panic at this realization. Did we hook up somewhere? Did I meet him in a French Concession bar, did he buy me a drink, did we sidle up to each other and put our hands on each other, did I do something I should regret? But I'm shaking my head as soon as I think this, rolling my eyes at my inner drama queen who secretly wishes for a juicy past. Instead, I was practical, unadventurous, a proper Chinese Malaysian daughter who embraced the role. No nights out, no dancing, no drunken fumbles in corners with strange men. Just one Mr. Right and a diamond ring two years later, a different kind of adventure.

"I met you two years ago," he says, snapping me out of my thoughts, prodding me to remember our history. "At Wujiaochang. You lived near there. I work in a language school, do you remember?"

There it is, his "do you remember" again, as if the more he repeats it, the sooner I will recall who he is. Give me more clues, I say, and he repeats *Wujiaochang, language school, two years ago.* But his repetition appears to work because the memory does come, though it is vague at first, like many memories of my first year in Shanghai, that time of uncertainty and hesitation and change.

*

In my mind's eye I see myself in a black coat on the corner of Zhengtong Lu and Songhu Lu, waiting for the light to change. It is April 2010 and I am standing with a guy I am very attracted to. We've just had Thai food for lunch, the green curry still burning my tongue. This is date number—ten? eleven? I can't remember—and I haven't slept with him, and I wonder if I ever will. I've never slept with anybody in the modern sense, declining romance for a path that included global travel and two master's degrees. But then I came to shiny, otherworldly Shanghai, and felt something I hadn't experienced living in Kuala Lumpur, Toronto, or London: the complete freedom of being in the majority, just another dark-haired speck in the crowd as long as I didn't open my mouth. The city moved at such a fast pace and heaved with such a seemingly endless flow of humanity that, for the first time in my life, I was certain I couldn't avoid meeting The One. Those first two months here, I daydreamed about my tall, tan, brown-eyed future partner-in-crime.

This guy beside me is short, pasty, and blue-eyed; this is irony's jest. *This can't be him*, I thought, initially fighting the attraction. *He's not Chinese.* But I've read enough to know that good things rarely come in predictable packages, especially in a peripatetic life. I like spending time with him and he makes me laugh, so here we are, slowly taking a chance, standing together, but also apart: I'm still careful to keep my distance, not wanting to force an intimacy just yet, no brushing of arm against arm or my breasts against his back. I'm sneaking looks at this man who will become my husband when I feel a strong grip on my shoulder.

I whirl around, ready to snarl, but a pleasant face smiles at me. Wavy black hair, bright round eyes, nose and lips like mine. He has flyers in his hand, and he asks me in Mandarin whether I want to enroll at an English school. It is early enough in my China life that I'm still excessively proud of my English, and I tell him I speak it fluently, thank you very much, and turn away.

I can't find my date. I stand on tiptoes and scan the crowd that's suddenly appeared before me, looking for a curly brown head amongst a sea of black. The man with the flyers is still watching me from two arms' length away; he reaches for my shoulder once more to get my attention, and peppers with me questions in English: where are you from, what do you do? His eyes are earnest, his smile sincere; he is good-looking, I think, too good-looking to be working this corner. His attention seems harmless and friendly and when he thrusts his business card in my face, I reluctantly accept it with both hands, not wanting to be rude. Overly mindful of Chinese etiquette, I quickly hand him mine in return, a simple scrap of off-white cardboard with my cell phone number, my Chinese name, and an email address I rarely use. "Let's keep in touch," he calls out when I finally spot the one I'm looking for and walk away.

David called me three days later. I was at my new boyfriend's apartment. We were a couple now; we'd settled on that. Back then I immediately recognized the man on the phone, his face and that hand on my shoulder still fresh in my mind. "Let's go out," he said, "let's meet again." Clear, direct, a little too commanding for my liking. I might have agreed if I hadn't been sitting on the same couch that I'm sitting on now as I write this. I might have said *why not?* if I hadn't been cuddled up against the same man I said "I do" to seven months ago. But if I'd been single, I might also have said the same thing: "No, thank you. I don't think so. But thanks for calling, have a good weekend." Because he was too eager, too persistent, too unnerving. "But I think we should meet now, soon," he'd repeated before I firmly said goodbye.

He kept calling that week. After the first few calls—*Let's go out, let's meet again*—I stopped answering. Why should I? I'd said no. I'd been polite. We'd had nothing more than a three-minute conversation on a busy street corner, honking cars and yelling children punctuating that brief exchange. Surely I hadn't led him on in three minutes. Surely he knew that handing him my business card was a mere act of politeness, not a foreign harlot's come-on. Had I made a cultural mistake? I fumed, and my boyfriend told me to calm down. David finally stopped calling, and that was that.

*

Now, two and a half years later, he is back. "Are you in Shanghai?" he asks. "Maybe we can hang out and have dinner. Where are you? What are you doing now?"

"Yes, I'm in Shanghai," I hear myself say.

"I can cook for you, would you like that?" he asks.

"Um, well," I say.

"You are very free these days, aren't you?" he says, pressing on.

How does he know this? Can he tell I'm in bed at noon? He's starting to scare me when he says, "Surely you're not busy now, let's see each other." He speaks quickly and seems to gain confidence as he says these things to me, these things that really make no sense since we're strangers. We've never known each other. He can't know how I feel.

My bedside lamp flickers and I'm distracted again, slowly turning my head to the right. The copy of *The Blue Jay's Dance: A Memoir of Early Motherhood* by Louise Erdrich is still sitting on the narrow table, the little blue bird on the cover solemnly staring back at me. My husband gave me that book the night he returned from a work trip to his native Minneapolis. "I got it from the bookstore owned by Louise herself," he said. "Her sister sold it to me, offered her congratulations, and laughed at the surprise on my face. 'You're not the first father-to-be who's come looking for this book,' she explained. And that's when it hit me, how real this is." He stroked my back as I happily flipped through the pages, planning to read it before my early motherhood began.

I never finished the book.

David is waiting for a reply.

"I can't meet you. I'm very busy," I say, staring at my pajama bottoms. My head pounds from last night's marathon. "I have a lot of work."

"Really?" He doesn't believe me. "What do you do?"

Only one thing, one lie, comes to mind. "I'm a writer." I think of my abandoned blog, which I ran from in panic after an anonymous hate-filled message about the eventual rape and murder of traitorous Asian women like me and our filthy mixed-blood monsters escaped my blog filters and left me sobbing for days, images of bloody, bleeding children haunting my dreams and exacerbating my depression in the months when my empty body felt most raw. I think of my incomplete manuscript, the sixty thousand words that need so many more. "I write now," I hear myself saying, wishing it were true.

"Ah, okay," he says.

I wonder why I am still talking to him, prolonging this awkward, pointless thing.

"Well, where are you?" he asks again as if he has a right to know, and I don't want to do this anymore.

"I'm at home with my husband. I got married." There's another long silence before a bright *Congratulations!* rings out. Maybe I'm imagining that it's tinged with hurt. David says my husband and I can both come over and we'll all cook together like one happy, mixed-up family. I don't think he even knows what he's saying. I gently tell him that I'm sorry. "Take care and goodbye, okay?" And though he still asks me, begs me to keep in touch and call him, I hang up. I hold my breath, waiting for another call, a follow-up text, but there's nothing.

*

I crawl out of bed and jam my feet into my furry slippers, walking through the home that hasn't felt like a home since the day Dr. Fu, a middle-aged Chinese woman with stilted English and a stern expression, smeared jelly on my belly then coolly informed me that my baby had no heartbeat and had stopped developing an estimated three weeks prior. Her sentences had combined into a sad haiku:

> *Baby far too small*
> *No movement in the belly*
> *Definitely gone*

To miscarry at any time is difficult. Miscarrying in China in the Year of the Dragon, however, seems especially cruel. Baby fever is high. People long for a child that belongs to the Chinese zodiac's most powerful, dramatic, auspicious sign. I was probably one of a handful who hadn't purposely set out to conceive a lucky baby, but nonetheless I felt proud and blessed. I tapped on my stomach nearly every morning, imagining that I was communicating with my daughter through an infant Morse code. *Tap tap,* how are you this morning, kiddo? *Tap tap,* thanks for not making mommy throw up.

My final ultrasound was in a hospital so packed with radiant dragon mamas-to-be that I waited three hours to confirm my empty uterus. For months I felt like I couldn't escape the countless articles reminding couples to conceive by a certain date to ensure their babies will be born before the Year of the Snake takes over, because who wants a snake if they can have a lucky little dragon? *Lucky, dragon babies are lucky.* I hear this so often that I'm becoming superstitious, suspecting that my dragon baby's demise means I am cursed. If dragon children are bringers of good fortune, surely the loss of mine is a bad omen, all my good luck wrenched away.

*

I wonder about David's luck. Two and a half years since that day on the corner. Something must have happened to him in that time, the kind of life event that compels someone to dig through a collection of old business cards, looking for a connection from a three-minute conversation on a crowded sidewalk years back in Yangpu district. I imagine a recent broken love affair, and a deep loneliness as he lies in bed each night, thinking that all you need to be happy is someone beside you. I can't help David, and I'm sorry. I hope he finds the connection he's looking for, but we both know it's not going to be from a married woman with a different kind of hurting heart.

Christine Tan has lived in Canada, Malaysia, Singapore, and England. A graduate of the London School of Economics-Fudan

University program in Global Media and Communications, she has written for CNN Travel, Matador Network, chinaSMACK, and The Atlantic. She and her husband currently divide their time between Shanghai, Kuala Lumpur, and Minneapolis. www.shanghaishiok. com.

HOW TO MARRY A MOONIE

By Catherine Rose Torres

ONCE, at a wedding party, I joined a table where people were talking about how expensive it had gotten to get married. "Of course, you could always go for a Moonie wedding," a friend quipped. Everyone laughed except me, and I saw my friend throw an anxious glance my way. Afterwards, she came up to me while I was getting some sweets from the dessert table and apologized for the joke. I looked at the wedding cake and imagined how nice the chocolate frosting would look on her lilac dress. I was not offended by her joke, or at least, not as much as I was by her apparent expectation that I should be. As if being Korean like Reverend Moon, the founder of the Unification Church, which is notorious for its mass weddings, automatically made my husband a Moonie.

Jay and I met in 1999, a few years after news reports began circulating about Filipino women being lured to South Korea to marry Moonie husbands, and the term *moonie* came to mean all Korean men seeking mail-order brides from poor countries like the Philippines. But I expected my friends to know the difference—to know I wasn't mail-order bride material. My husband didn't find my name and photograph among hundreds of other women in a catalogue or a website. We met in Japan when we were both still in college and had earned places in a month-long cultural exchange program with thirty-four other students from ten different countries by writing essays on "Asian coexistence." Looking back, it's suspiciously like one of those reality shows that are a dime a dozen these days. The organizers were probably thinking, *great essays, kids, now let's see if you can walk the talk and coexist.* And we did. We coexisted so well, the three dozen of us, that by summer's end, there were several international couples in the group.

Jay and I were not among the "official" love teams, although there was a strong undercurrent of attraction between us from the start. I was drawn to his quiet and reserve—he'd be engrossed in a book or magazine while the other guys clowned around. Later, I would learn that he'd just finished his mandatory military service, which I think might account for his seeming seriousness and maturity. In fact, he and the other male delegate from Korea were the oldest in the group (Jay was twenty-four and Jun twenty-five, while most of us were between nineteen and twenty-two) since they had to serve twenty-six months in the military between their college years. I myself am the bookish, introverted type, so I guess you could say Jay and I were compatible. This shared aspect of our personality was probably the thing that kept us from coming out as a couple, although we were the only one that would eventually get married among the love teams in the group.

Our marriage took place seven years later in Changwon, Jay's hometown, in spring. The winter before, I had finally met Jay's parents. Before leaving our hotel in Busan, Jay taught me how to do the ceremonial kowtow, which is traditionally done before your elders. You begin by standing with your legs together, then place your right leg forward, get down on your left knee as if genuflecting, place the other knee alongside it on the floor, and bow down with your hands in front of you, your forehead brushing the back of your hand. Jay and I practiced together, he reflexively, having had thirty years of practice, and I with the dead seriousness of a klutz practicing a dance routine for PE class. Thankfully, the whole thing consisted of no more than five steps so I soon got the hang of it, though I still had to count under my breath to keep time.

A friend of Jay's, together with his pretty wife and their adorable baby girl, offered to drive us up to Changwon from Busan, and the animated conversation they kept up during the ride, with an occasional English phrase thrown in for my benefit, helped keep my mind off my impending meeting with my future in-laws. An hour later, Jay announced that we were in Changwon. I felt my stomach churning as he pointed out the local sights. I was white as a radish being salted for kimchi by the time we pulled up in front of a two-story brick house on a street of lookalike dwellings. A small middle-aged woman with a short perm stepped out of the gate. The wife of Jay's friend, probably sensing my nervousness, led me to Jay's mother, who guided me up the stairs to the living room, where his unsmiling father waited to receive our bows. At Jay's cue, we went through the synchronized movements that I'd carefully rehearsed, and as I touched my forehead to my hand on the floor, I wished I could stay in that pose forever so I wouldn't have to look up and face his grave-looking father. Fortunately, I escaped his scrutiny because Jay's mother hurried off to the kitchen to prepare our food and I followed, offering, in sign language, to help her. Jay's parents didn't speak English, nor I Korean, so this was how we would communicate for the rest of our visit.

That same day, we all went to a fortune-teller to have our wedding date chosen. I was surprised when we reached the place to see an electronic signboard hanging from a wall. Red LED lights flashed the number of the client whose turn it was to be told about his marriage prospects or the odds of hitting the lotto jackpot. I wondered if it was a ploy to make people think that the guy was much sought after—after all, we were the only ones there when we visited. There was no queue of fidgeting customers, much less a jostling crowd that would necessitate an automated queue system. Instead, we were ushered right into the fortune-teller's inner sanctum. Jay and I were asked to sit on the floor across from him as he drew figures on a piece of paper with a calligraphy brush, all the while shooting questions to my fiancé and future in-laws. Not understanding a word of what was being said, I stole glances around me, taking in the dark wooden chests inlaid with mother-of-pearl, the offerings of oranges and other fruits on top of what looked like an altar, the wisps of smoke wafting up from the incense sticks. The guy didn't measure up to my notion of a seer. I had expected a wizened old man with wild white hair garbed in roughly spun robes, whose eyes, peering from behind a curtain of wrinkles, would pierce your very soul. You would have dismissed this guy for a salaryman if you had seen him on the street dressed in a suit and tie.

After what felt like an eternity, our salaryman/soothsayer folded up the piece of paper and handed it to Jay's mother. As we slipped out of the house, or rather, his mansion—Korean fortune-tellers clearly had their bread well-buttered—Jay explained to me that he had chosen the 16th of April the following year for our wedding. Later, I would find out that this was Easter Sunday. It helped salve my guilt over the superstitious manner in which our wedding date had been chosen, and the fact that it wasn't going to be a church wedding. Of course, it didn't change the fact that April 16th was barely four months away.

Another bride-to-be would have balked at that short time for preparations. Many brides I know are hands-on, obsessive-compulsive even, planning every detail of their big day, from the shade and texture of the paper to be used for the invitations down to the type of sauce for the pasta to be served at the reception. I was the complete opposite: I might have been a spectator at my own wedding. And in a sense, I was. I'd never been to a Korean wedding, and didn't know how it was done. So I let Jay's family take me to Lotte Department Store and pick out a dress for me to wear at the reception. I let his sister, a nurse, give me vitamins through an IV drip on the eve of the wedding, supposedly to get my skin glowing as befits a radiant bride. I looked away from the table outside the wedding hall where the guests formed queues to hand over cash envelopes to one of Jay's relatives, who religiously recorded in a ledger their names and how much they gave—useful, Jay explained to me later, in determining how much to give when it was the guest's turn to be married, or his son or daughter's.

Our wedding had two parts. For the "modern" ceremony, I walked up the aisle in a gown plucked off the wedding hall's rack to the strains of Pachelbel's *Canon*, the one aspect of the wedding that was mine, alone, to decide. It never occurred to me then to complain why I wasn't asked about more aspects of the wedding. I guess, at the time, I was just thankful that there was even a wedding at all, since I wasn't sure that Jay's father would allow it. Years before, when Jay had wanted to visit me in Manila, his father had opposed the trip and Jay had left their home. This might also be why the proceedings held a vague sense of unreality for me, especially the traditional ceremony that followed.

For this part of the wedding, I had to wear an embroidered red silk robe over my made-to-order *hanbok*, plus a headdress that made it impossible to do the ceremonial bow before my newly minted in-laws without the aid of two of Jay's friends. Things got stranger and stranger as the ceremony progressed. Jay's mother had to dance with a tray on her head. Jay had to carry me piggyback. My mother-in-law had to throw some chestnuts and jujubes over her shoulder while my husband and I stood behind her with a piece of cloth stretched out between us. My smile turned into a frown as the meaning of the ritual was explained to me: no, we wouldn't be getting prizes for the three chestnuts and three jujubes that we managed to catch; the number of chestnuts that fell on the cloth was how many daughters we would have, and the jujubes, sons.

The traditional rites left me with mixed feelings. On the one hand, I was grateful that our friends, including some from our summer in Tokyo who'd flown in from different countries, were allowed to witness what was traditionally reserved for family members. This meant a lot to me since only my parents were there from my side of the family. And I could tell our friends enjoyed the spectacle, as if they were watching scenes from a Korean period drama. But I didn't want our marriage to be a spectacle. I didn't want it to seem any different from, even any more interesting than, other marriages just because Jay and I held different passports.

I was relieved when the ceremony ended. I was eager for us to leave for our honeymoon in the Philippines, where, I felt sure, things would be different—normal, that is. By then, most of the guests had had their fill from the buffet, and after nibbling some morsels and having more pictures taken, we found ourselves in the silver Chrysler PT Cruiser a friend of Jay's had lent to us as a gift, caught in a bottleneck of wedding cars bound for Gimhae Airport, where we were to catch our flight. Apparently, our fortune-teller had consulted the same almanac as hundreds of others in the business. Of course, you could say that they prescribed the same wedding date to hundreds of other couples because they were reading from the same stars. So we stood in the departure hall, surrounded by dozens of other newlyweds in their matching "couple shirts." Jay did not insist that we dress alike, to my relief, as that would have been the point where I'd put my foot down.

Looking back, I am struck by how acquiescent I was. Having seen my sisters and several friends plan their weddings, I know it's usually the bride who runs the show, especially before "wedding planner" became an acceptable answer to the question "What do you want to be when you grow up?". Perhaps I knew it was part of the package of marrying a foreigner in a foreign land. Or perhaps I simply didn't know enough Korean to express my preferences or argue with anyone about theirs.

Jay had majored in English Language and Literature in college and was posted on a US base in Seoul for his mandatory military service, so his English often surprised people used to the stilted English of most Koreans. The downside of this was that I wasn't forced to learn Korean, and he, Tagalog, since we had a common second language to fall back on. To my credit, I took basic Korean as an elective in my last year of college, and attempted a few times to continue learning through books and CDs. But though I could attest to the simplicity and logic of the Korean alphabet, Hangeul, being able to read and write it to this day, speaking and under-standing the language is a different matter. I've failed to progress beyond the basic greetings in that department.

Still, my schooling in Korean culture continued, conducted by means of sign language. Omonim, my mother-in-law, showed me how to make cabbage kimchi, and cook *doenjang jjiggae, japchae,* and *bulgogi.* I grew accustomed to drinking barley water instead of plain water and snacking on rice cakes instead of pastries. I became an expert at using metal chopsticks and eating off a low table with my legs tucked beneath me in a way that wouldn't give me pins and needles. I learned to keep my camera and film rolls—before I went digital—off the floor, lest they get toasted by the piped-in *ondol* heating.

I met dozens of Jay's relatives, who scrutinized and discussed me openly. At the wedding, it was as if I was in a bubble, beyond their reach. But now, I would be sitting with Jay and I would hear my name spoken loudly by someone across the room. I would turn, thinking they were calling me, but they would simply carry on their conversation. I could have taken umbrage, but it was done so candidly, I could see no reason to take offense. The truth was, part of me was charmed by these people, how unabashed they were, how uninhibited.

Of course, these were the same qualities that feed the image of the ugly Korean. The tourists who chatter (and dress) loudly. The ones who get drunk and curse. With more Koreans coming to the Philippines, I've heard people grumble how rude, coarse, and arrogant they can be. And when they learn that I am married to a Korean, they either pipe down (to resume their ranting later with someone else) or complain louder, as if I were personally responsible for the faults of my husband's compatriots. Even my own relatives had their reservations. Is it true Korean men hit their wives, one of my aunts asked me. Don't they often get smashed? So not only did I have to convince people that my husband was not a Moonie, but also that he wasn't a hooligan.

It makes me wonder if Jay, too, finds himself constantly having to explain me to other people, and if this is something that afflicts only cross-cultural couples. Having married a foreigner, I wonder what it would be like to be married to another Filipino. Is it necessarily simpler, automatically easier? Or do the individual qualities of the other person outweigh, in the end, what his ethnic and cultural background brings to the marriage? But could you divorce the two? Isn't a person what his social milieu makes him? When I come home loaded with grocery bags and Jay does not make a move to relieve me of some of them when he opens the door, I think that a Filipino husband would surely know better. Ditto when we cross the road and he walks on the safer side instead of nearer the oncoming traffic. At the same time, I'm sure there are also times when he slaps his forehead and thinks he should have married a fellow Korean, like when I put too much salt on the kimchi or let it ferment for too long.

But I would be exaggerating if I overdramatize my marriage. The truth is, it is pretty boring if you compare it with what you see in those Korean TV dramas. This surprises, and disappoints, a lot of people. They expect something juicier from an international marriage, nothing short of a culture clash. And when they ask me how we manage it, all I can tell them is that it suits us, me and Jay. There's a word for it in Tagalog: *hiyang*. It means simply that there are people who are naturally suited or inclined towards certain things. Me, I happen to be *hiyang* to a mixed marriage.

There was a proverb my dad used to tell my sisters and me when we were young, which I did not take to heart until I got older: love me, love my dog. And the dog need not be an actual four-legged creature that barks and sheds fur; it is anything that each person brings into the relationship, consciously or not. What is marriage, after all, but a version of those reality shows where they throw people together to see how long they can stand each other? Looking back, I guess this is why I behaved the way I did at our wedding: I was starring in the first episode of my very own reality show.

And in that show, it isn't so much what you are—Filipino or Korean, Martian or Moonie—that matters, but how much maturity and responsibility you have to deal with the consequences of choosing each other for company, instead of someone else. You can call it coexistence, or you can call it love.

Catherine Rose Torres's prose has appeared in anthologies and periodicals in the Philippines, Singapore, and the United States, including The Philippines Graphic, TAYO Literary Magazine, Tomo: Friendship Through Fiction, *and* Motherhood Statements. *Her work as a diplomat has taken her to postings in New Delhi and Singapore, together with her husband, Sohn Suk Joo, a Korean scholar and translator, and their son, Samuel. She is at work on her first collection of short stories.*

HUANGSHAN HONEYMOON

By Jocelyn Eikenburg

I F rain on your wedding day is bad fortune, then what about rain on your honeymoon?

The rainfall began after we checked into a hotel at the foot of Huangshan—Yellow Mountain—in China's Anhui Province. By 9:00 pm, we could still hear the steady drip outside our window. And forecasts expected the rain to last for several more days, well after we had planned to climb the mountain.

Just as the wet weather dampened the landscape outside the window, so it dampened our prospects of actually seeing the mountain. My heart sank every time I imagined the foggy mist surrounding Huangshan, blocking panoramic views of its jagged granite peaks. This ethereal scenery, often captured in classical Chinese paintings, was the epitome of beauty among China's mountains—so much so that according to a Chinese saying, after visiting Huangshan, you need not visit China's Five Great Mountains (or any other mountain, for that matter). Thanks to the showers outside, chances were I would never get to experience Huangshan in all of its beauty.

But the rain was just one more symptom of something gone wrong. It was like my runny nose and headache that had started that evening, the first signs that I had caught the flu, and the odor of sweaty socks that invaded our three-person suite. I felt our bad fortune stemmed from the fact that we had asked Jun's father—who only brought one pair of socks for the entire trip—to join us on our honeymoon.

As I lay in my twin bed that evening, not even my stuffy nose could shield me from the stench of clothing that desperately needed a good wash. I grimaced with every breath.

"This room smells." I said it in English so that the man we both called Laoba, the Chinese term for *father* that Jun and his family preferred, couldn't understand.

"You're tired. You should sleep." My husband Jun always saw beyond my crabby moods to the exhaustion, illness, or even PMS hidden behind my words.

"I can't. I feel horrible... this room feels horrible."

He picked up the box of Tylenol from the nightstand between our beds and handed it to me. "Here, take one."

My husband, who usually cringed when I took painkillers for premenstrual cramps, wanted me to have the Tylenol? I popped a pill out of the package. As I reached for a glass of water, I glanced towards the far end of the room, where Laoba sat on the edge of his bed watching a Chinese news show, still wearing a cheap polyester polo shirt the color of dirty cement. The glare of the TV reflected off his face, still smeared with the sweat and oil that he hadn't bothered to wash off yet. Salt-and-pepper stubble protruded from his upper lip and chin as if he hadn't shaved for days. The very sight of this man in our room, a man who couldn't be bothered to bring more than one pair of socks on a trip, made me burn with frustration. The pill might relieve my symptoms for the evening, but no pill could ever relieve me of a father-in-law who piggybacked on our honeymoon.

I still couldn't believe I had agreed to this.

In China, the government allows every married couple a two-week honeymoon away from work. Jun and I had decided to take our official honeymoon just after he graduated from his master's degree program in psychology in June 2005. But we had been living together since March 2003 in Shanghai, where I worked as a copywriter and we shared an apartment like a married couple. By the time the summer of 2005 arrived, we had already enjoyed our share of honeymoon-like excursions during China's week-long national holidays—from lounging on islands in the azure waters of the Gulf of Thailand, to snorkeling in the ocean off Bali's pristine white beaches. We had also already registered our marriage at the Shanghai Marriage Registry Bureau by then, the equivalent of an engagement to his friends and family, and expected to plan our official wedding ceremony in China in the next few years. So with all of the time we'd spent together, and all of the romantic getaways we already savored, I didn't take our official two weeks of state-sanctioned honeymoon all that seriously. That's why I proposed that we spend our honeymoon a little closer to home, in China. And I suggested Huangshan, a mountain I had been longing to visit from the moment I first moved to China in 1999 to live and work—years before I even met Jun.

But the moment I mentioned it, my husband said, "We should take Laoba with us."

To Jun—and his father—Huangshan wasn't just one of China's ultimate mountain experiences or another big tourist destination to cross off your bucket list. Huangshan was something personal. Laoba could trace his ancestors back to Huizhou, the cultural region that includes Huangshan, and had even grown up in what you could arguably call the foothills of Huangshan. The importance of this was obvious to anyone who visited the family home. In the foyer, flanked by photographs of Laoba's father and mother, hung a gaudy Graceland version of a Huangshan landscape with Day-Glo cranes and the wizened silhouette and windswept branches of the

Welcoming Guests Pine. To Laoba and his son, visiting Huangshan would be like a personal genealogy tour, where part of the thrill came from rediscovering the very lands their predecessors once called home. So how could we possibly travel there without Jun's father?

The American side of me seemed skeptical about this bride's nightmare—taking your father-in-law with you on your honeymoon. Who would actually allow this?

But certain traditional Confucian values weighed upon me. When you're married to a Chinese man, you soon learn the importance of filial piety, perhaps the most pervasive of these values in modern China. Filial piety roughly translates into respect for your parents and ancestors. This value is why it's almost unheard of for Chinese children to put their parents into nursing homes in their old age. It's also why you might hear of sons in China who send money to their parents to support them. But supporting your parents depends on what they really need in life. While Laoba received a generous pension after his retirement from teaching, he rarely had the opportunity to travel—a favorite pastime of his not shared by his wife, a woman prone to motion sickness who preferred staying at home. Jun understood that offering a chance to travel, especially to a place so close to his heart, was perhaps the most filial thing we could do for Laoba.

Instead of protesting Jun's suggestion, I tucked away my American doubts behind a smile. "Yes, what a great idea!"

The truth is, my past with Laoba weighed upon me as much as filial piety itself. I thirsted for an opportunity to prove to Laoba that I could be a filial daughter-in-law. The memories of three years before still haunted me—a time when this man had serious reservations about my relationship with his son.

I'll never forget the way Jun bounded into our apartment in Hangzhou, China back in September 2002. He had just returned from a week-long stay with his family, who lived in a rural village in Zhejiang province only hours away from Hangzhou.

"I'm so glad you're back," I said as I hugged him. "So, how did it go?" I thought I didn't even need to ask, certain I could read the answer in his grin.

"I told my parents that we're dating," he said.

His words startled me, and not without reason. My previous Chinese boyfriend never had the chance to tell his parents about us—he claimed they could never accept him dating a foreign woman. Their opposition to having foreigners in the family forced him to break off our relationship in June 2002, an experience still fresh in my mind when Jun returned on that September day.

"So, uh, what did they say?"

"Laoba said, 'You can be friends with a foreign woman, but not date her.'" Jun smiled as he said it, as though he had actually returned home with his parents' blessing.

My heart pounded as tears welled up in my eyes.

But Jun put his arm around me. "Don't worry, it's fine, I'm not leaving."

"No, no, it's not fine," I said, shaking my head as I sobbed. I couldn't get past the parental opposition with my previous boyfriend. How would Jun and I ever get past his father?

But in fact, we did. In the months that followed, Jun and I stayed together. And in February 2003, Jun brought me home with him to spend Chinese New Year with his family, a visit that put me face-to-face with the very man who opposed our relationship.

If you've ever been married, engaged, or in a serious relationship, then you know just how nerve-wracking it is to meet your potential in-laws for the first time. But just imagine doing that in a different culture and language, with people who already have rather unflattering preconceived notions about you (in China, people often think foreign women are as loose and licentious as the seductresses and hookers in Hollywood movies). So when I walked in the door and saw Laoba, who nodded at me with a guarded smile, my stomach churned, my chest tightened, and my heart even seemed to palpitate.

For the next few days, Laoba appeared as cold as the near-freezing temperatures in their unheated home. But then, on Jun's suggestion, I showed his father an album of my family photos—from trips to Yosemite and Barcelona to my college graduation day. That photo album somehow magically flipped a switch within this man, and he lit up with all of the endearing wonder of a child. Soon, he started spinning tales of his childhood in Tanxia Village in the foothills of Huangshan, and shared with me his very own pencil sketches that immortalized the town he cherished as a boy. With every moment by his side, I could feel relief pouring over me like the afternoon sunshine on those winter days. How could this man, who now seemed to embrace this new relationship with me, be the very same person who had once threatened my own relationship with Jun?

As Jun and I rode back to Hangzhou in a rickety minibus that creaked and groaned with every bump, and had barely enough heat to thaw my numb toes, the thought of how much progress I made with Jun's father warmed me—and left me smiling all the way back.

"I still can't believe that was the same man who said I couldn't date you," I said to Jun while sitting on the bus.

"He probably just thought, you know, all foreigners are a little *luan*," or promiscuous. "But my father realized you were different, that you weren't what he thought."

I had come to a similar realization when I first arrived in China and suddenly noticed all the handsome Chinese men on the streets. As a college student, I had never entertained the thought of dating any of the Asian men I met. Was it simply because I studied at an overwhelmingly white university in West Virginia with few Asians? Or did I have some subconscious bias against dating Asian men, somehow believing they weren't attractive? All I know is I just shared cafeteria tables or cups of tea with them, and never gave them a chance to transcend the boundaries of friendship. Only when I came to China did things really change, just as only when I came to Jun's home did his father really change his mind.

But there in that hotel at the foot of Huangshan, the tight, uncomfortable feeling that spread through my body was more than just my growing illness and exhaustion, or some reaction to the lingering stench of dirty socks. Before when I visited with Laoba, we interacted with each other in predictable and brief moments—a talk over lunch or dinner, a short discussion in his study as he unveiled a new painting or drawing, a rooftop conversation as we watched the stars come out. I could always get him to flash a youthful grin, or break into a story about life growing up in Tanxia Village. It felt so easy to be the good, filial daughter-in-law—the antithesis of what he considered foreign women to be—when I only spent a few minutes with him here and there.

Yet as I lay in bed with tissues strewn all around me, only moments away from denouncing Laoba's personal hygiene, I realized just how worried I was. Would I lose my temper and suddenly yell at him, shattering the fragile image of the good, filial daughter-in-law I had worked so hard to cultivate? Would I regret that we brought Laoba along with us after all? These questions weighed upon me like my headache, and made sleep even more elusive that evening.

*

When we arrived at the foot of Huangshan the following morning, the mist of rain that clouded the forest canopy somehow echoed the exhaustion that seemed to cloud my body. I shivered even though I wore a raincoat with a fleece jacket and long-sleeved shirt underneath it. My symptoms now included a sore throat and clogged sinuses—worsened, no doubt, by a restless night of tossing and turning.

"I don't think I can climb it. I feel too sick," I said.

I felt a pang of regret and let a tear go. In the past, I had ruined many a family vacation when I balked at climbing to the top, including on New England's White Mountain and at the granite cliffs of Yosemite Valley. Before, I had always claimed I felt too tired and lacked the strength to move on. Yet a part of me knew that, deep down, I probably could have climbed anything if I believed I could. Still, as we stood at the foot of Huangshan, I had to admit that my illness sapped me of something—strength or will, I couldn't tell.

"Don't worry, we'll take the cable car." Jun soothed me by rubbing my shoulder and smiling, more concerned for my health than our vacation plans gone awry.

But Laoba said nothing in response, and my nerves remained unsettled. Had I ruined his journey to Huangshan? What did he think of me now, a daughter-in-law who was robbing him of the opportunity to finally climb his beloved mountain?

Those worries followed me as we waited for nearly an hour in the serpentine queue for the cable car, which most tourists rode up the mountain. I stood nearly catatonic in that line as I listened to Jun and his father chatting away in their local language, a Chinese dialect I still struggled to understand. The mist clung to Huangshan with tenacity, translating into a visibility of only a few yards at best. Our one day to summit the mountain and the heavens responded with the worst-possible viewing conditions. Was this a sort of punishment for all my unfilial moments, when I had privately chastised my father-in-law over those socks?

The three of us, along with a handful of other tourists, finally squeezed into the cable car, which quickly glided up into the air. Fifty feet up, a hundred feet up, and beyond: it soared into the sky, dangling from the cable. Below us sat the mountain fringed in clouds like a cotton-candy trim. Here and there, jagged spires—which looked like pale yellow sandstone—poked through the clouds, dotted with trees whose trunks seemed no larger than toothpicks from our vantage point.

As I gazed down at the scenery and realized the actual height of our car, I felt a wave of nausea, and my heart started to pound. My fear of heights, something that hadn't kept me from ascending Shanghai's Jinmao Tower a little over a year before, suddenly paralyzed me in that cable car. Worries flooded my mind: What if the car snapped off the cable? What if we tumbled onto those sharp ridges below us? What if this was the last thing I ever saw? My breaths became more shallow and hurried, and my palms started to sweat.

"Oh god, this is too high up!"

"Don't worry, it's okay, you're safe," said Jun. But Laoba stood between him and me, and so many other tourists packed the cable car that Jun couldn't put his arm around me or hold my hand.

Suddenly, two hands reached out for mine. "No problem, you're fine!"

Laoba. When I looked up at him, he flashed me an avuncular smile, one that reminded me of my father when he wanted to soothe my fears. And he even stroked my hands in an attempt to comfort me.

Whenever I saw Laoba at the family home, he never touched his wife, children, or any other relatives in public—not to kiss, not to hold hands, not even to suggest the affection that he held for them in his heart. Yet he held my hands without concern for what anyone else in the cable car thought about it.

I could feel my heart hammering against my chest. I had no idea if it was the height or the shock that Laoba held my hands.

"*Duibuqi,*" I said to him—*sorry* in Mandarin—as I felt a tear fall down my cheeks. Sorry for making a spectacle of myself in the cable car. Sorry that I forced us to take this cable car in the first place. Sorry for ruining the vacation—a vacation that, in some of my worst moments, I actually believed he had ruined for us. Sorry for not being the daughter-in-law he had hoped for.

But Laoba smiled as if I had never needed to apologize for anything—as if he couldn't have been happier than to be sitting right next to me, holding my hands. "*Ai*, don't be polite."

Jun once told me that no one ever said "thank you," "you're welcome," or even "I love you" in his home. These things were implied and understood, because you were part of a family and that's what you did for one another. And somehow, the way Laoba took my hands in his, the way he smiled at me—despite everything I had done—said everything I needed to know.

So I leaned on Laoba's shoulder, closed my eyes, and rested for the remainder of the ride up to the summit.

*

"Laoba, did you leave your socks in the bathroom?"

We had just checked into a guesthouse at the foot of Huangshan. It was one day after our cable car ride to the summit, where we spent the night before walking down by foot and catching a bus to this guesthouse. It offered one of the most comfortable rooms of our trip—soft maroon comforters and clean beige carpeting in the bedroom, and glistening marble countertops and white tiles in the bathroom. But I felt certain that a damp—and rank—pair of grey socks next to the bathroom sink didn't come standard with the booking.

"*Ai*, I washed them." Jun's father called out from the bedroom, where he had been lounging on one of those soft comforters while watching the news channel on China Central Television.

"But did you use soap?"

"No need!"

I had lived long enough with his son—who had inherited the very same penchant for smelly feet—to know that I needed to dispense with the politeness in this moment. "If we don't wash these with soap, I think the odor will make me faint."

Laoba giggled with embarrassment—a giggle that sounded a lot like Jun whenever I teased him about his feet—as he wandered over to the bathroom. "I'll wash again."

But before he could pick up the pair of grey socks, I snatched them away. "No, I'll wash them."

"*Aiya*, no need. It's trouble!"

I met his glance with a smile—the smile of a daughter-in-law who didn't mind holding some of the most disgusting grey socks she ever encountered in her bare hands. "No trouble. Now, go, get out of here! Watch the news!"

I shooed him out of the bathroom with my free hand until he retreated to the bedroom. Maybe it was a little rude to throw him out like that. But as I looked at the grey socks in my hand—and the bar of soap on the counter that I would use to scrub them clean—I realized that, even if it was rude and the socks were crude, I had never felt closer to Laoba.

Jocelyn Eikenburg is the writer behind Speaking of China, *a unique blog focused on love, family, and relationships in China which was inspired by her own marriage to a Chinese national. Her essay "Red Couplets" was published in the anthology* Unsavory Elements and other true stories of foreigners on the loose in China. *A Cleveland, Ohio native, Jocelyn discovered her passion for the written word while living and working in China, and has resided in the cities of Zhengzhou, Hangzhou, and Shanghai.*

THE RAINIEST SEASON

By India Harris

"**W**HAT the hell is going on here?" I shout, slamming my dive bag onto the welcome mat of our small rental house in the Philippines. My American husband and Filipina housemaid stare down at me from the loft bedroom, surprise flashing across their faces. Why are they hanging the master bed sheets on the indoor clothesline together?

"What would possess you to wash the sheets in the middle of the afternoon?" I direct the question at Edward, for I can never bring myself to yell at this ditzy maid. The queen-sized sheets, the only ones we own, drip water onto the living room floor. Does she not have the sense to spin them dry? And why on earth would she do laundry during a brownout? *What does this stupid girl think we will sleep on tonight?*

I dislike this maid, cringing at her careless rattling of my plates in the kitchen sink and the sight of her mop whirling in circles that always seem to be within earshot of private conversations. Is there a reason why my favorite ceramic dishes are now chipped and cracked? Does she resent our refrigerator full of food? Hate me for a closet bursting with clothes? Sense my antipathy? Or does she simply not care?

Baby has been with us for three months, hired initially to clean up during my family's five-week visit from Canada earlier this year. Now I'm stuck with her, my days carefully regulated by gardening or cooking projects—how can I lie on the sofa reading novels while

Baby crawls across my floors, scrubbing away our dirt? I freely admit that my cleaning skills are no match for the geckoes, spiders, ants, beetles, and tree frogs that seem as enthralled with our tropical house as we are, but I would dearly love to fire this woman who raises every hackle along my neck.

Unfortunately, we are Baby's only source of income. Abandoned by her husband, she is the sole provider for their seven-year-old daughter, so without a legitimate reason to let her go, I must continue to use more glasses and saucepans and cutlery than necessary, manufacturing chores to keep her busy day after day.

"Relax, sweetheart," Edward says, smiling at my angry face. "Is this any way to greet your long-lost husband?"

*

The next five days pass quickly, Edward and I cooking elaborate meals together, walking our silly, energetic puppy along the beach, enjoying quiet time in our pretty white house on the edge of the jungle. I am very much in love with our life here.

Since we sailed into the resort town of Puerto Galera on our ten-meter yacht three years ago, I've grown very attached to this beautiful island, its good-natured people, and the thriving garden I created with my own hands—the sensation of earth under my feet an enormous pleasure after seven years of floating on the back of the Pacific Ocean.

Though I wish he would stay longer, Edward is leaving in the morning for Subic Bay on the main island of Luzon—a seven-hour trip by ferry and car, including a drive through chaotic Manila—where he has spent most of the past two months overseeing minor repairs and general maintenance on *Feisty Lady*. I miss him when he's not here.

Tonight, as chicken bakes in the oven, we sit at the dining table, Edward drinking rum and mango juice, a drink that never bodes well for me.

"How long do you think you'll be away?" I ask.

"I have no idea. A while. Subic is a great place to get work done."

I remind him of my upcoming visa trip to Malaysian Borneo. Foreigners must leave the Philippines at least once a year and my year will end in two months.

Four years ago, over a romantic dinner on a South Pacific island, Edward suggested that we climb Borneo's Mount Kinabalu. It intrigued him, the idea of climbing the tallest mountain in Asia outside of the Himalayas. I had wanted him to join me on this trip and do the climb together, but he is no longer interested. Tonight I tell him that a friend has invited me to visit her in Brunei, which will add a few extra days to my trip, and of course, more money. Is that okay? Yes, it's fine. In the past he's always begrudged me any time away from him. I'm thrilled that he's allowing me to go on this holiday, which will be nearly four weeks long. I'm also grateful that he's being so uncharacteristically generous with his cash.

"Thank you!" I gush.

"Oh, by the way," he says, "I was talking to Baby and she has some sort of painful back problem. I told her she can come with me to Manila tomorrow and see a decent doctor, probably at Asian Hospital. I'll send her back here by bus."

She'll see a doctor on a Saturday? Well, I wasn't aware that Baby has been having any back problems, but the prospect of being rid of her for a day or two makes my spirits soar.

But Edward should not be spending money on a maid.

"Have you forgotten Bing?" I ask. Edward loaned our previous maid enough money to buy new front teeth. Truthfully, I hadn't noticed that hers were missing—I just thought she was too dour to smile. In the end, not only did Bing renege on the loan, she ran off to another island with a married tricycle driver, taking along our spare propane tank and one case of San Miguel beer.

"Once they start expecting handouts, it's the beginning of the end," I remind him. "I can't believe you're going to pay for Baby to have tests at Asian Hospital. Why would you do that?"

"Because she's poor and the fucking doctors on this island are useless. Unlike you, I don't mind helping people out. God, you're such a selfish bitch."

I am shocked at the resentment etched on his face.

*

In celebration of my forty-first birthday, I dive with friends, the four of us on a quest to spot sea horses. Two days have passed since Edward and Baby left. I have no idea how Baby's back is, but she called in sick this morning, a wonderful start to the day.

As I drift through the warm sea, I find it impossible to concentrate on the dive. My mind is on Borneo and climbing that damned mountain; I don't want to do it alone. I decide that I will invite my good friend Isabel to join me on the climb. She is the extremely athletic and adventurous Filipina who taught me to scuba dive eighteen months ago. Yes, Isabel would be the perfect companion.

The sea horses are predictably elusive, but our two dives are lovely, conditions perfect.

Back on shore, I pull out my cell phone, which remains frustratingly silent. Ten years we have been together. Is it too much to ask that Edward phone or text to wish me a happy birthday? Exactly one year ago he threw a lavish party for my fortieth birthday. This year, he has apparently forgotten all about me.

*

Seven weeks have passed since my forgotten birthday. Fully awake now, I climb out of bed and creep downstairs, leaving Edward in what I hope is a very deep sleep. I am determined to find out why my husband has become a rare visitor in our home, why he has emptied most of his clothing from his closet and dresser drawers, why his hair is now being cut so stylishly, why his clothes are new and expensive-looking.

My heart races as I pick up his cell phone and click onto his text inbox. I know that many people read their partners' text messages, but I have never, until this moment, been one of them. My husband has never given me a reason to distrust him—until now.

Far too easily I discover what I had feared. I read shocking messages from girls named Rose and Jasmine, Joy, and of course, Baby. His outbox reveals texts that were written by a new and unrecognizable Edward. Now understanding why he and Baby were washing my bed sheets in the middle of the afternoon, I lay down on the sofa and concentrate on only one thing—breathing.

In the morning, accusations are made; harsh words are spoken.

"But you like blondes!" I scream.

"People change."

"No they don't! They shouldn't! Not like this."

"Don't worry," he says vaguely, "I'll take care of you financially." My wedding ring is removed and Edward walks out the front door and down the front pathway, not looking back. Just like that, as though he were leaving to buy a carton of milk, he walks away from ten years of us, off to his new life, leaving me in his wake.

Edward has often ridiculed the white men who come to the Philippines and take up with young Filipinas. "God, they're stupid," he said.

"Who is stupid? The men or the girls?"

"Both," he replied.

So what happened to change the mind of my introverted, brilliant husband, an electronics engineer who holds two patents?

*

I am being asked to choose what color I would like the living room walls painted. Dante, our Filipino boatman, has taken care of *Feisty Lady* since we arrived in Puerto Galera. His skills are many: he can varnish and paint, change the oil and fuel filters, steer the boat, hoist and take down the sails. Four days ago, on a Sunday morning, Dante quietly knocked on my front door asking for work at the house; he has a family to support and no job.

I have always hated these stark white interior walls, but Edward would never let me paint them. Since he's gone, I guess I can do anything I want now. But what color do I like? It occurs to me that I should call Edward and ask him, but of course, I can't.

Since Edward left, I have found it hard to focus, often climbing the stairs to the bedroom only to forget the purpose of my trip. Familiar words and names regularly elude me. Once when I needed milk from the refrigerator I found my head in the freezer trying to remember what I was looking for. The smell of food turns my stomach. Only when my legs feel shaky and weak do I force myself to eat instant noodles.

There is fear in my solar plexus. What will happen to me, to my carefully built world? Will I be alone for the rest of my life? Each morning I take a tricycle to an Internet café and check the balance of our joint bank account. Will this be the day Edward empties the account, leaving me too penniless to hire a lawyer? *Should* I hire a lawyer? Oh, why didn't I open an account of my own? I should have made sure I had my own money; I should have demanded or begged or stolen money from him while I had the chance. Now it's too late. The Philippines is no place to look for a job, unless I can survive on five dollars a day. Am I fated to return to the grey tundra of Canadian suburban life, to work in a beige cubicle, without windows?

My great-grandmother's early Christmas gifts of chemistry sets and history books flicker through my memory. She refused to give me the Barbie dolls that I weaseled out of my parents. When I grew up, her daughter sent me to law school. There was clearly a message there, which I obviously missed until now. I'm glad they can't see how pitifully dependent I have turned out to be.

Having Dante in the house every day helps. There is a reason to climb out of bed and get dressed, and I can no longer sit on the sofa, crying. I am cleaning my own house again since firing Baby. She sent one text, begging me to reconsider: *Please, ma'am, I need work. My daughter is hungry.*

I DON'T CARE. THAT'S YOUR PROBLEM. DON'T TEXT ME AGAIN.

And she hasn't.

Dante is careful not to mention Baby or Edward. But one day he says, "I heard that Edward isn't using the boat in Subic. Why don't you sail it back here?"

*

Isabel looks beautiful and radiant, and I would like to leap across the table and punch her in the mouth. *Pull yourself together. Isabel is your friend; she's an athlete, not a bar girl.* But all I can think of when I look at her dark eyes and long black hair is that she is what Edward dumped me for. Isabel happens to be in love with an Englishman, an Englishman who has a wife. This fact, which never bothered me before, now enrages me. Why doesn't anyone care about the wife? Oh, but Isabel is so sweet, so Asian, always asking me how I am, giving me helpful advice: "What you need is lots of exercise," she has said.

Well, we are going to have plenty of exercise. We are about to climb Mount Kinabalu, the 4,095-meter mountain that is the tallest peak between the Himalayas and New Guinea.

Isabel is in front, so much fitter than me. I've been an insomniac for weeks now, waking up in bed, harassed by visions of my husband fucking Baby or Rose or Jasmine or whatever young dancer or hunting girl he has hired for the night in a girlie bar. How does a nation, especially a Catholic one, justify pimping out its prettiest daughters and sisters and wives and mothers? How do women rationalize feeding their children with money earned by prostitution? How many Western men, outwardly conservative and respectable, visit Asian countries as sex tourists, taking advantage of this deep, endless poverty?

I don't think I can do this climb; my legs feel like they are made of cement. Apparently, even the Malaysian guide knows I've come unhinged. Within minutes of setting off he stopped, snapped off a branch from a tree and carved it into a walking stick for me.

Following Isabel up the Mesilau Trail, I am aware of ginger plants, bamboo trees, rhododendrons, and wild orchids clinging to lichen-streaked trees in mossy forests. But who cares? My husband is screwing maids and prostitutes. Does Baby think he is going to divorce me and marry her? Does she think she will be moving into my house, cooking rice and fish heads in my kitchen? Is she crazy enough to think she will be sailing on my boat? I want to take my walking stick and whack Isabel over the back of the head.

Oh yes, Filipinos are so religious, such good Catholics, ostentatiously crossing themselves every time they drive past a church. Well, whatever happened to *Thou shalt not commit adultery*? Do the rules of morality not apply to poor people? I would like to knock Isabel right off this goddamned mountain.

For hours the torture continues, Isabel taking photos of me beside the *Nepenthes rajah*, feeding me energy bars and butterscotch candies, smiling at me, unaware of my crazed animosity. Our lungs, so long accustomed to breathing at sea level, struggle to find oxygen in the thinning mountain air.

Finally, after nine hours of climbing the seven-and-a-half-kilometer trail, we reach our sleeping hut at 3,300 meters. Isabel's head has begun to ache. There are other people in our unheated room, apparently rolling around in aluminum foil to keep warm, the ceaseless crinkling distracting my exhausted mind from sleep. We are staying in backpacker lodges, my budget now reduced to that of a student. How dare Edward do this to me?

The guide knocks on our door at 2:00 am, summoning us for an unappetizing breakfast before we embark on the summit climb. Isabel feels terrible. It is freezing cold and pitch dark outside, and I want to quit and go back to bed. On the trail Isabel vomits. The guide takes me aside, announcing that Isabel has altitude sickness, but wants to continue the climb, slowly. He will stay with her.

"You must walk to the top alone," he says to me.

I am strangely invigorated by the notion that the mighty Isabel can be been felled by something as accidental as altitude sickness—and at a mere 3,300 meters! I stomp up the trail, angry that the guide has abandoned me in the dark, my cheap flashlight producing only a pale sliver of light. I am the only climber who is alone.

Pulling myself along guide ropes which have been chiseled into the steepest of the granite slopes leading to the summit, I concentrate on placing one foot in front of the other, counting out loud, "one-two-three-four, one-two-three-four." My body's reaction to the thin air is an unpleasant surprise. After every fourth step, I sit down on the granite and suck at the air, desperate for oxygen.

Edward has done this to me, as surely as if he had driven our car into a tree with me in the passenger seat, smashing my life into pieces, while he walked away unscratched.

Soon, I cannot walk more than three steps without resting.

You're never going to make it. Eventually, I am alarmed when I need to sit after only a single step, while other climbers steam past me. Again and again I see Edward lying on top of Baby in my bed. I know that I cannot continue like this. Exhausted by this infinite and tedious anger, I have a choice to make. Either I allow them to win—or I defeat them.

I begin to sob. There is a new voice inside my head, barely audible at first, but which becomes louder and more insistent: *You may have ruined my life, Edward, but I will not let you ruin this climb! I AM going to make it, you lying, cheating bastard!*

For three and a half hours I walk and sit and walk and sit— until scrambling over the final boulders before Low's Peak. I stand proudly on top of Borneo, observing what remains of a cloudless, peach-colored dawn. Though my fingers are numb, I continue to stand there, awaiting the arrival of the Malaysian guide, who, according to the rules, must witness me at the summit in order to credit me with the climb.

While I wait, I feel that something has changed inside of me. I am not the same person who set out on this journey yesterday morning. I don't know how, but Mount Kinabalu has transformed me in some strange and miraculous way. I can feel a new strength, both inner and outer. I can do anything!

I make a decision. I will fight for Edward, for my marriage, for my home—for everything that I value in my life. And I will win.

*

Back at home, I fly into action, determined to lose weight and get fit. In the decade that I've known him, Edward has always pressured me to stay slim. My recent lack of appetite has served me well, helping me to shed eight pounds already. I take up jogging and begin each day with sit-ups, push-ups, and toning exercises. I buy new clothes. Edward has always been attracted to me and I refuse to believe that he no longer wants me. When I look in the mirror, I like what I see.

But will he?

*

I watch the girl wrap her body around the pole on stage. I have lived in the Philippines for more than three years, yet this is my first time in a girlie bar. Tonight, my friends have suggested that we come here for a laugh.

I can't resist wanting to see what my husband sees. Some of the girls on stage look bored; a few seem inexperienced and awkward. The one slithering around the pole is clearly aware of and savoring her power over these men whose eyes remain glued to her every move. I wonder about the girls, how they have come to work in a place like this. I've been told that most have small children who are being raised by their families. This is one way to pay for diapers and milk.

I am surprised to see so many men that I know. I feel embarrassed, as though I have caught them in the act of masturbation. I look away from their faces when I begin to imagine Edward's eyes instead of theirs.

Money is paid to the *mama-san*; girls are led away for the night or the week or whatever length of time has been negotiated. Surprisingly, as a woman, I am not made to feel out of place. Waitresses are polite and smiling: "Ma'am, what would you like?" This is, after all, a business.

Does Edward believe that these young, beautiful girls are really attracted to him? Does he think that they are dying to go home and have sex with him? Watching the old men watching the dancing girls, I realize that a man's ego can convince him of anything.

"What would you like?" the waitresses keep asking.

I'd like my life back, please.

*

As each week passes, I find it easier to live on my own, knowing that it is only a matter of time until Edward comes back. I am ready to put this terrible episode in our relationship behind us. Eventually, he will tire of playing Hugh Hefner and come back to me.

Sure enough, three and a half months after he walked out of our house, he texts me that he wants to come for a visit. I am jubilant but nervous. Everything must be perfect. I clean the house until it shines; I plan meals and shop. On the morning of his arrival I put on a new dress, jewelry, and mascara.

He arrives in the early afternoon, smiling. I notice that he looks happier and more handsome than he has in years. I hope this is because he has come home, but I am wary: he is carrying no luggage. I cannot upset him, cannot interrogate him, cannot accuse him. I cannot live in limbo anymore; I cannot live in borderline poverty. I must get my life back.

He compliments me on my appearance and the changes I have made to the house. I serve wine as lamb shanks braise on the stove. He receives text message after text message, and is quick to answer them. I cannot ask questions. Foreboding creeps into my chest.

I light candles and serve dinner and he praises my food. The texts continue and my anxiety grows. He says he is tired and asks if he can sleep in our bed upstairs.

"Of course," I say. "Do you mind if I sleep there too?"

"That's fine, sweetheart," he says.

I climb into bed and seduce my husband, as I have planned, eager to show him that I can do anything those girls can do.

The next morning, I am triumphant. *Take that, you whores!* Might there be some irony in the victory?

At eleven o'clock his cell phone rings. When he answers, a woman's voice is loud and angry. He is placating, using a tone of voice I have only ever heard him use for me.

"I'll be back tomorrow afternoon, sweetheart," he says into his cellphone.

"Who is that?" I yell.

"A friend, that's all."

"A friend? You don't talk like that to a friend. Why is she calling you?"

"Okay, look, I didn't want to upset you, but I'm living with her in Subic. It's nothing serious, I've lived with a few girls in the past few months. I really just came down here to take back the electric oven."

*

It has been almost two months since Edward walked away with the electric oven, and I've tried to figure out where it all went wrong. After all, how can two people living inside the same relationship have two such completely different assessments of it? Why was I happy while Edward was not?

A faded memory emerges from my distant undergraduate past. Many years ago, I participated in a study conducted by my university's psychology department, designed to evaluate memory. I watched hundreds of slides, wrote tests, attended interviews. After all was said and done, I felt that I had performed very well. Until my exit interview, that is.

Apparently, the study was not about memory at all. It was about my perception of the world.

"You see the world through rose-colored glasses," I recall being told. "You are the complete opposite of depressed."

"Well, that's good, isn't it?" I asked. "Isn't it good to be happy?"

"There is a danger that you could become delusional. Being happy without a reason is not necessarily healthy."

Delusional? Who was this guy to imply that I had no reason to be happy?

I sat there, wondering if this was some kind of joke.

"I don't understand," I persisted. "What's wrong with feeling good?"

It was explained that I could be lacking emotional sensors. Kind of like the emotional equivalent of being able to walk on hot coals and not feel it. I may get badly burned.

What a crock of shit! What have these guys been smoking? Hey, I have no trouble functioning. I wake up in the morning feeling great. I pass my exams. I pay my bills on time. I have friends. What could possibly be wrong with that?

"Be careful" were the last words I heard as I escaped out the door.

Now, all these years later, it occurs to me that maybe those psychology students were right. Maybe I have been living in a rosy bubble. Maybe my marriage was always terrible. Maybe my whole life has been terrible. Maybe I have been deluded into believing I was happy because of some random chemicals flowing through my brain.

What is perception, anyway? Aren't we all influenced by brain chemistry?

*

Though it may only be a delusion, I believe I am on the road to recovery. I have met divorced middle-aged women who are terminally bitter. I don't wish to join their club. If I want my wounds to heal I must stop picking at them; it's time to move forward.

I've told my family that I won't be returning to Canada. In fact, I never even considered the possibility. I like Asia. Despite its flaws, I like the Philippines. There is an energy in this part of the world, a dynamism that speaks to me. This is where the future lies and where I want to be.

I phone Edward to discuss finances. I tell him that unless he wants to spend the rest of his life working the graveyard shift at a Seven-Eleven he'd better agree to support me financially. He does. I also tell him that I'd like to have *Feisty Lady* back with me, in Puerto Galera. I would like to sail to Palawan in a few months. Surprisingly, he agrees.

"But you need to come up to Subic and sail her back," he says.

*

A few weeks later, I arrive in Subic Bay, having sent Dante the boatman ahead to prepare the boat for the two-day, 105-nautical-mile sail.

This will be my first voyage as captain and I'm nervous. I don't want to be in charge—I much prefer being first mate. Will I be able to navigate correctly? Will I be able to find tomorrow night's anchorage before nightfall?

Watching Edward in his new element is hurtful. He introduces me to a few of his friends and we all go out to a floating bar, where girls sit on his lap, laughing and drinking the expensive "ladies' drinks" that he buys them. I cannot believe that this is my husband. At one point a girl asks who I am and he answers, "Oh, she's just a friend." *Just a friend?* Later, we go back to his house, where I smash a framed picture of his girlfriend. I hadn't wanted to behave badly and feel ashamed as I pick up the shards of broken glass. Edward stares at me, disgusted.

The night before we leave, Dante and I sleep on the boat. I toss and turn and wake up at 5:00 am with a head full of doubts. Do I really want the responsibility of taking care of this boat? Can I handle the expense? It's not too late to change my mind.

I've never sailed *Feisty Lady* without Edward on board, and it feels like he has died. It feels wrong to be sitting at his navigation table, punching waypoints into the GPS. He should be here. I didn't expect to feel so much grief. I want to tell Dante that I've changed my mind, that we'll take the bus back to Puerto Galera, but he pops his head through the hatch, cheerfully announcing that everything is ready up on deck. Though the sun is barely up, I am wearing sunglasses to cover the tears leaking from my eyes.

"Just a few more minutes, Dante," I say, and his head disappears.

If I'm going to take charge of my life, I need to do this. I can't be afraid anymore. At forty-one, it's time to grow up. Edward is not coming back to me. I'm an experienced sailor and I know how to manage this boat. I walk up the companionway steps into the cockpit outside.

"Okay, Dante," I say, starting the engine and taking the helm. "Throw off the dock lines."

We maneuver out of the marina and I don't look back.

After seven years and two adventurous crossings of the Pacific Ocean on a ten-meter yacht, Canadian India Harris sailed into the Philippines in 2001, fell in love with the country, and became a landlubber. When not at her seaside home which she shares with a menagerie of pets, India can usually be found in some other exotic part of the world with her camera. She has also lived in Tokyo, Paris, and Hawaii.

CROSS

By Saffron Marchant

September 2007
Hong Kong

SKYSCRAPER city: roads snaked with stone-wall trees; buildings clad in yellow, pink, green tiles, baking in the heat or sleek with rain. City-state hemmed by the busy waters of the South China Sea, immured by the jade-greenery of the mountains, immobilized by the concrete poured over the foothills so that the land won't slide.

A city of refuge. From war, famine, revolution. People have raced here through paddy fields in the black of night, swum through icy rivers with their children on their backs. They have boarded trains in Shanghai, Guangzhou, or Beijing, or boats in Saigon or Hanoi, with their money sewn into their clothes, no certainty they would get here.

I arrive in Hong Kong in the business-class section of a British Airways 747, on a one-way ticket bought by somebody else.

The air I step into from the air-conditioned frigidity of Chek Lap Kok is Irish to look at—misty, drizzly—but warm to the touch and deadly on the hair. The humidity is a damp skirt swishing around my legs, warm in my throat, hot across my chest and thighs. But by the time we've crossed the concourse to get the car to Central, the tropical sultriness has gone. It's sweat sliding through the crack in my buttocks, down my legs, out of my armpits and into my handbag.

Now, there are oceans and continents and seven hours between me and London and all those "when will you and Dave start a family" questions, or "you'll get there keep trying" from all those I-just-need-to-stand-next-to-him-and-I-fall women.

So far, at least, I'm not barren in Hong Kong.

*

We are tourists in Hong Kong for our first few days as residents. Dave has relocated with his bank; I'm a recovering solicitor, taking time out, a would-be maternity leave. We arrive on a public holiday. The Mid-Autumn Festival celebrates the full moon that brings the harvest. Lines of red lanterns are strung from the entrances to the apartment blocks; the supermarkets sell delicate mooncakes in red and yellow boxes. We puff our way around the walking trails on Lamma Island, pass the seafood restaurants, the fish morbidly swimming in the tanks, the tables packed with holidaymakers, scissoring chopsticks.

We visit the Tea, Space, and Heritage Museums, go to the bar at the very top floor of the Peninsula to watch the Festival of Light with cocktails at Felix, go downstairs again to eat a cheese fondue in Chesa. I almost lose a shoe on the steep climb on the tram up to The Peak, clutch my toes, press hard into the paneled floor, strain something, walk with a limp that annoys Dave.

We go to the Po Lin Monastery, take a cable car up high into the Lantau hills. "These things are always breaking down," says Dave as we lurch into the clouds. "Or falling from their moorings." I stare at the ground as we leave it behind and cross my fingers.

We eat a vegetarian lunch at the restaurant in the Buddhist monastery. My period comes in the restrooms under the Big Buddha.

October

Dr. Chan squeezes my breasts and tells me to take my knickers off. In any other circumstances this would be a slap-able offence.

Instead I clamber into the stirrups. The nurse places a pink nylon sheet over my splayed knees.

"Well, you have a nice clean cervix and your notes tell me that your tubes are clear, husband's sperm is fine. Come back to my office and we'll discuss."

The wall behind Dr. Chan is covered in photographs of nature-defying parents and their babies. The wall opposite the window is papered with thank-you cards. There is a plastic pelvis on his desk. Dr. Chan attends the women in the hospitals on Hong Kong Island in the mornings, those who have just given birth. He runs his clinic in Central from ten to two. After two, he performs the IVF procedures in the Sanatorium Hospital in Happy Valley. Frequently he is called away to a woman in labor. You would think this schedule would fall apart given the unpredictable nature of harvested eggs and at-term babies, but Dr. Chan is an acrobat, spinning through the air on the point of a needle.

"Let's do intra-uterine insemination. We will give you hormones to stimulate your ovaries to make eggs," says Dr. Chan. "Then we will monitor for ovulation, and when the eggs are just about to be released, we will pass the sperm into the uterine cavity. It's a very gentle procedure. The hormones are easier on the body than IVF because we don't want many eggs, just three or four. We'll do a couple of cycles, see where we are."

I'm grinning. I'm mentally writing the thank-you card. He has a calm authority and a plan.

"So, we'll just take some blood and start the hormones tomorrow. I'll need you to come in every day for an ultrasound so I can check your ovaries are not hyper-stimulating."

"I'm going to Vietnam tomorrow," I say. "It's our wedding anniversary."

Dr. Chan throws down his pencil, eyes flashing. "We have to abort this procedure unless you cancel your holiday."

"At the London clinic, I was tested five days into the hormone treatment."

"You hyper-stimulated at the London clinic."

We abort. I start to cry.

"A month's wait isn't so bad," says Dr. Chan softly.

He's wrong about that. A month is very long when you can't get pregnant. Every missed cycle is a step towards other options—donor eggs and surrogacy and adoption. I walk miserably past the paper offering shops of Sheung Wan, gifts for ancestors in their afterlife. Paper microwaves, paper cars, paper televisions. It's our second wedding anniversary. I thought I'd be a mother by now. Rock-paper-scissors.

I am going to Vietnam. When I'm ovulating. This could be it! It won't work it never—*Get over yourself you stupid cow and go shopping*. I buy two dresses from Vivienne Tam and tell Dave that I only bought one.

November

We make new friends, go on tentative first dates with couples who are friends of friends or colleagues of Dave's. We gossip in the cab home. *Did she seem really unhappy to you? Why was he constantly going to the toilet? I liked him. I liked her. Do you think they liked us?*

I like my new home, Hong Kong. The bauhinias are fuchsia lanterns strung through the trees on Victoria Road, or, once fallen, crimson streaks in the minibus tires, flattened to paper. There is so much nature here, slithering through the dark green hills or careening past my window with a mouse in its beak. Living in this heat means that nature gets indoors too. I jump in fright at the cockroach in my sink (the size of my elbow and levitating) or the scattering silverfish in my tea drawer. A dusk walk to the supermarket brings an ankle chain of insect bites, bruised and raised and dotted.

One afternoon Dave and I go to the beach at Deep Water Bay. It is a warm Sunday in November but the shore is deserted. Then a family appears, noisily settling close by. Blanket. Parasol. Deck chairs. Sun cream. They are all blonde. Dave smiles as he watches the toddler with the pale halo of curls and the crossbow smile. "He looks like us. He looks like he could be—"

"Jesus, there's no peace now that bunch have turned up," I say.

I'm cross because I've been diagnosed with ovarian cysts, common in women undergoing fertility treatment. The news is crushing: another delayed cycle. I haunt the Internet chat rooms, lurk and read the cysts threads silently, a non-contributor, tears on my cheeks.

December

The day of the IUI treatment. After two months' delay, I have Dave's sperm in a little pot between my boobs and am on my way to have it "washed." How quickly I have become used to Hong Kong: you don't drive to a doctor's surgery, you take an elevator. Dr. Chan does not provide the sperm-washing facility so he sends me to a clinic that does.

A man comes into the clinic and places a vial of white froth on the counter. "Here is my sperm!" he booms in a voice straight out of Hong Kong's colonial past. He is irritatingly proud of his specimen. I stare at his sperm with a flare of anxiety: he has produced way more than Dave.

*

I'm in the stirrups. The sperm is loaded into a catheter. It's done. A smear test is more painful.

"Take it easy. We'll test on Day 25."

*

My period comes on Day 24. I don't get out of bed.

Dave comes home from work to find me, curtains closed, bedroom humid. "Do you, do you think you've got depressed again? Shall we find you somebody in Hong Kong?"

We go out for dinner. I wear my nightshirt but put on a bra and jeans; comb and put up my hair; long, dangly earrings. Then there's the anti-pregnancy diet. Vodka martini with a coil of lemon peel, foie gras, steak medium-rare, goblets of Pinot Noir, and a blue cheese oozing mold and *listeria*. "I'm not going to bother with the turkey-basting business. I'm fat and flatulent from the hormones as it is." My vowels are slow, but my consonants rushed, a mouthful of gobstoppers.

Dave nods. "You're the one who has to go through the hormones."

The end of dinner. I'm drunk and we're going to tell Dr. Chan it's time to move to IVF.

*

I also give Traditional Chinese Medicine a try, availing myself of everything that Hong Kong has to offer. Tony Wong slips needles into my ears, between my eyes, across my belly, down my legs, and into my toes. He does this with a sleight of hand: he's a conjurer, a magician who can pull a baby out of a hat, turn hostile uteruses into cozy nests, an alchemist who can tweak cervical mucus with his herbs. He puts a heat lamp over my tummy, tells me to relax, and leaves the room.

Tony is a traditional Chinese doctor, hence his alchemy, borne of his heritage, his glass pots of dried sea horse, scorpion, and willow bark.

Borne.

Why does the B word creep into everything?

Baby, born, belly, bump.

Barren.

*

At a Spanish restaurant on Elgin Street, a heavily pregnant woman sits at a neighboring table. She is slow on her feet, her smile directed inward towards the watery home of her child. Pregnancy has puffed out her ankles and freckled her nose. I want all of the above. The retching and the aversion to smells and the gravitational shift, it's all real to me. I can taste it in the tapas.

*

I learn new beliefs. The Chinese believe in auspicious numbers. Two of anything is lucky; the word for the number three (*saam*) sounds like the character for *birth* and is considered lucky. The number four is inauspicious because it sounds like the word for *death*. I'd love to have a child, or three, a shape like my own family. I guess four eggs could be unlucky here. Is luck based on geography? Should I be more wary of four in Hong Kong than I was in London?

The Chinese believe in wind and water, feng shui, the correct orientation of a building to bring the best of luck. If your office has poor feng shui, you will not make money. Even those who don't believe will err on the cautious side and subscribe anyway, the same just-in-case mentality that prompts me to hang rosary beds above my bed. Thus a feng shui master decrees that the escalator in the new HSBC building has poor geomancy and the architect moves the stairwell. There are many gods here: gods of the sea and the kitchen, monkey gods, earth gods, gods of mercy and affluence, happiness, justice, long life. Spirits can be evil and the mirrors around doorways ward them off. Incense purifies the air on street corners, and rice and fruit are offered to gods outside the temples. Joss sticks burn on the ground in small red shrines, and at the festivals great feasts are eaten at the gravesides so that the whole family—the dead and the living—can dine together. Cars or microwaves or cigarette boxes made out of paper are burnt so that the deceased can enjoy them in the afterlife.

I have a new god.

The old God was wrathful; He punished the wicked. My old God made me barren. He punished me for my sins, whatever they might have been. Now I believe in the god of the embryo, of the welcoming womb, the Gonal F god.

I ward off the bad god, the period god, the god of the miscarriage and the cold womb, with science and alchemy. I move the mirror out of our bedroom because it's bad feng shui.

January

My sister, to my mother's despair, is moving to Melbourne and is taking the scenic route, through the Philippines. We meet her and Pete in Boracay.

Annie and I use our flip-flops as mini floats and swim amongst the diaphanous jellyfish. Annie asks about egg retrieval: does it hurt? How many eggs do they take? What about the anesthetic, is it general or local?

Then she says: "Pete and I were talking. If it comes to it, Saff, you can have some of my eggs."

I put my head under the water to muffle her voice. My thoughts scatter as my hair plumes out behind me. Then I focus. I am both enraged and touched. But more enraged. Even my family has given up on me.

March

The egg harvest. I go under to the sound of gentle Cantonese, Dr. Chan chatting to the nurses and the anesthesiologist, my left arm held out straight on a plinth, taped down, a needle in a vein, knickerless, my legs pulled apart by the stirrups.

I come round in the hospital ward. The curtains around my bed are closed. The woman opposite me, post anesthesia, is vomiting. We are the IVF "patients": we are not sick, but we are in hospital. We have had surgery but we have not been cut. We are here for different and varied reasons—blocked tubes, poor sperm quality, advanced age, unexplained infertility—but for each of us to be lying in these beds means that we have pretended, lied, bartered, and bargained, given something essential up, and, eventually, offered ourselves at our own cost to science.

Dr. Chan is surprised to find me sitting up and reading an Anne Enright novel, the one she won the Booker for, with the family of twelve shaped like my own Irish Catholic mother's. I look at Dr. Chan and think, twelve? He puts his hand on my leg. "Ten eggs. That's about right for your age. We'll see how they go."

The woman in the bed next to me has had twenty-two eggs extracted and crows about it to her partner. I look out at the racecourse of Happy Valley. A lone runner pounds the track.

*

Dave and I rush through a series of small victories. All ten of our eggs fertilize. I am glued to the Internet chat rooms; I read all the remarks without contributing, a cyber-ghost. It is rare for all of the eggs to fertilize. We are lucky.

We get luckier. The cells multiply.

All of the embryos make it to day five and are given a new name: *blastocysts.* They look like tiny cabbages.

We have left our future offspring across town. I dispatch my four dead grandparents to stand guard over the test tubes. I envision my impassive grandfathers shaking hands across the racks of test tubes, bewildered by the science of it all, fearing it ungodly. My grandmothers beam with excitement and peer at their genetic material in the vial marked *Marchant.*

*

I go back to the hospital in Happy Valley. The day of the embryo transfer. I put on the uniform: disposable knickers, a checked gown that is open at the back, white knee-length socks, and plastic slippers.

"Please drink lots of water. Your bladder must be full so that Dr. Chan can see the womb on the ultrasound," says the nurse.

Dave sits beside my bed. His thumbs move across the buttons on his BlackBerry. He looks up at me. "What?"

I ask him to refill my water bottle. He leaves the BlackBerry on my table. I think about smashing it on the floor or flushing it down the toilet or hiding it in the bedclothes but I decide not to. Dave needs to work to pay for the treatment.

"Is this you, Saffron Gretta Marchant?" The operating theatre nurses bark from behind facemasks. I peer at a label that wraps my wrist. "Yes." I stand up. My bladder is so full that my stomach is a hard dome. "I think I may have drunk too much water." I am ignored. "Is this your birth date?" I look at my own wrist once more.

Dave and I are escorted through several doors until we are in an office at the center of which is a computer. Dr. Chan is sitting at the desk wearing scrubs. His feet are tucked into rubber boots. "Here is your embryo, Saffron and Dave."

There is a brain-textured circle on the computer screen. I understand. "We only have one left?" I cannot say anything else.

"No you have plenty left. Let's see. You have nine left. We'll put three in—"

"Not four?" I want four. I want unlucky number four; I don't care about auspiciousness.

Dr. Chan laughs. "No, we won't put you through that. Too high a chance of multiples! We don't want you going through a reduction procedure."

I finally hear the message about the nine embryos. Euphoria. My elastic mood bounces skywards. "I have a really good feeling about this, Dr. Chan." Dave and the doctor exchange glances.

"We'll see," says the doctor.

"Dave's coming in with me?" I ask. The blue in Dave's tie matches his eyes.

"He's not scrubbed up." Dr. Chan shakes his head. "This will only take a few minutes. You won't be able to see much on the ultrasound anyway."

The nurses come in, shouting more questions about my wristband. Dave kisses me as my head is squashed into a cotton cap.

Two blastocysts are loaded into a catheter and put back inside me. They sail into my womb like tiny, oar-less rowing boats.

*

Ten long days.

I lie down and will implantation.

I am sore. I speak on the phone to my mother for hours each day. I take progesterone to ensure that my womb lining is thick enough to provide an ample bed for the embryos.

The hormones are cruel. They mimic early pregnancy: sensitive breasts; tears on the bus; a slouched, fat gut; a bigger bottom. I look pregnant, three months gone. I have been congratulated twice. In Central, I get so cross that I want to bite the office-workers slow-walking in impassable packs, punch the minibus-goading taxi driver, push the smug pregnant woman down the escalator. I attend an Anne Enright lecture at the university. She is witty, charming, clever. I want to bite her too.

*

"Your blood is bad. Your blood tests show it," Nurse Kelly says. For a pregnancy, human chorionic gonadotropin needs to be present in the blood. If it's not there, the blood is bad.

"I'm not pregnant?"

"Your period should come now. If it doesn't by next week, you need to come for more blood tests."

"Because if it does not come I might be pregnant?"

"No! It means that the baby is in the tubes. Ectopic."

"But I could still be pregnant—"

"There is no way that you can be pregnant because your blood is so bad... I'm sorry," Nurse Kelly repeats. "These are things that happen."

"Shit," says Dave softly. I listen to him breathe. I should not have called him at the office, he is surrounded by people. "I thought it would work."

I nod. Tears slide down my face and neck.

My mother and sister send texts of commiseration and posi-tivity. Then Dad calls. Dad never calls. He has had a fall outside a customer's factory and broken his glasses. He has cuts on his face. I ask him to repeat the name of the customer: Dad has unwittingly been making cushions for an up market London sex shop!

I spend an hour on the phone with Annie, describing to her the types of products available on the sex shop's web site. The bestsellers are jade cock rings, brass anal plugs, and long, tasseled whips.

I laugh hard.

*

My period is a week late. Bad blood takes time to leave. Today is Day 33, April 5, 2008. Today is the Ching Ming Festival, the grave-sweeping holiday, and we are holidaying at Sun Moon Lake in north Taiwan. In Hong Kong, Macau, and, for the first time since 1949, mainland China, the tomb-sweeping holiday was celebrated yesterday, April 4. We are surrounded by clusters of family groups, tiny sons and daughters run around the lake. We walk with them, no one-child policy in Taiwan, brothers in sunglasses and their tiny sisters, their hair swinging like cloth as they scooter away from their families. The grandparents carry broomsticks, the parents armfuls of red-and-purple-petaled flowers. Above the lake dance kites, two lions, and a rabbit.

I bleed but it is sparse, weird. That's IVF for you.

*

"Your period was two weeks ago, correct?" Dr. Chan asks. "There is absolutely no ovarian activity whatsoever. You haven't ovulated this month. It may be stress, but you usually ovulate." I stare at the dark patches on the ultrasound; it is an empty auditorium. Without any ovulation a frozen embryo transfer is pointless. Dr. Chan can trigger activity with more injections. I eagerly agree to this and have a blood test and go out for lunch with one of my new friends.

Two hours later Nurse Kelly calls. "When was your last period?"

Two weeks ago. Why?

"I'd like your permission to do a pregnancy test."

Pardon?

I am standing in the Armani Tower, my phone clamped to my ear, office workers stepping past. I can't be pregnant; I have just had two glasses of Chablis and an extremely strong latte. I look at Isabel, in whom I've just confided. *I might be pregnant.* She turns high octave: Do you feel sick? Why did the clinic not test before?

*

I'm pregnant.

I cancel tomorrow's highlights appointment. I drag Dave out of his office and flash him the pee stick, with its implausible cross.

"You see?" he says. He can't stop laughing.

I call Mum, who shouts with joy. I tell my dad and my sister and her husband and my brother. I tentatively try out new words: grandparent, uncle, aunt, nephew, niece. I hold steady and breathe.

*

I am knowingly pregnant for two days.

Then it's gone. I lose the tiny clot of cells.

I keep my positive pregnancy test in my handbag. In the plastic window shines a cross, a belief of sorts, or a promise.

Saffron Marchant read English Literature and Language at Oxford in the early 1990s. In 2007 she began to study Creative Writing at Hong Kong University, and eventually graduated with distinction from its inaugural Master of Fine Arts. In the intervening years, she studied and practiced law in London, Paris, and New York, but now terms herself a "recovering solicitor." She now lives in Hong Kong with her husband, son, and daughter.

MOVING TO THE TROPIC OF CANCER

By Philippa Ramsden

RAINY season in Burma[1] is spectacular. At night, I love to lie in bed, listening to the torrential rainfall drenching the earth and bringing life and vitality to the land. Between showers, the air is so thick that you can hear the moisture dripping from leaves and branches. And if you listen very carefully, you can almost hear the grass sighing and burbling with delight as it wallows in the rainwater. When the rains come down, they do so thick and fast. Even with an umbrella and raincoat you are quickly drenched. In the intervals between the downpours, it is hot, humid and sticky.

When I arrived in Burma in mid June of 2009 to start a new job, rainy season was in full force. Having lived in Asia for more than a decade, I have become close friends with the monsoons, which bring welcome respite from stifling heat and humidity. Being caught in a sudden downpour, or even listening to the rain from outside, brings energy and feels like a revitalising force. I have many fond memories of standing, drenched to the skin, grinning from ear to ear after only a few moments in an unexpected cloudburst. It helps that the rain is warm! Coming from Scotland, where the rain can be just

---

[1] Editor's Note: The publisher acknowledges the sensitive issues surrounding the naming of Burma/Myanmar. Signal 8 Press has chosen to use the name Burma in this collection.

as heavy but usually accompanied by grey skies and often a biting wind, I have never tired of this warm torrential rain.

When the rains make their first annual appearance, they usually arrive dramatically, and the world is transformed. There is a festive feeling; smiles and laughter return. The sight of children playing in the rain, splashing in puddles and letting the rain soak them through is ubiquitous. And not just children—adults too! The city turns green, mosquitoes hold crowded parties, and the frogs grow to such a size that they sound like male tigers as they croak in the night. The ground and pavements are covered with a layer of slippery, slimy moss in the hidden spaces which have not already turned to mud.

Such was Yangon when we arrived with our suitcases, papers, and a crate of enthusiasm, to take up a new life in this enigmatic country. It is quite an experience looking for a home in such a setting. We had a temporary place to live but were keen to settle and unpack properly. In those first weeks, we tramped round a number of potential homes, the mosquitoes nipping at our ankles and the rain teeming down.

It was not too long before my husband found the perfect place, a simple bungalow within walking distance from work. We made arrangements to view it, and the heavens opened shortly before the visit. The road outside the office flooded, and we had to wade through warm, murky water to get there. It was well worth the effort, though. The bungalow was indeed perfect: modest, but deceptively spacious. The wooden floors gave it a cosy warmth and the large, high windows made it feel light and optimistic. Unusually for Yangon, it had ceiling fans throughout. My fear of earthquakes was assuaged by the fact it was all on one level. The generous garden was gloriously tropical and mature, bounded by bamboo, mango trees, and hedging, and filled with pink, white, and yellow bougainvillea, crimson foliage, pink and purple hibiscus, and scented frangipani. It was ideal. We would share it with several families of geckos, some of which were the tiniest ones I have ever seen. They added to the nighttime chorus with their characteristic chirruping sound.

After a series of one-year postings in different countries in the South and Southeast Asian region, we were very happy at the prospect of a longer posting. We were keen to move into this peaceful space and finally unpack. Particularly back in 2009, Burma had an air of mystery, and were eager to learn about our new environment. We made arrangements to rent this house and moved in as soon as everything was in order. It was a marvelous feeling to be settling at last.

By late September, the rainy season had truly left its mark: the vegetation was lush and vibrant from the rains, clothes seemed to be neither clean nor dry, almost everything was growing a layer of mould, and the humidity made me feel constantly grimy.

One unremarkable evening, as another hot, sticky, and wet day was drawing to a close, I had my usual shower to refresh myself and clean off the day's grime. It was in the shower that I felt a hard, solid area where one should not have been, in my left breast.

I was instantly transported back in time twenty-six years to when I had found a lump one evening while bathing. I vividly remembered the sensation of sick fear as I checked that I had not imagined it. It had indeed been real all those years ago, and I had had it investigated promptly the next day with my local doctor. It had turned out to be nothing sinister and was shrinking by the time I had a hospital appointment a couple of weeks later. Although the lump at that time was not worrisome, the emotions and fear that I felt at that time were very real.

My reaction was different, however, on finding this lump all these years later. My stomach didn't sink in quite the same way. In the previous days, I had noticed some changes in my left breast, and was intending to seek medical advice. However, I believed these to be related to my age. When my fingers rested on the hard mass, I knew that the lump plus changes must constitute worrying signs. This really could be sinister this time. I comforted and contradicted myself, focusing on the fact that eighty percent of breast lumps are benign, and moreover, there was no history of cancer at all in my family.

I swallowed the sense of fear and uncertainty. My mind had to absorb the possibility that I might have cancer. And I was living in a new and foreign environment. I had no idea what the implications might be. The next morning, I found a recommended medical center and made an appointment to see the doctor.

Then I spent a ridiculous amount of time on the Internet, searching and searching and confusing myself with the wealth of information available. I frightened myself by searching the different diagnoses and the various types of treatment. The more I searched, the more I realised that my symptoms ticked a few of the "let's get worried" boxes. And the more I searched, the more I realised that the entity we know very simply as breast cancer is actually a massively complex beast. I was on the threshold of a very strange territory, both physically and mentally. I gripped tightly to the hope that I would not have to cross over into that unknown and terrifying place.

My appointment with the doctor was the next day. That day was rather surreal. I didn't feel as scared as I imagined I would; I felt myself shift to autopilot. My doctor confirmed my concerns: there was indeed some "asymmetry" and this should be checked out by a specialist. The regular protocol in Yangon is to be referred to Bangkok and have a diagnostic mammogram, ultrasound, and biopsy. She told me that I should do this as soon as feasible, and without doubt within two weeks.

At this stage I entered a strange limbo. I returned to work and quietly informed my boss and one colleague in an upbeat email, even though they sit next to me. Saying the words out loud would have been too difficult, and my mask might have cracked. I asked them to keep things low-key, in case it was nothing. I preferred people to think everything was "business as usual" until the limbo time was over.

In these waiting days, I mostly just got on with day-to-day matters and tried to put it to the back of my mind. I lurched from having an attitude of "well, this thing is not going to get me, if it is cancer" to lying awake worried sick in the night. At my most frightened moments, I believed that I would not be alive to see the coming Christmas.

The stress of not knowing whether I was harboring cancer was exacerbated by paperwork complications. We had to deal with the logistics and other difficulties and would be leaving Yangon on a one-way ticket. My husband's passport only entitled him to a fifteen-day visa for Thailand. We did not know if and when we would be able to return to Yangon, irrespective of whether or not the diagnosis turned out to be cancer. We knew we would be leaving our new home and life, and truly stepping into the unknown.

The strange period between finding the lump and traveling to Bangkok lasted barely a week, but feels much longer in my memory. The day we were to leave for Bangkok we headed to Yangon's spectacular and spiritual Shwe Dagon Temple for a barefoot circuit of the complex, slushing through ankle-deep water. Making offerings of flowers and pouring cups water over the Buddha's head at the shrine dedicated to the weekday of your birth brings blessings, and whispered prayers may be heard. I stood at the Saturday shrine in my bare feet on the slippery ground, pouring one cup of water for each of my years on this earth and placed a spray of flowers in the urn for that purpose. It is not difficult to guess the plea in those prayers.

Less than hour later, I was sitting chittering in Yangon airport with an anxious husband by my side. *Chittering* is a useful Scottish word which describes a trembling and shaking which is so violent that it makes the teeth chatter. The fear was manifesting itself physically.

On the short flight to Bangkok, I settled a bit, distractedly munched the nondescript in-flight whatever-it-was and filled in our landing cards. We landed in Bangkok in the late afternoon as the sun hovered on the horizon, heavy and red. A car was waiting for us at the other side to go straight to the hospital and the diagnostic tests. I knew that I was going to learn in a matter of hours whether or not my life was about to change.

When we arrived at the hospital, we were already late for the imaging appointments. Our liaison manager appeared magically and guided me gently and with great care and professionalism through the next hours. I was led straight into the imaging department and asked to change into a hospital gown for the first test—the mammogram. I chose to ignore the fact that the hospital gown was a nondescript beige, and in no way related to blue, my most auspicious color. The technician took an unbelievable number of pictures from all angles, and I felt as if I was doing Bollywood poses at times. I had been prepared for pain and discomfort as I was squashed between the Perspex plates, but although the procedure was not pleasant, it was not an ordeal. I think, though, that this may have been because my mind was in overdrive, trying to pick up clues (and hope) from anything—a gesture, a smile, a question, an auspicious gown color, an auspicious room number...

Auspiciousness plays an important part in life in this part of the world. The auspicious time for our Himalayan marriage rituals several years earlier was deemed to be 9:00 am on a particularly auspicious date. That is why we had pre-marriage blessings and my favourite snacks at 7:30 that misty December morning. And that is why I put my auspicious midnight-blue traditional marriage attire on before the sun rose that morning to become a daughter-in-law of the Himalayan Tamang people. It is now second nature to seek out auspicious signs and indications around me, particularly from colors and numbers. But in desperate times, such as during cancer tests, one may look for auspicious signs in anything.

During the mammogram procedure, I picked up the word *calcification* at one point and immediately latched hope onto that. It sounded logical, and not harmful to my lay mind, so my heart lurched with optimism. *Breasts are for producing milk, and milk is made of calcium, so calcification cannot then be sinister*, my mind decided.

Next was the ultrasound. I was escorted almost directly into the room and the young, gentle technician started the procedure. Again the investigation was very thorough. This time though I could see the screen and all sorts of weird ghostly shapes emerged as she methodically worked her way through the process. Again, I tried to pick up clues and hints. Soon I heard a very big clue.

"Left side—problem."

This was definitely not encouraging, but then, as I told myself, I knew there was a problem on the left side. I just needed to be told it was not sinister, thank you. The chittering started again.

"You need biopsy," was the next clue.

That started another round of violent chittering!

The technician was lovely—calm and professional but very matter-of-fact and clear. I told her that I was worried and scared, and she smiled kindly at me.

"Don't worry," she reassured me. My stomach and heart lurched again with hope, only to be dashed by the second half of her sentence: "Your doctor is a great specialist in breast surgery, and you are in the best of hands."

She then started pegging the dimensions of a shape she was seeing in the scan. I was compelled to watch, but kept looking away as she pegged a strange shape and clicked to save it. Then my stomach turned as she started to key in explanatory text. I saw the letters as they appeared on the screen one by one, spelling out *M-A-S-S*. That was a very big clue, and not a good one. My heart stopped as she continued to type and *N-O-1* appeared on the screen. I closed my eyes and swallowed: *Mass No 1*.

Oh. My. Dear. God. There was more than one lump in my breast.

I think it was around then that the surgeon himself appeared, his Bluetooth flashing in his ear, and he joined the party. Or maybe it was a training workshop because he had a magic marker in his hand, and he methodically started to draw on my shivering chest. He and the technician reassured me that they were not going to hurt me, just draw on me! These were the markings for the biopsy.

Eventually the drawing was complete, the ultrasound images all recorded, and I knew that the time was coming for biopsy and review of the scans.

I changed from the gown back into my clothes and headed back to the waiting area. I was about to down when I was ushered into Room 59, the surgeon's consulting room. Even at that stage, I seemed to have developed a strong sense of trust and faith in my doctor. That might have been connected with the fact that he had trained in Scotland. Of course, I grasped another auspicious sign in that. He examined me again, and all the while the biopsy instruments glinted at me wickedly. I knew that the biopsy procedure would be painful as well as frightening.

He invited me to sit down and started to talk through the findings of the mammogram and ultrasound. He talked about the calcification a bit, but I could not really make sense of his words. It seemed that calcification was not as innocent as I had assumed and hoped. He highlighted aspects from the mammogram, including large areas of calcification. Then he moved quickly on and focused on one of the masses from the ultrasound. The mass highlighted on his large computer screen was cigar-shaped, and he pointed out to me that it was irregular in form and growing in different directions.

He paused, turned away from the screen and looked directly at me.

Gently, irrevocably, he told me, "This is highly suspicious of cancer."

At that single, defining moment, my life changed forever. I stepped into a new world, a world in the Tropic of Cancer and of tropical cancer. I could feel myself shrinking, detaching from reality, as his words danced in the air around me, rushing, echoing as they gathered speed and volume, pounding, thundering down all around me, just like a tropical rainstorm.

Epilogue

That day, October 2nd 2009, I did indeed step over into a different world. My official diagnosis came three days later, when I had major surgery and the pathology confirmed cancer in two of the three masses, as well as in my lymph nodes. This started a journey of acute treatment as I became a wheelchair-using, mask-wearing, single-breasted frequent flier commuting between Yangon and Bangkok during treatment and recovery.

The fact that I am telling this story today confirms that I am very much alive and kicking, albeit living with a fear and paranoia of recurrence and a cocktail of after-effects and side-effects from long term medications. I am wonderfully cared for by my medical team in Yangon and Bangkok who have seen me through a few bumps in the road, and whom I unashamedly adore!

I am still living and working in Myanmar/Burma in a different and changing context, still finding it a fascinating environment rich in inspiration, and still smiling when the monsoon rains pound down outside.

Scotswoman Philippa Ramsden is a development and humanitarian professional, writing in any leisure time. She had been to Asia only once when she stepped off a plane in Kathmandu in 2000 to take up a new job, with no idea what to expect—and has been in Asia ever since. She has lived and worked in Nepal, Mongolia, India, Sri Lanka, and Burma/Myanmar. She is currently working on a memoir, and blogs as Feisty Blue Gecko.

FIVE WEEKS ON

By Nicola Chilton

THE Japanese used to believe that earthquakes were caused by a giant catfish, the *namazu*, who lived in the mud under the surface of the earth. Guarded by the god Kashima, he was held down by a powerful, magical rock that kept him under control. But when Kashima let down his guard, the giant catfish writhed around in his underground lair in an attempt to escape, causing violent tremors and earthquakes on the surface.

*

In Tokyo, the first signs that things weren't quite normal were in the shops. The supply of batteries was limited to one pack per person. It was the same for candles. And milk. Half of the lights in the supermarkets were switched off, as were the Family Mart and 7-11 signs. But everyday life, on the surface, seemed to carry on as usual. Harried-looking salarymen with grey faces and grey suits hurried to their next meetings. Women with perfect hair and perfect make-up balanced on their heels as they went from department store to department store. In Tokyo, beer was still drunk, karaoke was still sung, taxi drivers still proudly polished their cars, and the cogs and wheels driving the city still turned. Life went on almost as usual. If you could ignore the aftershocks, that is.

It was a very different story up north. The Tohoku Expressway was much quieter than usual that Sunday night. This is the road to the northernmost prefectures of Honshu, home to people known for their stoicism, their ruggedness, their resilience to the region's harsh weather. The expressway was dark, lights switched off to save electricity. There weren't many vehicles on the road, but those that were making the journey north had signs announcing that they were delivering aid to the disaster zones. Police cars from all over the country and Self Defense Force trucks and jeeps made up the rest of the traffic.

There was a sense of foreboding as we made the journey northwards, through Saitama and Tochigi Prefectures, towards Fukushima, home of the embattled Fukushima Daiichi Nuclear Plant, still spewing who knew how much radiation into the ocean and air five weeks after the disaster. The 20km exclusion zone had just been extended to 30km, although the British government advised against traveling within 60km of the reactor, and the US government insisted that anything within 80km was potentially hazardous. As we drove north through the night, we talked, we laughed nervously at times, we listened to music.

We traveled in two vehicles—a two-ton refrigerated truck full of fresh food, preserved fish, vegetables, fruit, beer, all donated by friends, supporters, and members of the Japanese surfing community who wanted to do something to help the people of the coastline they loved. The other van was filled with non-perishable items: clothes donated by surf-brand sponsors, trainers, underwear, children's books, crayons, colored pencils, and tents, sleeping bags, water and food for ourselves. The aid mission had been coordinated by a Hawaiian pro surfer, Kirby Fukunaga. There was a strange irony in an aid mission organised by a pro surfer to a region decimated by waves.

We stopped at the service area for hot coffee, cookies, chocolate. We looked at maps, spoke about where we should go, where most aid was needed. We all had a sense of purpose, a mission that needed to be accomplished. We were about to head into the aftermath of one of the worst natural disasters the world had ever seen, and we tried to remain focused. I didn't tell anyone that I was worried how I'd react when we got there and I got my first glimpse of the devastation. I had lived in Sendai for three years and felt a desperate need to do something to help the people in what was once my hometown. I'd tried not to tell people where I was going and what I'd be doing. I was worried that somehow I'd make this personal, that somehow I'd make it all about me. I didn't tell anyone that I was afraid I might break down at the wrong moment. That I was afraid I might not break down at all. That the reality might feel no different from watching the coverage of the disaster on CNN.

We drove on for a couple more hours. The surface of the road started to get uneven as we entered Fukushima prefecture, the magnitude 9.0 earthquake that shook the country on March 11th, 2011 having twisted, cracked, and torn the asphalt. A quick repair job had temporarily fixed the worst cracks, but the road still had dips and troughs every few hundred meters. We bounced along, banging our heads on the roof of the van at times. Vehicles slowed to avoid damaging the precious cargoes of supplies being transported to the north, and for the first time, I felt that I was witnessing the truly terrifying power of nature.

I had seen the earthquake and tsunami unfold in my office in Bangkok, watching the helicopter footage of the waves racing towards the shore and the oblivious drivers in their cars, the images of boats being swept onto bridges, of elderly people trying to outrun the waters to higher ground. The casualty figures started to come in slowly, small numbers at first. It was impossible to believe that the numbers would remain that small, but it was impossible to imagine just how enormous the final figures would be. My immediate fears were for my friends and their families, for old colleagues. There were no telephones, no electricity, no ways for people to be contacted.

The news continued, the figures remained small, and I went home from work to pack for a weekend of what seemed like unbelievable frivolity in light of the disaster that was unfolding in a place that was once my home—I flew to the Golden Triangle to take part in an elephant-polo competition. For the next two days I was in and out of mobile-phone range, snatching snippets of news where and when I could, constantly distracted, seeing the death toll grow. By the middle of the following week, I'd managed to trace all but a handful of friends and their families, all physically unharmed. It was another ten days until I found the last ones, alive and well, but without water or gas.

The aftershocks were unsettling. Throughout the seven days of my journey I felt many. After years spent living in Japan my body had become accustomed to earthquakes, and I'd learnt how to feel them. At first, even the slightest tremble was terrifying. I'd wake in the night with a feeling of blind panic, call friends, asking if they felt it too, waiting for another, stronger rumble. But after you've experienced a few, you learn to wait, to stay in bed until it gets stronger, to pull the covers over your head. In the dead of night I had an unflinching confidence in the power of my duvet—unless the earthquake got much stronger, the duvet would keep me safe. Apart from a few CDs tumbling off shelves and the TV falling on the floor one day, I never experienced anything more powerful. But during those few days in Tohoku, the earth creaked and groaned. One evening, sitting on the ground around a campfire in what remained of a fishing village, I felt a rolling, angry, growling rumble under the surface of the earth. I'd never felt anything like it, and with my body in direct contact with the ground, it felt even more real, yet unreal at the same time. And there was the sound, almost imperceptible, impossible to define, but very much there.

Nothing can quite prepare you for that first glimpse of the devastation left by those waves, no matter how many times you've seen it on TV, recycled every thirty minutes by the twenty-four-hour news media who supply the public with a constant flow of disaster porn, something to make us gasp in horror, to give us a frisson of morbid excitement, to make us thankful it wasn't us. And the truth is, I felt that frisson too. My first glimpse of the destruction was of rice fields that were now full of debris. I'd watched the footage over and over again on the news. I'd read all the newspapers, witnessed horrifying images of bodies partially submerged in the mud, of the devastated relatives left behind. And now, seeing it for the first time, I was shocked, horrified, speechless, strangely excitedly nervous, yet numb. Something in the brain disengages to let you get on with what you're doing—the initial shock doesn't last long. I suppose it is what's called the human coping mechanism. But it kicks in surprisingly quickly. At least, it did for me. The usual clichés are the easiest to grasp onto, the "it-looks-like-a-warzone," "it-looks-like-a-tornado-hit-it" type of comments. But it looks exactly like what it is—the aftermath of a devastating tsunami. Huge stretches of flat land dotted here and there with crushed cars, a fishing boat lying on its side two miles from the sea, towering electricity pylons crushed into the ground as if by an invisible hand. It was difficult to connect the surreal landscape that I was witnessing with the people who had perished in this very spot.

During the first couple of days, I felt strange being there. I felt like a tourist. I wanted to take photos so that I wouldn't forget, and so that the people I showed them to wouldn't forget the need for help. But at the same time it felt strange, almost as if I was collecting memories, images of other people's misery, for my own use.

We didn't stay in the disaster areas most nights. We didn't want to put a strain on the limited resources available there, nor did we want to put ourselves at risk. The likelihood of another magnitude 8 earthquake was high during those days. So every day, we commuted. We would leave the disaster areas in the evening, driving away

towards the normality of life only ten, fifteen kilometers away. We'd
stay in cheap hotels where we were guaranteed a hot shower, electricity, food. In the morning, we'd wake up early and get in the vans,
driving back towards the ocean, music on the radio, wifi switched
on in the car so that we could follow the news on our laptops and
phones. But the normality very soon turned into devastation once
again. The difference between the areas that were practically unaf-
fected and those areas that were completely destroyed was as sudden
as turning a corner. We drove down streets where houses still stood
intact, rubbish carefully piled up at the side of the road, but we'd turn
at a junction and once again be plunged into scenes of destruction.

The survivors were doing everything they could to make the
lives of their fellow survivors less difficult. People like the three
teachers from the local school who were cautiously navigating the
piles of debris in Kitaizumi, looking for memories of the now broken
homes of their students. Kitaizumi used to be a popular surf point in
Fukushima. One of the teachers pointed vaguely to a pile of timber,
futons, and blankets that looked very much like all of the other piles
of rubble, and said that one of his students' fathers died there. There
was nothing left of his home. On another of these piles someone
had made a memorial to a lost surfer—a skateboard, wetsuit, and
a clock stopped at 3:39 pm, the exact moment at which the world
changed. But amazingly, amongst the rubble, photographs survived,
CDs, books. Items that had somehow miraculously escaped the
waters, and were now waiting for their owners to come and find
them.

Walking along the seafront, I looked out at the ocean, quiet
now, gentle waves softly washing over the beach, as if embarrassed
by the wreckage they had caused. But five weeks on, huge blocks of
concrete designed to reduce the force of incoming waves lay scattered throughout the rice fields. Concrete foundations remained
where houses no longer stood, their timbers smashed to splinters.

Clothes, shoes, handbags, underwear, letters, teddy bears. Thousands of carefully guarded private lives turned inside out and laid out in the open for strangers to see. But others had already been there. Photographs, school albums, books, and toys had been carefully and lovingly retrieved from the dirt and placed in boxes along the side of the road, in the hope that their owners may still be alive, and may one day soon come and collect them.

At my feet was a box containing a water-damaged photo of a man smiling at a party, a small running shoe, a girl's rubber boot, negatives that had been carefully placed under rocks so they wouldn't blow away, and a Winnie the Pooh soft toy, gazing expectantly upwards, waiting to be picked up by the child who had lost him to the waters.

We drove south, stopping to deliver food and supplies to makeshift evacuation centers, getting closer and closer to the invisible, sinister shadow that was impacting the rescue effort more than any of the other visible, physical aspects. Five weeks after the tsunami, the small city of Minami Soma, once famous for its thousand-year-old samurai horse-racing festival, was a much quieter place than it should have been. With a population of seventy-five thousand, it should have been a bustling town, with people working, shopping, going to school. But it wasn't. A closer look revealed that the convenience stores were closed, their windows covered with newspaper to hide the empty shelves within. The few people visible in the streets were dressed in the dark green uniforms and helmets of Japan's Self Defense Forces. Restaurants were closed indefinitely, as were the supermarkets. Cars were few and far between. This was the outer circle of the Nuclear Exclusion Zone. The center of Minami Soma is about twenty-five kilometers from the Fukushima Daiichi Nuclear Plant, but other parts of the town are well within the twenty-kilometer zone. Residents within the thirty-kilometer area were told to stay inside their homes. Residents of the twenty-kilometer area had already been evacuated, and at the stroke of midnight on April 22nd, a new law was introduced making it illegal for anyone to enter the twenty-kilometer exclusion zone, resident or not. Each household was given two hours to send one member inside to retrieve items from their homes, before being ordered back to the evacuation centers. As of midnight, anyone attempting to enter the zone would be fined JPY 100,000 and face possible arrest. In spite of the stern warnings, there was no information made available to let people know when they would be allowed to return to their homes. And there were still countless bodies within the exclusion zone, as well as abandoned pets and livestock.

Our journey next took us north, further up the coast. On an icy cold, wet Monday afternoon in the small town of Namiitakaigan, we met Mr. Sugimoto, the owner of a surf shop, K's Surf, named after his son. Five weeks on, all that remained of his shop was a tangle of wires, a pile of broken wood, and a surfboard snapped in two. Everything else was lost, his business erased from the coastline that had once made his living for him. Mr. Sugimoto was in his shop when the earthquake hit, and having lived by the sea all his life, he knew that a tsunami was likely to follow. He got into his car and drove up to the highest ground he could find, a small hill on the road above his shop. And as he sat in his car, he saw the waves roll in, an unimaginable volume of water, traveling at unimaginable speeds, eating up everything in its path. The waters came up higher than anyone could have expected, engulfing the first three floors of the hotel that stood next to his shop. Five weeks after the tsunami swept away his livelihood, Mr. Sugimoto wanted to show us where his shop had once stood, and we walked together through the icy rain to see if anything of his business still remained. He made his way slowly over the piles of rubbish in rubber boots, eyes scouring the ground as he stepped over planks of wood, twisted metal, telegraph poles, and suddenly exclaimed, "It's my fax machine!" The fax machine had survived, along with the credit-card machine and the telephone wires. But that was all he found. A stand of pine trees separates the beach from the former site of K's Surf. And about thirty feet above the ground, a panel of wood is clearly visible, impaled on one of the branches, clearly indicating the height that the waves reached that day.

After the quake, Mr. Sugimoto stayed in his car for two days and nights, braving freezing winter temperatures, with no knowledge of whether his wife, children, and other family members were safe. Fortunately, they were. The waters stopped a few meters away from his house, leaving a trail of destruction and destroyed lives in their wake, but leaving the Sugimoto family home untouched.

We followed the coastline back towards the south again, through driving rain and desolate landscapes. Five weeks after March 11th, the Self Defense Forces could still be seen scouring the river banks through the mist and rain, a line of dark figures with sticks in their hands, walking slowly in single file as they searched for the hundreds of unclaimed bodies waiting to be taken home for a final goodbye.

We reached Ishinomaki, one of Japan's major fishing ports, and stood at the top of Hikarigaoka Hill, one of the city's most popular viewpoints, and one of the best places for cherry-blossom viewing. The *sakura* hadn't quite blossomed yet, but the buds were pink on the branches, and in places the delicate petals, so pale they're almost white, had burst through to welcome the new season. A sign of life where so many lives had just ended. Below, the scene was a charred mess of metal, wood, broken tiles, cars, iron girders, and the lonely remains of the handful of buildings that managed to withstand the waves. The pitched roof of a temple and a lush pine tree still stood, reminders of the community that once lived here. The Self Defense Forces still searched for the missing, estimated to total two thousand seven hundred in this town alone. A few bunches of wilted flowers paid silent witness to the scenes below. Bulldozers worked their way through the wreckage. After the tsunami, Ishinomaki had burned. There was still a faint smell of smoke in the air. And all around, cars, tires, cooking pots, cupboards, a plastic waste-paper bin with a cartoon frog, a heater, plastic piping, a children's story book, a blanket, vital at this time of year when snow still falls, a mirror, a crash helmet, a cracked teacup, a rice bowl, a mattress, a sweater, a child's car seat, a tube of sunscreen, a lone slipper, a pair of skis. All the trivial items of everyday life.

We carried on south, making deliveries of supplies along the way, and entered Miyagi prefecture, my home for three years, and the Oshika Peninsula, an area of outstanding natural beauty, dotted with small fishing villages, and the gateway to the sacred island of Kinkazan. I used to go for drives there, taking the boat to the island to feed the deer, stopping at the small villages to see what local produce was for sale and to take a moment to appreciate the beauty of this extraordinary place. Oshika was the part of Honshu closest to the epicenter of the March 11th earthquake, and one of the areas hardest hit. The beauty of the peninsula was wiped out that afternoon, the one main road buckled and cracked, huge fishing boats tossed ashore, entire villages wiped away. On March 14th, three days after the quake, a thousand bodies had washed up on Oshika's beaches. And five weeks later, the police were still discovering more. We drove along the coastal road, and as I looked out of the window, I saw something I hadn't seen before. A line of people in white uniforms, pushing a stretcher on a trolley, with a blue body bag on it. I started seeing the debris around me differently. This wasn't just the wreckage of houses, this was a graveyard for people who still hadn't been found. My mind started playing tricks on me: a piece of wood sticking out of a house now looked like a broken arm, the trousers lying on the ground still had someone in them, a rock sticking out of the mud looked like a submerged back.

Electricity had been restored to parts of the peninsula, but there was no gas, and water was limited. There were numerous makeshift evacuation centers. One small garage in Kobuchihama was now home to fifteen people. The fifteen inhabitants of the garage huddled around a fire in an oil drum to try and keep warm in the chilly early morning air on a sunny day that, in any other place at any other time, would have been considered beautiful. They rolled out futons on the floor at night, sleeping closely together, not only to keep warm, but also because there was not enough space for all of them. Kobuchihama was one of the main centers for oyster cultivation in the region, the harbor sheltering the twenty-four fishing boats used by the men of the village. But five weeks on, only seven remained. One of the fishermen told me that when the earthquake struck, he got in his boat and headed far out to sea. He stayed out at sea for two days and two nights, not knowing what he would find upon his return. And when he came home, after the tsunami warnings had been canceled, he found that all that remained of his village was a handful of houses just high enough to escape the reach of the waters. Everything else was gone.

Amid the wreckage, there was laughter, smiles. It was astonishing to see that humor still thrived here. The survivors have survived, and continued to do all they could to survive. The people of the north are strong, practical, pragmatic. On a sunny morning, five weeks after the tsunami washed away everything they had, the oyster farmers of Kobuchihama were combing the debris to find items they could still use. The tsunami had destroyed everything, but a large part of the wreckage was made up of huge rusted iron anchors, items that could be used again if salvaged. These anchors were heavy enough to need four grown men to lift them, but seemingly light enough to be tossed about by the waves at will. We asked a group of fishermen, relatives of the inhabitants of the garage, if we could help them. They looked at us uncertainly, before handing us serrated metal hooks. One of them handed me his pink Hello Kitty gloves—to protect my hands. With no real idea of what the task was going to be, and with the vague instructions of "go over there, you'll work it out," I stepped through the wreckage and walked to where the work was going on. The men were using the serrated edges of the hooks to cut through the tangles of rope, fishing nets, and electricity cables that now tied the anchors together. One of them pointed to the electricity cables, and told me that they could make money out of them, the copper running through them being a valuable commodity. These were the anchors that the oysters were grown on, the seeds being planted on scallop shells bought from Aomori and Hokkaido, and taken out to sea to let the oysters quietly grow in the rich waters. It takes two to three years for the oysters to be ready to eat. And it will take at least five years from now for the men to be able to harvest their first oysters since the disaster. They don't know what they'll do in the meantime, but for now, they're salvaging what they can to start working again. Anchors, thick ropes, buoys. And all the time, smiles, laughter. One of the oyster farmers slipped on a piece of wood and fell heavily to the ground, twisting his leg awkwardly beneath him. He was motionless for a few moments, and then let out a cry of pain. "My bum's split in two," he cried, and the men smiled and laughed, pulling him to his feet.

I was working alongside Mr. Kimura, one of the younger oyster farmers. A husband and father, he hadn't seen his wife or son since the day of the tsunami. She had gone to pick him up from school in her car. But they never came home. Five weeks on, Mr. Kimura was still waiting for them, as were his daughters. And until the day that they find their bodies, his daughters will always live with the belief that one day their mother and brother will come back to them. As he told me this, Mr. Kimura looked into the distance and smiled. "But I can't sit around crying all day," he said. "What would my daughters think?" And he carried on with his work, cutting ropes, carrying anchors, retrieving the tools that will help the town live again. My eyes were stinging. I made it my duty to go and collect buoys from further along the harbor, away from everyone else. The weather was glorious, the sun was shining, the sky a perfect spring blue. I turned my face upwards so as not to let my tears fall, not wanting to be weak when everyone else was being so strong. I looked back at the men working in the sunshine, and for a moment it looked like a normal scene. But of course it wasn't.

As I walked back, carrying two salvaged buoys in my arms, and knowing that the following day I'd be on a plane flying home to the normality of my world, I made a promise to come back here. Before we left, I told Mr. Kimura that I'd return to eat their first harvest of oysters, five years from now. "Please do," he said, "if you don't mind the radiation." He laughed, I smiled, we returned to our vans, and we carried on to the next village.

Originally from Yorkshire, Nicola Chilton has lived and worked in Asia since 2008, with stints in Japan, Hong Kong, and currently Bangkok. "Five Weeks On" is based on a seven-day journey to Tohoku in northern Japan to deliver food and clothing to villages devastated by the March 11 earthquake and tsunami. The trip was organised by Kirby Fukunaga and a group of friends who all had a connection to Tohoku, and who all felt a need to do something to help. At the time, none of the major aid organisations was accepting volunteers, but there were still thousands of people struggling to live from day to day without the basic necessities.

TOKEN

By Edna Zhou

THE conversations always went the same way.

"Where are you from?" The taxi driver—or the waiter, the sales clerk, or nosy bystander—would ask upon hearing my accented, not-quite-perfect Mandarin. "Korea? Japan?"

"*Wo shi mei guo ren*" (I'm American), I'd reply—often with a sigh, because I knew what was coming next.

"*Mei guo ren?*" American?

I'd nod, bracing myself for the inevitable.

"But you don't look American." Sometimes, this was said in a sincerely confused way. Sometimes it was said cruelly, as if accusing me of lies.

"Well, I am," I'd assert through gritted teeth.

"Okay... but where are your parents from?"

With Westerners, the conversation went a little differently, but we still ended up in the same place.

"Wow, your English is really good!" the new coworker would say, or the guy at the bar, or the lost tourist who asked me for directions.

"Well, it should be," I'd reply coolly. "I'm American."

Sometimes, they'd leave it at that. But sometimes they would press on:

"Oh, but... where are you from *really*?"

Where am I from? I was born in Ohio and I grew up in Pennsylvania. I smile with all my teeth, pepper my speech with far too many *awesome*s, and ask for weather in Fahrenheit.

Where am I really from? I'm really from America. And for me, that label doesn't come with any associations of color.

Yet when I moved to China, hearing those two phrases—getting complimented on my English and then being pressured to reveal my "real" country of origin—constantly reminded me that I was different, and not in a good way. That all people could see was my Asian face.

Those taxi drivers and nosy strangers and guys at the bar would never stop asking me questions until we arrived at the final destination: "Ah, you're a *hua qiao*," (*an overseas Chinese*), they'd say, finally satisfied that they could peg me into one of their preconceived labels—as if accepting that I was truly an American who just happened to have Asian features was too far outside the realm of possibility. Knowing I had Chinese parents helped them make their world make sense. But why did it have to get to that point every time? Why couldn't I just be an American?

My greatest frustration in moving to China wasn't the public spitting, the censorship, or the pollution. I was used to all that because (exasperated sigh) *yes*, it is indeed the country of my heritage, and I'd spent countless summers in Shanghai growing up. No, my greatest frustration came from the number of encounters I had with people who could not separate my looks from my passport, my ethnicity from my nationality.

My first-ever move abroad found me in Dalian, a second-tier city in northern China, in 2008 between my second and third years of university. I was eighteen at the time and had had very little experience living amongst an Asian population. Though I'd traveled to Shanghai with my family every summer, I'd been kept in an English bubble; I mostly just visited relatives and spoke to my parents, who translated everything for me. On top of that, my family speaks Shanghai dialect, so I picked up that language as a child. So I arrived in Dalian knowing very little Mandarin, and with very little knowledge of how to be in China on my own.

Instead, I brought with me eighteen years of experience as the "token Asian" in a small suburban part of Pennsylvania. I grew up in a mostly Caucasian town and went to very Caucasian-dominated schools and university. While I was cognizant of the fact that there was something different about my looks, I embraced that difference—friends jokingly referred to me as the "token Asian" and I even had T-shirts with that nickname printed on the back; to me it was a source of humor, not an actual defining characteristic. That, plus the fact that I was not treated any differently by my peers because of my looks, meant a part of me never truly comprehended that I did not look like my white friends. Thus, like a duck raised in a family of swans who then believes he *is* a swan, when I looked in the mirror, I did not see myself as someone who looks Chinese.

So to arrive in China and suddenly become *invisible*—to feel everyone's eyes just go straight through me, because I suddenly looked the same as *1.3 billion* other people—was soul-crushing. After eighteen years of believing I was a swan, it broke my heart to blend in and realize I was, in fact, a duck.

I would use any excuse possible—loud phone calls at the coffee shop, large-font English books held out in plain view on the metro—as often as possible to let the foreigners around me know that I wasn't a local; that there was in fact someone around them who could understand their embarrassing, confidential private conversations carried out in loud English.

Upon settling down in China, I immediately began to notice a difference in the way I was treated by the locals, in comparison to the Caucasian friends I hung out with. As the whole intention behind my move had been to study Mandarin, many of my first friends were fellow American students, and later my circle extended into the local English-teacher community—many of whom were American or British, all non-Asian.

Whenever we went out, their smallest attempts at Chinese— even just mustering a *ni hao* or *xie xie*—would be met with a big smile and an enthusiastic, "Wow, your Chinese is so good!" Even friends who were Asian but not Chinese—Korean, Japanese, Thai— would be complimented on their language skills.

Then I would follow up with a few sentences in decent, albeit accented, Mandarin. Or sometimes, like when asking for special requests in a restaurant or giving specific directions in a taxi, I'd point to my friend and say, "Please ask them—their *Putonghua* is better than mine." And in each scenario, I would watch as the person's face changed from being impressed by the foreigner who speaks Mandarin to disgusted at the Chinese girl whose tones weren't perfect. I could imagine their thought process as they realized something was not quite right about me: *Wait, you don't speak Chinese? Wait, aren't you Chinese? No, stop saying you're American. You look Chinese, so you are Chinese. So… why don't you speak Chinese?*

Walking down the streets of any Chinese city, surrounded by advertisements for whitening creams and streets full of Audis and BMWs, I can't say I didn't understand where all the Asian-on-Asian racism was coming from. The country has spent the last couple of decades gunning for a prime position on the world stage, and its citizens want to keep up with the Joneses. Cars from Germany, wine from France, purses from Italy: foreign is perceived to be better, and that extends to appearance.

It's why my Caucasian friends were constantly sought out for gigs where all they had to do was speak a couple lines in English in a commercial; one was even offered a large sum of money just to be seen with a company's product for one afternoon at an open house. Meanwhile, other Asian-American friends were offered less money in their English-teaching contracts than their Caucasian counterparts, and some were outright denied positions based on their appearance.

Everywhere I went in China, I saw my Caucasian friends getting preferential treatment. Yet I was almost never on the receiving end of these perks and accolades, simply because I didn't *look* like a stereotypical American.

For example: for a few months, to supplement my travel habit, I worked as a substitute teacher at various English schools around Dalian. Each time I stepped into a new classroom, parents would look visibly concerned when they saw that someone who looked like *them* was teaching their children English. Then they'd start looking around as if I'd simply hidden the usual Caucasian teacher in a nearby closet.

Another time, a friend took me with him on a job at a local university; they needed two Americans to record audiotapes to accompany their English conversation books. After taping a few practice lines, the woman in charge claimed my American voice was "exactly" what they needed. She left to retrieve our payment, but then returned with the school director a few minutes later and suddenly rescinded her offer, claiming my speech on the tapes had a *Chinese* accent. I was flabbergasted: my accent is as neutrally American as they come (so I've been told by many a Brit and Aussie), yet she was letting my appearance affect how she heard and interpreted the sound of my voice.

Dating in Asia also opened up new opportunities for judgment. When I hung out with platonic male friends who happened to be Caucasian, there were times I was mistaken for a hooker or scammer trying to target a Westerner. After I met my (very pale and ginger) British fiancé, whenever we traveled together I could see the sneering looks, the staring accusations, all screaming, *gold-digger.*

We are constantly being judged, and the ten-year age gap between us doesn't help: people assume I'm only with him because I'm after his bank account and a green card.

My Caucasian friends in China complained frequently about being stared at in public, singled out by touts, and overcharged by vendors; they always voiced their desires to blend in like I did. It's a classic grass-is-greener argument. Maybe it's just my ego speaking, but I'd prefer being put on a pedestal than being looked down upon.

All of the judging, the assumptions, the condescension, the racism—it's all very tiring and leads to a major identity crisis. In slang terms I'm referred to as a "banana," or someone who is "yellow on the outside and white on the inside." However, there are still a few Chinese characteristics and cultural traditions I've inherited from my parents, so I very much feel like a first-generation American, not someone whose identity has been firmly cemented in the country for decades or centuries. Yet I'm definitely American enough that I do not feel like I could be called Chinese; with my mindset, attitude, and habits, I do not fit in in China. So I'm too Chinese for Americans, too American for the Chinese—where do I belong?

People often ask me why I moved abroad at such a young age and why I love it so. Why do I insist on moving to a new country every other year? Why don't I have any immediate plans to return to the States—especially considering the stress that being on my guard against racism puts upon me? The US is the only place where I've felt accepted without question, so why don't I just go back?

Some days, I don't know the answer to that question. But one large reason to stay is the nature of the expat. The expatriate life attracts a certain type of person. Moving abroad, especially to Asia, requires an open mind, and that lifestyle appeals to the type of person who knows better than to jump to conclusions or stand by

stereotypes. Living abroad forces someone to throw any preconceived notions they had out the window; an expat in Asia learns not
to be fazed by many things, least of all a person who comes from
mixed cultures.

So in each city I move to, I always end up finding at least a
few friends from similar backgrounds, who can relate to my story—
from Chinese-Australian to Swedish-Lebanese—or friends who at
least aren't confused by their friends' mixed heritages, and are who
understanding and patient when we experience the occasional identity crisis. No matter which city I live in, I always find friends who
don't see me as Chinese or American; they see me as a combination
of everywhere I've been, everything I've done, and everything I've
learned up to that point. They just see me as Edna.

After that first year in Dalian, I went on to live in Shanghai, and
then moved to Singapore after graduating from university in 2010.
After spending a total of three years in Asia, in 2012, I moved to
Paris (where the racism persisted, but in a totally different and in
some ways even more condescending manner). Moving to Europe
made me realize that Asia is my true love; I long to wake up each
day surrounded by the sounds and the smells, the colors and the
chaos of Shanghai, of Singapore—yet each time I consider moving
back, I wonder if I'm ready to face the judgment and presumptions
again, the daily battles with taxi drivers; if I'm prepared to have my
guard up at all times, to once more be on the defensive with loud
phone calls and large English books. But I think about all the friends
I've made over the years in Asia: other children of immigrants, of
mixed heritage, of dual nationalities, who know their identity does
not define them. I think about all the friends I've met who could not
care less where someone is from. And I know the answer.

Where do I belong? I belong wherever I want to belong, because
those taxi drivers don't define me, just like my looks and my passport

don't define me. I know this is a battle that won't be resolved in my lifetime; there are still far too many preconceived notions to fight. I know that whenever I do decide to move back, it won't be easy. I'll still get compliments on my English; I'll still get frustrated and angry. But I can hope that eventually, one day, just saying, "I am American" will be good enough.

Edna Zhou is an American sports journalist and serial expat who first moved abroad at 18, then just kept moving. She has lived and worked in China, Singapore, Paris, and Italy, and is always thinking about the next place to call home. She writes about her adventures at <u>www.expatedna.com</u>.

NINETY MINUTES IN TSIM SHA TSUI

By Susan Blumberg-Kason

I froze in front of Hankow Center. As if in a trance, I stepped into the building's open-air ground floor. There I found the directory, in the same place it had been sixteen years earlier when I lived in Hong Kong. My eyes scanned the names: J, K, L… and there she was, my former doctor. Seeing her name again pulled me back to a place I had tried to escape long ago. I blinked back tears.

It had been a Saturday in October, the day warm and dry, as it always is that time of year in Hong Kong. My doctor, a British woman named Sally, had placed her hand on my shoulder while I stood in a daze in the middle of her office. Even now I could still hear her words.

"You have an infection that is usually sexually transmitted. Please know that in Chinese culture husbands might cheat, but it doesn't mean they don't love their wives."

It felt as if Sally had punched me in the stomach. Tottering back against the examining table, I softly asked, "Could I have gotten it from something else? Swimming or a toilet seat?"

"I suppose that's possible, but it's not common."

No, it couldn't have been Li. It must have come from the YMCA where I swam most mornings. Maybe I had unknowingly placed my suit on an infected area in the changing room. Just twenty-six then and going on my second year of marriage, I not only wanted to stay married to the mainland Chinese man who had wooed me during my first semester in graduate school, but I also couldn't imagine leaving Hong Kong. I hadn't planned to stay there for just a couple years while I studied; I wanted to spend all of my adult life there. When I confronted Li over the phone a couple days later—he was in China for a few months to extend his student visa and passport—I believed him when he insisted that he didn't have a girlfriend. For years after that I kept quiet, fearing that my family, friends, and doctor would convince me to return to the US if I allowed it to become real. It was easier to be in denial than face the ramifications of the truth.

For a moment, staring at the white letters that spelled Sally's name and office number on the black directory board, I pictured taking the ramshackle elevator upstairs to see her. I could wait in the reception area, flipping through Hong Kong gossip magazines just like old times, until she had a few free moments. My new husband Tom was napping back at the hotel and wasn't expecting me for an hour or two. But instead of walking toward the elevator, I found myself turning away from the building, from the cramped jewelry stores and bank branches on the ground floor, in the same zombie state I had been the day Sally told me that Li had cheated.

Sally probably wouldn't remember me. It had been so long ago, a year before the Handover. And if she did, what would I say? *I was in the neighborhood and thought I would say hello. You were right all those years ago. I'm sorry I didn't believe you then, but wanted to tell you that I'm happy now, a mother of three and married to a man who treats me as an equal. Thank you for trying to talk some sense into me.*

But it seemed silly and sentimental to go back there after all this time, not just to see Sally, but also to revisit the pain I had kept inside for years until I finally gained the courage to leave Li. Since my divorce, I had learned to stand up for myself and trust my instincts. Or so I thought. For the last decade, my interactions with him—by phone, by email, or in person—were all conducted in America. I had been back to San Francisco a couple times since I left Li there, and had lived in Chicago for the twelve years since our divorce came through. But this was the first time I had returned to Hong Kong or anywhere in Asia since I had left my expat life—still married to Li—a decade and a half ago.

After I returned to the US, I often wondered if I would ever make it back to Hong Kong. The city wasn't just a fleeting stop. It was where I had come of age, arriving as an innocent college student who had never had a boyfriend, and leaving as a married woman, pregnant with my first child. When I repatriated to San Francisco at twenty-seven, I was hopeful for my future. Now at forty-one, I still had hope, but also security and the knowledge that my bills would be paid on time and that my kids were safe in Chicago. I didn't have to worry that their father would whisk them off to another country without telling me.

Not too long after our divorce, Li had moved back to Hong Kong for a few years. During that time, the territory was plagued with SARS, bird flu, and swine flu; there always seemed to be a reason to stay away. It wasn't until my youngest child was two that I thought Tom and I could sneak away for a quick trip to Hong Kong while my mom watched the kids. Li had returned to China and was remarried, too.

*

Drifting away from Hankow Center, I found the underground walkway to cross Kowloon Park Drive. When I reemerged on dazzling Canton Road, I saw that it had transformed over the years from a street of electronics and souvenir shops to one packed with European and American luxury boutiques. I made my way to a

Hong Kong home ware and clothing shop that I'd hoped to visit on this trip. While I perused the store for almost an hour, the emotions that had welled up in front of Sally's building seemed to dissipate.

But back on the street, I paused again. As throngs of shoppers strolled by, I stared across Canton Road, a street I had traversed hundreds of times during my expat years. A street where Li's other family suddenly came to life again.

I felt as if I was back in the mid-'90s, accompanying Li to the ferry terminal across the street. China Hong Kong City, it was called. The first time I sent Li off to southern China to visit his ex-wife Wei Ling and daughter Ting-Ting, many questions raced through my mind. How would he interact with his ex-wife? Would his daughter take to him after a three-year absence? I was doing the right thing in supporting this reunion, wasn't I? These were heavy issues for a twenty-four-year-old newlywed.

I had wanted to greet Li at the terminal when he returned that Sunday, and thought the two of us could stroll along Canton Road toward the MTR station, perhaps stopping in our favorite food court in the Tsim Sha Tsui district before boarding the train back to our campus apartment up by the China border. I usually ordered a large bowl of Japanese udon soup and Li a Chinese-Western hybrid dish like thin pork chops served over white rice, topped with a ladle of gravy. But Li had insisted I wait for him in our dorm room. He didn't want to trouble me.

"It's no trouble," I said. "You know I love going into Kowloon. We could hang out there a bit. It'd be a nice change of pace."

Li wouldn't hear of me schlepping forty-five minutes to meet him. At the time, I just thought he didn't want me to take out two hours from studying to travel to the ferry pier and back. Later on I would gradually realize that Li preferred to compartmentalize his life, including me in some things and not in others. As he was getting ready for his first trip to see his daughter, I didn't want to make a big deal about it and agreed to wait for him in our dorm room.

When he arrived home from that trip, he seemed refreshed and encouraged by his reunion with his then six-year-old daughter. I sat next to him as he pulled out a small album of prints he had developed at a one-hour photo store in Zhuhai. Ting-Ting looked bashfully at the camera and to my surprise, resembled not Li but both of his parents. That was all the more apparent when Li flipped the page and I came face to face with Wei Ling, her almond eyes and gentle smile illuminating the page. His rundown of the weekend confirmed that Ting-Ting took up his attention in Zhuhai, not Wei Ling. I felt secure enough to see him off a couple more times to visit his daughter and ex-wife, trips where again I accompanied him to the ferry pier but went no further.

*

Looking around Canton Road, I could almost picture the day I spent with Wei Ling and Ting-Ting. Any one of the red taxis cruising down the street could have been the one we shared all those years ago.

When Li learned that Wei Ling and Ting-Ting would be passing through Hong Kong after a group tour to Thailand, I volunteered to take them out to lunch. He would already be back in China because of an expired Hong Kong student visa, a month before we were to move to San Francisco. I was four months pregnant with my oldest son and only child with Li. Nervous and afraid that Wei Ling would be cold and closed off, I planned to spend only an hour with them, enough time to eat lunch and give Ting-Ting a few art supplies and a money envelope from Li.

But the moment I met Wei Ling, my feelings changed. She seemed nothing like the plain, selfish woman Li had described over the years. Instead, Wei Ling had big brown eyes and a petite, slender frame. Her warm smile and soft-spoken words had a calming influence on me that day.

After lunch at a hotel buffet in Mongkok, Wei Ling turned to me. "Would you have time to go with us to the ferry pier? We could talk a bit more in the taxi."

"That would be wonderful," I said, relieved to hear this. I was just getting to know Wei Ling and Ting-Ting, so it seemed premature to end our afternoon together quite yet.

Once we arrived on Canton Road, I playfully argued with Wei Ling over who would pay for the cab ride. I won in the end, with Wei Ling promising to pay next time. Next time, I told her, perhaps we would meet in San Francisco.

"It would be great if Ting-Ting could visit us after we have the baby and settle in," I said, presuming the latter would come true.

Wei Ling peered up at me sheepishly. "Thank you. That sounds like a great idea. Being a single mother is so tiring."

As an overhead announcer called for their boat to board, I understood that Wei Ling would accompany Ting-Ting on the long flight when the time came, at least on that first trip. And that was fine with me. It was a weird relationship, I knew, but Ting-Ting was Li's daughter. Plus, I liked Wei Ling. I hugged her tightly and turned to Ting-Ting to do the same. After we let go, she waved as she and her mother headed for the door that led to the boat ramp.

That meeting turned out to be the only time I saw Wei Ling and Ting-Ting. Settling into San Francisco never happened, and Li and I never followed up with Ting-Ting about visiting us. That day I met Wei Ling, neither of us spoke much about Li. Over the years I wished I had asked her about her marriage to him. But I knew if I had, I would be admitting that mine had problems, too.

Now back on Canton Road after all these years, I wished I could go back and freeze time. Shoulder-to-shoulder shoppers crammed the streets, their faces and bodies a blur. Even so, for the first time in years I could see my twenty-six-year-old self. She might appear confident on the outside, but inside she was struggling to stay afloat in a complicated, confusing marriage for which she was ill-prepared. Yes, if I could stop time, I would embrace her tightly because no one had done so for me back then. That was because I never confided in anyone, not my best friends, my mother, or close coworkers. And when Sally tried to warn me, I refused to listen. Now I longed to go back and tell my younger self to have confidence, trust your instincts, and put yourself first.

I felt tears fall down my cheeks, but made no effort to wipe them away. In true Hong Kong fashion the passersby left me alone, either letting me save face or perhaps not even noticing me. It was only now at forty-one, back in Hong Kong, in Tsim Sha Tsui, on Canton Road that I remembered how alone I had felt back then.

How could I have been so naïve to think that these memories were just a thing of the past? Just because I had moved on from Li didn't mean I had reconciled my issues with my twenty-something self. The choices I made, the problems I ignored, the stories I told myself to sustain my marriage to Li—they all resurfaced here on the tip of the Kowloon peninsula.

There was still time before Tom and I were to meet a friend for dinner. While I had planned to stay out a bit longer, wandering through the narrow streets in Tsim Sha Tsui as the sun went down and the neon signs illuminated the area, that all seemed trivial now. Tom was back in the hotel room and I wanted nothing more than to crawl under the covers next to him until dinner. I finally wiped my tears and rushed back to the hotel, putting to an end that part of my past once and for all.

Susan Blumberg-Kason is the author Good Chinese Wife (Sourcebooks, 2014), a memoir of her five-year marriage to a musician from central

China and how she tried to adapt to Chinese family life as a wife, daughter-in-law, and mother. She is also the books editor of Asian Jewish Life magazine and can be found online at <u>www.susanbkason. com</u>. Remarried, Susan lives in suburban Chicago with her husband, three children, and a clingy cat.

HERE COMES THE SUN

By Leza Lowitz

First Meeting

HIROO Orphanage is a pink industrial-looking building in a posh section of western Tokyo. The emperor founded this orphanage after the war. My husband Shogo and I are going there to meet our son.

On February 9th, we take the subway through the city. When we walk through the big glass doors, holding hands, I'm more nervous than I was on our wedding day.

We're led into the entrance hall, where there's a giant stuffed panda slumped over on a bench in the waiting area. There are no kids around. It's very quiet and orderly. *Where is everyone?* I think. We're allowed into the playground behind the main building. My heart pounds in my chest. I've waited ten years to meet my son. What will he look like? Will he smile when he sees us? Laugh? Cry? Will he like me?

A woman leads us down a hall and into a courtyard. Yuto is pointed out to us. He's chubby and wears a dirty blue down jacket that makes him look even bigger. His hair is cut in a rice-bowl that sits above his red, ruddy cheeks. His pants are too big and rolled up to his ankles, and they seem filthy, too. We look at him and wave. He doesn't smile. Instead, he runs the opposite direction and hides in the corner. He doesn't want to have anything to do with us.

Shogo and I exchange glances. Wordlessly, we agree. Who could blame him? He's been down this path before. Why should he trust us?

We don't chase after him. Instead, we approach the other kids in the playground and start to play with them in sandbox, push them in the swings, play hide-and-go seek. Gradually, Yuto comes over to us, observing in a cautious way. His eyes are brown and the whites have small brown spots on them. I wonder if he's sick.

Soon our hour is up. He hasn't approached us once.

We go back to our car. Shogo reaches over and touches my hand. "Don't worry. It's going to be okay," he says.

Yuto is not what I imagined my child would be. I don't know exactly what I imagined, but somehow, it's not this. Some kind of joyful greeting, where he runs into my arms like a movie? Right. When has my life ever looked like that? I take a deep breath and try to put myself in his shoes. I'm sure I'm not the picture he had in mind for his mother, either. For one, I'm white. Foreign. American.

This is not going to work, I know it, I think. *How stupid of me to think I could even try.* I try to stifle my tears, but the more I try to push them down, the more forcefully they arise. Is this grief? Is it okay to feel grief? Shouldn't I feel happy, overjoyed now that we have a son after twelve years of marriage, half of it spent trying to start a family?

I try to express all this to Shogo.

"It's okay. Just feel what you feel," he says, squeezing my hand. He's in it for the long run. To him, this is it. There's no Plan B. He's not uncomfortable with sadness, or with silence, or with any of it, it seems.

I want to be strong like Shogo, a samurai. But I'm not. I'm an American girl from San Francisco, trying to understand how life has brought me here.

Like The Lotus

Like many women of my generation, especially those from broken families, I've been ambivalent about starting a family for so long that when I wake up and realize it is too late, it is, in fact, too late.

But is it?

Before I had a child, there were a few things I wanted. I wanted to have a strong, solid relationship. I wanted to establish my career. I wanted to see the world. I wanted to heal my relationship with my own father and mother. Last but not least, I wanted to find myself. I considered these prerequisites for having children. The items on this list weren't frivolous. To me, those prerequisite steps would spell the success or failure of the endeavor.

I'd seen my mother sacrifice her own needs, desires, and dreams to raise her children, and I'd seen the toll that had taken on all of us—when she was forty, she woke up and realized she didn't know who she was. Granted, it was the seventies, and we lived in Berkeley, California—a hotbed of radicalism and social change. She'd done what most women of her generation did—had families, not careers—and when we were old enough to take care of ourselves, she decided it was time to take care of herself. I agreed, but the decision led to divorce. Watching her, I thought that starting a family would be something I'd do after I'd "gotten my shit together." And I thought, as many do, that "if it's meant to be, it will be."

For so long, I didn't want to have a family of my own because I didn't want to bring anyone into such a dysfunctional family. That feeling held me back for years. Then I met my husband, who loved me for who I was—Jewish neurosis and all.

*

I met Shogo at a jazz bar in Yokohama where mutual friends had a gig. He was a poet and a martial artist, and we shared a love of literature and mind-body traditions. But I'd just come off a long relationship, and getting together with a Japanese man was as far from my mind as Timbuktu.

One night I was sitting on the couch in my apartment, enjoying my independence yet bemoaning one too many bad dates set up by well-meaning friends. I'd positioned myself perfectly under the light of the single lamp in my tatami room and was reading Galway Kinnell's poem "After Making Love We Hear Footsteps."

The phone rang, breaking the silence.

It was Shogo, a month after our meeting at the jazz club, wanting to know if I wanted to see a movie with him.

I liked him, and his gentle, wise manner drew me in. Still, doomsday thoughts arose from the recesses of my mind like bad Japlish T-shirts: *Cross-cultural relationships are doomed to fail. A woman needs a man like a fish needs a bicycle.*

Whoa. Did I really say yes to this fresh-faced Japanese man in a polo shirt and sockless Dockers who liked Kundera and knew how to make a Hollandaise sauce? And why wasn't he married at 33? Was he gay?

"Just picky," he said. And he hadn't met a Japanese woman who "matched" him.

Did I "match" him, I wondered? We were so different. He's not my type. He's not my race. He's not my religion, though I hardly practice it myself. He's not so many things.

Maybe that's okay, I realized. Because he was so many other things on my list of "perfect partner." Patient, wise, independent, smart, and he called me on my shit. He was someone with whom I felt I could grow. And I could help him grow, too. It wasn't long before he quietly swept me off my feet.

A year later, we married.

"Let's enjoy being newly-wet," he said. I didn't correct him. It seemed like just the right word.

He helped me see that because of the muddy waters I'd come up from, like the lotus, I could grow stronger, more resilient, and also more compassionate and vulnerable. Wasn't it ironic that all the muck I'd tried to wash off was really fertilizer to create a richer soil? But I still had work to do before "starting a family" was on my radar.

*

Ten years go by. We try to have a child, and fail. I do a few Western treatments and many Eastern approaches, including acupuncture (Chinese style, dagger-like thick needles, not thin Japanese ones), Qi Gong, Chinese herbs, past-life regression, lymph drainage, and a host of other alternative therapies. I dive deep into yoga for healing. It helps me calm my mind and body. Even if I don't get pregnant, I don't get as stressed out about failing, and that's progress.

As time goes by, with no child on the horizon, I try not to get discouraged, to see the lesson, to build my relationship and community. It certainly isn't the first test I've faced, and it won't be the last.

With Shogo's help, I open a yoga studio in Tokyo, and even though I'm not yet a mother myself, I take heart in mothering others who come there to heal. I get a lot of practice being motherly. There are many like the tall, young Japanese kid who comes to try yoga for the first time. He's stiff and nervous. We stretch, shake, sweat, and do partner yoga. He loosens up and laughs.

After class, he comes up and takes me aside. He says he's having emotional problems, and as he talks, surprisingly, he starts to cry. I give him a hug. He holds onto me for a long time and starts to sob like a baby. Hugging a stranger, and being emotional in this way is very unusual, especially in Japan, especially in front of the whole class. But it's a good thing that he feels comfortable enough to release his feelings, or maybe he's just so deeply distraught that he can't close the floodgates. When he recovers enough to compose himself, he bows and thanks me, and says he'll be back.

I'm sure I'll never see him again.

I already feel like a mother.

I think I can love anyone now.

Hello

One of the teachers at my yoga studio, a British woman named Em, occasionally reads tabloids like *Hello* and *Us*, which she gets from a teacher at the international school. When she's done, she passes them on to me. It's our preferred form of mindless entertainment, and I'm hooked on them, too.

In one issue of *Hello*, there is an article about Angelina Jolie and Brad Pitt planning to adopt a little boy from Vietnam named Pax. The article mentions a woman named Dr. Jane Aronson, who helps people with foreign adoptions. I get on the web and google her. She has two adopted children herself. I take a deep breath and email her asking for referrals, not expecting a reply. To my enormous surprise, she emails me right away (she is online at the same time!) with the names of two agencies who do international adoptions for people living abroad.

I write her right back, thanking her for being there, for helping me, for hearing me, for acknowledging my existence. This is a busy woman, a famous woman, an amazing woman. Who am I to her? I tell her I'd given up hope of ever having kids, but she's rekindled it in me. To my surprise, she emails me right back again. *You will adopt. You will move on*, she writes. I can feel the power in this woman through these seven simple words. I believe her. I sit at the computer and cry. I love this woman, though we've never met and probably never will, I think. *Thank you*, I write. *Thank you*. Someone has "gotten" me.

Her faith gives me more faith. I soldier on. Shogo stays by my side. We celebrate our twelfth wedding anniversary. Seems we're in it for the long haul.

Adoption: First Step

After that, another friend tells me of the government agency's Child Guidance Center—Jido Sodan Jo. There are offices in each of Tokyo's twenty-three wards. The CGC handles adoptions, though adoption is uncommon in Japan.

There's a long-standing stigma about adoption, a reluctance of birth parents or extended family to relinquish rights even when they cannot take care of a child. There are comparatively few healthy and young kids available. That year there are only 1,320 adoptions—less than half of those between unrelated children and parents. Compare this to the US, where there are approximately 127,000 annual adoptions and where 1.7 million households have an adopted child. Adoption in Japan is rare and difficult. I should give up. But I know my child is out there, and I'm determined to find him.

We apply through the CGC, though the odds are daunting. The application asks questions like: Why do you want a child? What kind of upbringing and education would you give your child? What are the most important values you would share with a child? What about religion?

Filling out the application is challenging, but it's an opportunity to become very clear on what our values are and what kind of parents we see ourselves being. We talk about issues most parents don't address until they come up, if then. It feels good to sort these things out in advance in a calm, organized way. Just the same, having these discussions pulls at my heartstrings.

Will we ever get through the logistics and just get to be parents?

Bloodlines

Slowly and with caution, we tell our friends that we're hoping to adopt. Partly it's to ease the pain of the constant barrage of questions, such as "When are you having kids?" Or "Why don't you have children yet?" But then we have to deal with more careless comments. People, it turns out, have strong opinions on adoption, especially people who have naturally born children. "Oh, we'd love to adopt too, someday," or "We considered adoption, too," and so on.

One thing everyone agrees on is this: "Japan is a difficult country to adopt from."

Not only are there few children up for adoption, but it's the only country in the world where you need to get the extended family's approval for the process. Bloodlines are seen as all-important: one's ancestors are one's link to the past. The family registry, or *koseki*, goes back generations and lists each birth and marriage tying family to family. I remember that when we got married, keeping my own name had created a problem with the *koseki*.

Once again, doubts start to flood my mind. If we succeed in this adoption, I'll be bucking the system again. I know how difficult it is to raise a child, let alone one who is adopted in a country that is not particularly "open" to adoption. In Japan, most adoptions are kept secret. Some children don't even find out until their parents die.

So we brace ourselves and ask my father-in-law for permission. I find out, to my surprise, that his own father—Shogo's grandfather—was adopted. His parents were samurai on one side, gangster on the other. My husband has them all in his ancestry—geisha, gangster, samurai, rickshaw driver. This assortment of characters pleases me, makes me feel less strange for my difference, more welcome. My father-in-law says yes.

We're already a rainbow family, he with his long hair and stay-at-home job, me with my red streaks and funky yoga studio, not to mention our strange pit-bull mutt and his family's eccentric lineage. In a conservative neighborhood in a conservative country, we already stand out as freaks. Why try to fit in when we clearly can't?

Why not embrace our differences completely?

Low Priority

Our application is approved. I'm overjoyed, and a bit surprised. Could our dream finally be coming true? Soon, the interviews and home visits begin. We remain optimistic, though the CGC prioritizes according to age and we are very low priority. I am forty-four and Shogo is forty-eight.

We attend an all-day lecture with fifty other couples who are hoping to adopt—and those are only applicants for this season. There are hundreds of others who have previously applied and are waiting. I try not to think about this as we prepare to visit Nazareth House, an orphanage in Takadanobaba, a university town where I used to shop at The Blue Parrot, one of Tokyo's best English bookstores.

Before our trip, we go to Kiddieland—a bustling three-story toy shop in ultra-trendy Harajuku with lots of Disney, Hello Kitty, and other big-brand characters shouting out to be purchased. The shop is a cacophony of bells, whistles, motors, and mechanized voices. It gives me a headache. I buy finger puppets, the most low-tech thing there. I'm surprised the shop even has them. We plan to bring them to the orphanage. It's something inconspicuous and quiet.

We listen to a lecture on life in the orphanage, and how the kids there get accustomed to institutional ways and are different from kids who grow up in "normal" families. I wonder about these potential adoptive parents. Each of them has a journey, a story like ours. Some are way younger than us, dressed in hip clothes, and appear to be in their twenties. Others are older, more conservative. Many, like us, seem to be in long-term marriages. I can tell by the way they relate, hopeful but wary. They've been on a long journey.

We wait until the kids finish eating lunch. When the meal is over, the kids play in the playground. The staff lets the prospective parents in for ten minutes, all as a group. While some approach the children confidently, others are hesitant, moving slowly towards the children, with a mixture of hope and fear.

I step back and look at myself from the child's point of view. I see what they see. We are strangers. We are strange. I'd be scared too.

It's a revelation to see their faces. Waiting. Wanting. Just like us.

An oversize boy runs around terrorizing the others. Another boy, who appears to be half Japanese and half Middle Eastern, won't stop crying.

I think: *Could I love him? Could he be my child some day?*

And if I was his mom, could he love me back?

The Baby Box

In November, the CGC calls and says there's a girl available for adoption. Are we interested? We say yes. They say they will get back to us, but they also say they are considering six other couples for the same girl. And there is a priority list.

Three weeks go by and nothing happens. Shogo calls the orphanage, and they say the girl has been placed with another family.

Would they have called us to tell us?

We're definitely on our own here, and it's unknown territory. I'm not very good with uncertainty. I'm getting better; I've had to. But still, it's not my favorite place to be.

In December, the CGC calls about a boy. They ask if we are interested in adopting him. We say yes, They say they will get back to us. They don't.

We wait some more.

I ask Shogo to call them, and he does. They say they have placed the child with another family.

Many younger couples are waiting to adopt. By now, my fierce optimism has begun to wane.

Perpetual Yes

January brings a new year. We go to our neighborhood temple and ring the bell one hundred and eight times, one for every earthly desire. I have at least that many. I still want to have a child. I still feel its soul out there, calling me. Why can't I find it?

A few more telephone calls come from the CGC, telling us there's another child available and asking if we are interested, only to have no further contact.

I have to do something proactive. I am fiercely committed to living my dreams. If I'm not, who else will be? I ask myself: Am I going to live the life I want to live, how I want to live it? Or am I forever going to be living by others' dictates, rules, and limitations? Not when I can avoid it, I decide. I make Shogo call the orphanage. I insist that he tell them to stop calling us every month to ask if we are interested in a different child.

"Tell them to put a perpetual 'yes' on our file, okay? Tell them that whatever child they have available, we are interested."

"Whatever child?" he repeats.

"Yes. Whatever child," I say firmly.

I want to say things like "It isn't fair" and "Why us?" but I already know the answers to those questions—that there are no answers. This is our fate, our journey, our path. There is nothing to do but trust, and let go.

And then it happens. Our placement. Our child. And all the years of waiting, wanting, trying vanish in an instant. I wouldn't take back any of it, not at all.

Home Study

We go back to visit the orphanage. Yuto cautiously approaches us in the lobby, hiding behind the giant stuffed panda, then runs away. His caretaker, Kirita-san, a kind young woman who's been carrying Yuto on her back since he was a baby, tells us that he's doing great. He's so happy, she assures us. Shogo nods optimistically. We decide that we're going to go to the orphanage every day for the next few months, even if just for half an hour, until he comes home with us forever.

We make a breakthrough when we ask if we can bring our dog, Aska. If Yuto's going to be our child, we reason, then he has to meet the other member of the family too. "She's our daughter," I say to the staff, risking ridicule. But to our surprise, the orphanage agrees to let us bring her.

The following day, we load Aska in the car and drive to the orphanage. We park and take her to the back alley that runs beside the orphanage grounds by the playground. The children line up at the fence to reach their hands through to pet her. When we get closer, some stay back, some run away. Those who stay at the fence make a neat line. Yuto stays at the fence. He has no fear. Aska goes down the line, sniffing their shoes. She stops at Yuto. She's been smelling his scent on us for weeks. She knows who he is. Her tail starts to wag. She makes a smile that frightens some of the children, seems strange and menacing. But Yuto smiles back. His face lights up in a way I've never seen it do before. He loves her! He sticks his fingers through the fence. She licks them. He tries to pet her through the fence.

We ask the orphanage staff if we can take Yuto on a walk with Aska on the street, away from the orphanage.

Not yet.

We put her back in the car while we go inside to visit with him.

He shares a room with three other kids, two girls and one boy. The other kids jump on us and cling to us when we come in the room. We play with blocks, puzzles, toy food, and Legos.

Of the hundred kids in the orphanage, only one is available for adoption—Yuto. The rest remain in limbo, without parents but legally unable to be placed with families who will care for them. It's a tragic situation with so many people waiting to adopt, and so many kids just sitting in foster homes and orphanages because the government holds out hope that their blood relatives will claim them. Most don't. The kids grow up in the foster system, many never meeting their birth parents or having the experience of family or home.

It's heartbreaking. I want to adopt them all.

Flying Bird

The next time we visit the orphanage, Yuto asks where our dog is: "Where's *wan-wan?*"

"Her name is Aska," we say. "It means Flying Bird."

He laughs. "I want to see her."

"We'll bring her next time," I say.

The anticipation is good. He climbs on my lap, lets me read him a picture book. Then he plays ball with Shogo, dancing and happy. He goes to the window and holds the windowsill, dropping back to the floor in a backbend. He's a yogi!

"Has he always done that?" I ask.

"Always," they say.

From then on, we bring Aska every visit. Each time, Yuto warms up to us a little bit more. Finally, we can take him out of the orphanage for a walk. Since it's our first time to take him off the orphanage grounds, we've been asked not to bring Aska. He's disappointed, but we take him to a nearby park which has a duck pond. He loves throwing bread into the pond. There's also a Baskin-Robbins nearby. We discover his two great loves in the same hour—animals and ice cream.

On the street, he talks to everyone. Construction workers, old ladies, teenagers. It turns out that he's not shy at all. Slowly but surely, my heart begins to wrap itself around this little boy.

Oyatsu

Weeks go by, and we're all getting more comfortable with each other. One day, we're taken into a special room to feed him *oyatsu*, a snack. It's really to see if he'll eat without his familiar caretakers like Kirita-san around.

The first time, he doesn't touch his food. Maybe he feels too much pressure with all eyes on him. For all I know, he's been through this before. How much does he remember? I can tell he's a very smart boy, and observes everything intently.

We don't force it.

The next time we come and sit down with him to have his snack, he sips his milk. The time after that, he drinks the whole cup. Finally, he drinks the milk and takes a bite of his cream puff, but only eats half of it. He's starting to trust us. Progress! I never thought I'd be so excited about a half-eaten cream puff. Kirita-san says he loves them. Now I know why he's so chubby.

The next visit, he eats the entire pastry. Even though I'm not thrilled about him eating a cream puff, this is very good news. It means we'll be able to bring him to our house for a day visit, and that means he's one step closer to coming home.

Day Visit

I spend the week cleaning the house from top to bottom as if preparing for a visit from a head of state. But when the day comes to bring him home for a few hours, my happiness is dampened when I notice scratches on his face and bite marks on his arms.

"Did he scratch himself?" I ask.

"We don't know," the orphanage staff says.

I have a theory—one of the girls in his room has been acting out. "Why does he have visitors—a mommy and daddy—and I don't?" she asked me one day. My heart aches for her.

"Are you sure she's not available for adoption?" I ask. The staff shake their heads. I'm making it harder by asking, I know.

The staff prepare a day pack for him in case he won't eat at our house. Towels, a change of clothes, a rice ball, and a Thermos. We take him in our car. He's never ridden in a car before, and he's excited and scared. On the way to our house, he notices everything, calls out the names of what he sees: birds, flowers, construction cranes, trucks, buses, cars, airplanes, helicopters, ambulances.

After having lived mainly within the walls of an orphange for the first two years of his life, the outside world is a symphony of sounds and sights and smells. Everything is new, scary, and exciting.

Everything is possible.

Home Visit

On March 25th, finally, we can bring Yuto home for an overnight visit.

He sleeps in the same bed with me, tossing and turning. Of course, he would be scared. There are so many new sights, sounds, smells, and in my case, even a new language. And though Hiroo is an orphanage, it's still his home. It's familiar and comforting. It's all he's ever known.

Aska sleeps at his feet.

Finally, he closes his eyes.

Listening to them breathing softly together, I bask in the joy of the moment, but I don't want to get my hopes up too high yet. Anything can happen.

So we take each day as it comes. We read to him, play with him. He eats Shogo's soba, slurping it happily. He asks for seconds. He's a big eater. That's a good sign, too.

He celebrates his second birthday at the orphanage, dressed in a suit and tie. He blows candles out on a cake. We clap and sing.

Is it ever going to be time to bring him home forever?

Home

On April 19th, weeks after Yuto's second birthday, we get the green light to bring him home forever—or at least for six months before the court renders its final judgment and he's legally our child.

We bring Ai-Ai, a stuffed monkey, to comfort him in the car. First, we bring it into the orphanage, and he takes it and hugs it, holding it tightly in his arms. Kirita-san, the woman who's been taking care of him since he was brought there two days after being born, cries inconsolably. She is happy, she says, waving her hand in front of her face, but I can feel how hard it is for her. I don't know this then, but Yuto is the first child she has ever taken care of at the orphanage, and she's raised him as her own. She gives us a huge bag filled with toys, clothes, books, all lovingly bought and wrapped. I am sure this is totally against orphanage regulations, but no one stops her from giving it and we graciously accept.

She sees us all the way out the door, bowing as we leave.

Yuto tries to leave Ai-Ai behind in the foyer, placing him next to the giant panda. We have to convince him that he can keep it: he's never had a single thing of his own and doesn't quite know what to do with it.

As we pull away from the orphanage, Kirita-san is still bowing and waving until we are no longer in sight.

Mama Papa Yuto Aska

Though we're in Japan, I offer a Jewish blessing for bringing home a child. I light a candle at the Japanese altar of Shogo's ancestors and say the blessing when we bring Yuto and his bag of gifts home:

> *May our home always be a mikdash ma'at, a small sanctuary filled*
> *with your presence.*
> *May we reach out to each other in love.*
> *May our hearts be turned to one another*
> *May we create bonds of trust and care*
> *that will keep us close as we grow together as a family.*
> *Bless us, Source of Life, all of us together with the Light of Your*
> *presence.*

I think the prayer must be working. At home, Yuto is so polite. He helps me with the dishes. He carries my bags. He follows me into the bathroom. He asks before he does anything. Is it okay? *Ii desu ka?* Can I eat? Can I get up from the table? *Ii desu ka?* Can I pet the dog? *Ii desu ka?* I know this asking for permission will soon be a thing of the past, and I savor it. It's clear he's on his best behavior. His desire to please us is so beautiful it breaks my heart. He hardly has to try.

He's no longer chubby, and somehow, he's incredibly handsome. Is this the same child we saw at the orphange months before?

At night in bed, after I read him a bedtime story and before he drifts off to sleep, he says "Mama, Papa, Aska, Yuto" over and over, as a question, as if wrapping his head around this new unit, branding them into his heart.

"Mama, Papa, Aska, Yuto?" he asks.

"Hai," I reply, over and over until he falls asleep.

It's our mantra.

We are a family. We will stay together.

Mama, Papa, Aska, Yuto.

I say Yuto's blessing in my mind, repeating our names, stitching them together in my heart.

We are here for each other.

Forever.

Excerpted from a memoir-in-progress entitled *Here Comes the Sun: A Memoir of Adoption, Yoga, and the Samurai Spirit.*

Leza Lowitz is a writer and yoga teacher in Tokyo. Her debut young adult novel, Jet Black and the Ninja Wind *(Tuttle, 2013), received the Asian/Pacific American Award for Literature in the Young Adult category. Portions of her memoir in progress have appeared in the* New York Times *online,* The Huffington Post, Shambhala Sun, Best Buddhist Writing 2011, *and* Yoga Journal. *Lowitz's* Yoga Poems: Lines to Unfold By, *was a #1 Amazon bestseller. www.lezalowitz.com*

CHINESE STONEWALLS

By Ember Swift

GUO Jian and I had climbed the eastern gate of the walled city of Dali, located in southern China's Yunnan province. We looked out on the traditional rooflines of the city in the foreground, a shimmering mountain in the background. Behind us lay a wide-open lake. The remaining traditional architecture in China always takes my breath away, as if I've been whisked back a few centuries in the span of a single moment. But, on that day, the breathlessness was also related to nerves.

We sat down on the west-facing outer ledge to watch the setting sun, its warmth a contrast to the chilly early December we had left behind in Beijing. Golden light glinted off of tiled rooftops with their eaves intricately carved with dragons and spirit gods. My eyes traced several roof corners, finding centuries-old figures illuminated by the sunset, one after another, all frozen in upturned poses of strength. It was as though they were there to reinforce my resolve. My heart started beating much too fast for such a peaceful moment. I closed my eyes. This was long overdue.

With the sun on our faces and my heart in my throat, I choked out these words in a raspy Mandarin whisper: *"Nǐ zhīdào wǒ yībàn gēn nǚrén zài yīqǐ ma?"* (*You know that I am usually only with women, right?*)

We'd taken a spontaneous trip south. It was our last few days together before I had to return to Canada, where my life was established—a life that didn't include Guo Jian. In the past few weeks, our relationship had progressed to that mountain of bliss only two people falling in love can scale. We were high from it, buzzing. We walked the streets of Dali as though levitating on love. The more intense our feelings grew, the more I had stalled.

Until that moment, I had never really come out to him. I could blame it on my limited Chinese, but that's just denial. I was afraid. How could I be in love with someone whose views on homosexuality I had not yet even heard? What if he was a homophobe? What if the feeling of floating on perfection was, in fact, hiding a deep, dark prejudice? Was I about to descend into a specifically *Chinese* version of homophobia? I gulped after I said the words. I could see only orange spots on the inside of my eyelids. I held my breath and bit down on my lower lip.

At that time, I had spent five months in total in China—three months on my first trip, two on my second. Now that I live in Beijing, it's hard to believe that I was ever temporary here. Back then, though, China was a mystery whose pages I was thumbing through eagerly, impatiently. I wanted so much to fit in—to convince China to accept me; I wanted to understand this world. My sexual identity seemed the only thing at odds with this place. Everything else had a resonance that made me lose my balance, like a bell clanging in my spirit. I was "China-charmed."

On my first journey to Beijing, the spring of that same year, I had met a lesbian woman whose chosen English name was Rain. She took a fancy to me and, despite the attraction being one-sided, I enjoyed being shown a world of quiet, back-alley bars where other women-who-love-women congregated. One confessional evening, Rain told me that most of her friends were "fake married" to gay men in order to make their families happy.

"Chinese parents don't believe gayness even exists," she said, practically screaming over speakers blaring Ace of Bass's "I Saw The Sign," a hit from 1993. "Those who do consider it a disease." It made my heart ache. She was well over thirty and continued to lie to her family about her life. "It's the only way," she said, taking another long gulp of her beer.

Later in the night, amidst the smoky haze of suspendered tomboys, or "T"s, in crew cuts holding hands with "P" girls in two-inch heels and red lipstick, Rain's eyes widened like full moons when I told her that gay marriage had been legalized in Canada. I had already attended a few of my friends' same-sex weddings, I said. Homesickness washed over me as I spoke, coated with a sadness that made me think Rain had chosen her name wisely. How could I feel so connected to this country when my very presence in a women's bar was considered illicit? What does a queer like me have in common with a reputedly repressed society (at least in "sexual revolution" terms) where gay marriage, for instance, is a long, long march away? Why did I want to be here so much again? I asked myself.

After that conversation, I made my way back to my dorm room at the university in which I was enrolled as a three-month language student. I slouched in the taxi like a despondent castaway who had mistakenly washed up on eastern shores. Could this all have been a mistake?

The first time I stepped onto Chinese soil had been just a month earlier, in the spring of 2007. I got off the plane and stood at the baggage carousel, groggy from the flight and dazed to finally be in the country that I had considered my "dream destination" for over a decade. As the luggage began to cascade toward our gang of weary travelers, the identical baggage tags caught my eye. There in big black print were three capital letters: PEK. My heart nearly stopped. I looked around for an explanation, like I might be hallucinating or dreaming while upright, but no one seemed bothered by anything. Was I the only one who could see those matching tags?

Ten years earlier, when I decided to put my dream to go to

China aside for a career in music, I had sat in a garage in British Columbia midway through my first national tour with my band. There, perched on an abandoned wheel well and leaning against the bumper of a classic car, I let my guitar echo off the tin roof as I wrote an instrumental song. I had just graduated from university with a degree in East Asian Studies, and this piece was a plaintive yearning for China in musical form—a place whose calling I was choosing to ignore. Little did I know that this song would become a signature song and remain on my band's set list for over a decade. The song was called "PĒK," named after the phonetic spelling of three separate words whose combined meanings seemed to embody this calling: *peak*, *peek*, and *pique*.

I quickly realized that PEK was the airport's acronym, harkening back to a time when Beijing was called Peking, but at the moment of my arrival, standing at the baggage carousel, those three letters signaled that I had truly found my long-awaited destination. That was the first of the many tolling bells.

Recovering from my surprise, I had gathered my bags and hauled them into my first of many Beijing taxis, en route to the hotel whose address I gripped tightly in my hand. That's when the remembering started. The smells, the sounds, the language in my ears and on my lips, and even the stonework of the buildings we passed—it all seemed to vibrate in my bones as familiar. *I've been here before*, I thought. *I know this place.*

No, coming to China couldn't have been a mistake. The signs told me I was meant to be here. In Chinese, they call it *yuánfèn* (fate).

The night I met Guo Jian, I was in a music venue in Beijing called Mao Live House, at the tail end of that first trip to China. I couldn't stop staring at a beautiful, tall, lean Chinese woman on the other side of the lobby dressed in Thai fisherman's pants and a blue floral jacket. She stood straight-backed with long dreadlocks tied neatly at the nape of her neck. In her profile, I could see high cheekbones and the hint of a dimple. Perfect skin. She was stunning. It wasn't until she turned and glanced in our direction that I saw *his* goatee. I almost fell off the bar stool in surprise. I had just spent several minutes lusting after *a man*, and yet, I couldn't stop. I had to admit it, *he* was one of the most beautiful human beings I had ever seen.

If you break down the differences in physical traits, Han Chinese men (Han being the ethnic majority in China) are slighter than Western men, on average, and are mostly hairless unless they sport wispy goatees or light moustaches. Many have the fine facial features we associate with femininity like high cheekbones, full lips, and smooth skin. He wasn't the first man that I had mistakenly thought was a woman since coming to China that spring. I've always been attracted to the sexiness of androgyny, so I watched him approvingly from across the room, giddy with the strange liberty of exploring attraction for a man without it being a challenge to my established identity.

Shortly thereafter, my American friend Traci introduced us, explaining that we were fellow musicians, but I didn't catch his name before he moved on to talk to others. My eyes trailed after him. At that time, Chinese names took me several tries to remember, so I nicknamed him "Dimple Boy." I winked at Traci when I told her that I thought Dimple Boy was pretty cute. She winked back.

It's true that people express gender differently across cultures, but I noticed Dimple Boy was different from other Chinese boys—more flamboyant and colorful, confident, careless—so different, in fact, that I distinctly remember wondering if he was gay and liking the thought of that. I felt a connection with him. Maybe we were both two queers floating in a straight sea? Maybe we needed to be friends.

The second time I met Guo Jian was on my second journey to China, less than six months after the first. It was three days into my trip. I had arranged to meet Traci at a popular folk bar called Jiang Jin Jiu. Walking up the narrow *hútòng* (alley) on foot, I found her waiting for me outside with a big smile of welcome.

As we swung open the wide wooden doors of the pub, the aroma of sweet popcorn mixed with the sharp smell of cigarette smoke rolled over us like an ocean wave. Traci immediately called out a greeting to friends. By then, I was convinced Traci knew every musician in the city, and we found ourselves seated at one end of a long wooden table with a local band. There were three scruffy guys and beers on offer. Traci was translating. Within ten minutes, two more guys rolled in, laughing and shoving each other like school kids— the last two members of the band.

And there he was: Dimple Boy.

I froze, beer bottle halfway to my lips. He was more beautiful than I had remembered. We were introduced again, and he nodded at me with recognition and then immediately left his four bandmates and disappeared to the opposite end of the table, joining another group of people. I self-consciously continued drinking and laughing with the people we were sitting with. We didn't speak all night. For me, Dimple Boy was simply an acknowledgment of the rare attraction I have for men, nothing more. At least, that's what I told myself in the moment. After all, I'm queer.

As the night progressed, even with Traci's translation I was oblivious to the fact that one of the scruffy guys was flirting with me. Not having spent my early adulthood being socialized in a heterosexual world, straight signals are a complete mystery to me. I did notice, eventually, but only because Traci impersonated his raised eyebrows and the fluttery spark in his eye after he had asked me a question. It took seeing a *woman* flirting with me in mocking, delayed duplication for me to realize that *a man* had been flirting with me in real-time.

Seeing me recoil, Traci quickly suggested I play some music. It was sort of an open jam, and the place had about twenty people in it, scattered about. There was a guitar propped against a chair on the stage that had just become empty. The flirty guy at our table seconded Traci's suggestion, raising his eyebrows at me again. I may have lunged five steps to the stage and picked up the guitar just to get away from him.

Traci moved up to an empty front table and I laughingly blurted out that I had *"hē duō le"* (drunk too much). She quipped back, *"měi wèntí"* (no problem), and then added, *"wǒmen yě shì"* (so have we!) while gesturing toward the guys behind her. They all laughed.

I played three songs. She sang along to the ones she remembered from my first trip. I noticed Dimple Boy moving closer to a table behind Traci's, further back and to the left, and sitting there alone in the shadows. I wondered why he had broken off from his friends and thought it strange he didn't join Traci, a person he obviously knew. But the beer and the music were distracting. When I looked around for him after I came off stage, he was gone.

Looking back at that night, I remember struggling to explain to everyone, including myself, why I had come back to Beijing so soon after my first journey. More language study felt like a superficial excuse. The city had this ineffable magnetic force and I was powerless to resist it. Now, I think I may have come back to find him. Maybe I was powerless to resist *him*.

Was it because he was so pretty, I asked myself? Was it the charming way he sought me out (again, through my friend Traci) and then started to show up at places he knew I would be? Was it the dimples? Was it his patience with my Mandarin and his pleasure in teaching me about the culture that I loved so much? Maybe he just became a symbol of China, the country I was already in love with? Despite the many questions I asked myself, my head still couldn't understand what my heart had already decided.

I was grateful to be so far away from the women's community

who would surely notice this *man* in my heart. I worried that I would
be seen as a traitor. Or worse, that I would be viewed as betraying
the LGBTQ movement—a heartbreaking thought for someone
who had spent her life and career as an activist. What would my
friends and fans think of me for looking forward to his knock on my
rented room's door, or poring over his Chinese text messages with
my dictionary, not wanting to miss a single subtlety?

I focused on the friendship we started building, sweeping aside
the ever-increasing attraction I felt for him. A month went by in
which we spent a lot of time using music as our common language
and sharing platonic space. We proved that words are overrated; our
mutual *musical* fluency linked us. We jammed together and played
songs for each other and those conversations flowed beautifully.
They rose and fell in intensity and emotion. They spoke without
needing to.

Being inept at heterosexual courting practices—those pesky
straight signals—I was unsure of his feelings towards me beyond
friendship and musical camaraderie. I could see the crescendo
of attraction growing between us, but I had rationalized it away,
because surely he must be gay, I told myself. Aren't most of the
beautiful men gay?

We had spent the whole night jamming. We were switching
between instruments (guitar, bass, hand drums, keyboards), and
he'd been showing me how to pluck the *gǔzhēng,* a traditional
Chinese zither. Guo Jian had also pulled out a gorgeous traditional
tea service—tray, mini teapot, utensils, the works—and had been
endlessly refilling my mini tea cup with *pǔ'ěr,* a deep and intense
black tea filled with enough caffeine to chase yawns away. Each time
he filled it, I politely sipped it back in one or two gulps before it
got cold. It wasn't long before the dim light of dawn was sneaking
around the curtains.

I stood up, gesturing at the morning light, placing both my palms together and then laying my head sideways against them like they were a pillow—the universal symbol for needing to sleep. "*Wǒ hěn kùn*" (I'm sleepy), I said, adding a playful pout. He stood up, too, contesting my departure in one of his solid English words ("No, No, No!") and reaching for my arm.

I didn't expect the kiss, even when he leaned his face forward and found my eyes with his. It wasn't until his smooth lips were against mine, dreadlocks cascading around my face and enclosing our kiss like a curtain, that I acknowledged what had been happening between us all those weeks. All of the longhaired women I've kissed came to mind with fondness. I immediately relaxed.

After our blissful trip to southern China, we returned to Beijing and then, two days later, I boarded a plane for Canada with a teary goodbye and a promise to stay in touch. Predictably, when I returned to my home country, an identity crisis attacked me with cold winter winds. Some things were clear: I am queer. I love women. I prefer women. I love the company and community of women. But I had fallen in love with a man. Proud queer or not, he was in my heart. Multiple truths had managed to maneuver themselves into my life and I couldn't deny any of them. The mirror was mocking me. *Who am I,* I kept asking myself?

*

While I weathered the winter winds of questioning, memories of climbing the Dali gate in the sunset glow kept my heart from freezing over. City gates in China used to serve as guard towers where straight-backed young men watched over the city threshold. Their role was to keep outsiders out. It was about safety. We build walls to keep ourselves safe, but when we open gates to risk, great learning often greets us. What's more, new cultures don't always overtake and transform us; sometimes they strengthen us, widening our perspectives, expanding our identities.

After I spoke those fateful words and bit my lip in waiting, the orange light in the inside of my eyelids held me suspended for a few stretched seconds, the echo of my whisper floating in the breathlessness between us.

"*Wǒ zhīdào, wǒ zǎo zhīdào le,*" he said, telling me knew and had always known. Then he took my hand. When I opened my eyes and found his, they were as warm as the dusk. I could settle into those eyes, I thought. I sighed into their brown depths as the anxiety rose from my shoulders and fell away from the tower, disappearing into the perfect evening air.

His eyes were open—he was open—wide. To me.

Ember Swift is a Canadian musician, songwriter, performer, and writer. She has released eleven independent album recordings since 1996, one live DVD project, and continues to perform regularly in both North America and China. Now based in Beijing with her Chinese husband and two children, she maintains three popular blogs through her website: www.emberswift.com and is a contributing writer for Women in China Magazine, Herizon's Magazine, Mami Magazine, Beijing Kids Magazine, China.org, *and* InCulture Parent, *an online portal for cross-cultural parenting.*

WAITING FOR INSPIRATION

By Coco Richter

IT'S 11:00 am and I'm sitting on my sofa, tapping my fingers on the creamy brown leather. I've already been to the gym, read two newspapers, and downed three cups of coffee. I'm starting to regret declining that lunch invitation until I think of the ever-growing bulge forming in my midsection.

My kids are at school. They stream out the door five days a week with backpacks weighing twenty kilos, one with a violin, the other with a trombone, forging into the lift with such determination. They will not miss the school bus, not because I'd mind driving them to school but because the school bus is where they get their best information.

As I sit, Zeny is no doubt scrubbing the bathroom tiles for the third time this week. When I came in from the gym, she was vacuuming the already-spotless living room floor. Zeny's phone rings and the sound of Tagalog fills the flat. It's a thundering loud language filled with staccatos, more Hispanic to my ear than Asian. Zeny has lots of friends: the ones she walks the dog with in the morning; the ones she meets at the grocery store; an expansive network of friends she gathers with on Sundays at the malls and cinemas, parks and beaches. She's been in Hong Kong nearly twenty years. It's more home to her than her native Philippines and yet can never truly be her home.

I try not to think too much about the fine line between her world and mine. The one that allows me to sit here enjoying an unobstructed view of Repulse Bay while she inhales fumes from the bathroom cleanser so that she can send a chunk of her wages home to an ever-growing circle of siblings, cousins, nieces, and nephews. I chew on my lower lip as the next thought inevitably arrives. Zeny's days have purpose while mine do not.

I look away, the sun now beaming into the room with laser-like focus. I draw the sheer curtains, preparing my defense. My days have purpose, but that purpose is less defined than it was a year or so ago, before I moved here, when I had a job, a title, an income, an office, file cabinets, a computer network, a webpage, secretary, book-keeper, client meetings, lunch engagements, professional seminars, and a leather desk chair on wheels. My nails dig into the sofa. I've left a mark—a gouge really—the sliver of a moon shape, a marking of expat angst.

I'm about ready to get up and do something—just what, I haven't quite gotten to—when my mobile phone rings. I wait to pick it up until it's rung three times, feigning breathlessness. It's my husband. He calls me several times a day, just to be sure I'm still here, that I haven't packed it up and moved back to Boston in the three hours since he left for work. It's sweet. He knows it's hard to start over, to build a life from scratch without a network of friends or family in the same time zone. I assure him I'm fine, that I've already been out of the house, and that I have plans for the afternoon. I hope he doesn't ask me what they are because I'm making this up as I go.

"So that rash I told you about," he says, "you know the one on my arms?"

"Hmm," I say, vaguely recalling an outbreak the day before.

"Well, it's really painful now. It feels like pins sticking into me, and it's spreading."

"Really?" I say. My husband is a bit of a hypochondriac. Whenever he gets the flu, he thinks he has cancer and may only have three weeks to live. "Maybe you should see the doctor," I say, knowing he'll agree.

"I have an appointment this afternoon," he says. "It's really weird. Are rashes supposed to do that?"

"Do what?" I ask.

"Spread."

"I'm sure it's fine," I say, knowing he's headed toward a global pandemic. "Probably just an allergic reaction to something. Did you use a new soap or skin cream?"

"No," he says, "I've done nothing different. It's just completely out of the blue."

Without any further thoughts on the source or migration patterns of his rash, I tell him I've got to run, and, fortunately, he doesn't ask me why. No sooner have I put the phone down when it rings again.

"Itchy fingers too?" I say.

A woman's voice comes over the line. It's Helen, the mother of a friend of my daughter's. She doesn't ask about itchy fingers and I don't offer an explanation. After a minute of chitchat, she gets to the point.

"I work for a headhunting firm," she says.

"Hmm," I say, trying to remember if I'd ever seen her wearing anything other than yoga pants.

"I don't usually cover the legal sector but something just came up and I immediately thought of you, given your legal background."

"Really?" I say, trying to sound more casual than I feel.

"It's a part-time role," she says.

This is getting better by the minute.

"It's to head the training department for a large UK firm.

Essentially you'd be preparing training materials and sessions for their young lawyers in Hong Kong. What do you think?" she asks.

Where do I sign, I want to say, but instead I play it cool. "It could be interesting."

"I think it would be a great role for you, particularly since it's part-time and, let me tell you, part-time roles are hard to find in Hong Kong."

"Hmm," I say.

"If you're interested at all, why don't you come by my office tomorrow and talk with Yuki. She's the one handling the search for us."

Yuki? I debate telling her I'm busy for a half-second before eagerly agreeing to see Yuki the next day. As soon as I put the phone down, I grab my computer, typing in the firm's name, absorbing everything there is to know about them from a Google search. Four hundred lawyers with offices in four cities, everyone smiling in conference rooms kitted out with complete book sets of statutory laws and judicial opinions, looking more like Brooks Brothers models than any lawyers I've ever known. I envy them their suits and office towers, their days filled with meetings and deadlines.

I run to my closet, assessing my wardrobe. Two suits hang at the far end, one navy and one black, a fine layer of dust resting along the top of the shoulders. I select the black one and try brushing off the dust. It doesn't move. It's now a film that's seeped into the fabric. I take a damp cloth and scrub the film away. Nothing can stand in my way. I pair it with a silk blouse, royal blue in color. I'm ready. I can already see myself, coffee cup in hand, glasses perched on my nose, pontificating to eager young faces about the perils of cross-examination.

My phone rings again. It's nearly one and I'm meant to be out. I answer it just before it goes to voicemail. It's my husband again.

"You're never going to believe this," he says.

"Try me," I say.

"Well, the rash has now spread all along my sides. I look like a leper," he says.

"Hmm," I say.

"Anyways, I went to the doctor and he kept asking me if I had a new laundry or bath soap, or shower gel, and I told him no, nothing was new. So after like thirty minutes of this he says to me, 'Do you work a lot on the computer?' and I tell him yes, and he asks me if I have a new desk!"

I eye the custom-made wood desk he purchased from a high-end furniture store on Hollywood Road the week before.

"Can you believe it?" he asks. "That blasted new desk of mine, it's coated in Chinese lacquer and the doctor thinks I'm allergic to it. That's why the rash is concentrated on the underside of my arms."

"Of course," I say.

"So can you get rid of it?"

"Get rid of what?" I ask.

"The desk," he says.

This seems extreme, not to mention wasteful, but I wasn't going to debate it with him. He has pins digging into his skin and a doctor's diagnosis in his pocket so I tell him I'll take care of it.

Zeny helps me carry the desk from the bedroom into the living room. It's an attractive piece, much like an architect's drawing table in a dark, glossy wood. I think it could work as a buffet in the dining room or a credenza behind the sofa. We try it both ways and agree it looks best against the wall as a buffet. I place some decorative items on top. A gold-and-white porcelain elephant from Thailand, a tribal man in stone from the Philippines, and a brightly painted wood carving of a Japanese girl. I'm pleased, briefly pondering a career in home decoration until one of my kids walks through the door.

"Hey, what's Dad's desk doing in the dining room?" she asks.

"It's a buffet table now," I say.

"Whatever," she says.

Minutes later her sister comes in with more helpful commentary. "The desk looks weird there," she says.

The next morning, I'm up earlier than usual, eager for the kids to head off to school so I can get ready. I haven't mentioned my meeting. I'm not ready to field questions about it or, more particularly, about me. The meeting's not until 10:30 a.m. but I leave the house at nine, just to be safe. I drive my car, the master of my own destiny. After parking at IFC, I'm still forty-five minutes early, so I window-shop along Queen's Road Central. Catching my reflection in a shop window, I realize my blouse puffs out from the top of my skirt, making me look like I'm growing a bubble. I tuck it back in but a few steps later, the bubble's back.

Not wanting the blouse to stand between me and my future, I stride into a shop and browse the racks, locating a form-fitting grey sweater. I try it on and it fits nicely. I move around in the small dressing room, raising and lowering my arms. The sweater's like glue. It adheres to my skin without bubbling. The sales clerk snips the tags and I emerge from the shop feeling great. I'm on the cusp of a professional life in this new city of mine. Goodbye tai-tai lunches and monthly shopping bazaars. My future awaits me.

Checking my watch, it's time to make my way into the building. My heels click against the white marble flooring. The musty scent of law, finance, and insurance fills the air. This is a serious building for people with serious lives. This is where I belong. I enter the elevator, confidently punching the button for the seventeenth floor. Scores of people file in after me, packing the elevator car. When it reaches the seventeenth floor, everyone files out. It seems we're all going to the same place, and though I was the first in the car, I now find myself the last in a long line of people checking in with the receptionist.

Stacks of brown clipboards sit on her desk, and she dispenses them like a Vegas card dealer. When I finally reach her, she flings one toward me. I put my hand up and explain that I have an appointment. The young woman thrusts the clipboard into my hand.

"Everyone must first fill out the form," she says.

I begrudgingly take it from her and squeeze myself onto the sofa between two others who are studiously filling out their form. I put my handbag on the floor and root around it to locate my glasses. *Application for Employment*, the form says in large block letters. I flip through its six pages containing all manner of questions about my prior work experience. I rise from the sofa, explaining again that Yuki is expecting me.

"You want a job, we need the form. That's how it works," she says, forcing a smile.

I retreat, reclaiming my spot on the sofa. My neighbors appear to be nearly finished with their forms. Fifteen minutes later, I'm done and am now the only one still in the reception room waiting to be called. When the reception girl finally calls me, I jump up and follow her down the hall, past rows of thin cubicles, each containing one of my elevator friends in the midst of a sales pitch about their background. At the end of the hall, I'm deposited into one of the very same cubicles with walls rising three-quarters of the way to the ceiling. A cacophony of voices fills the air.

"I am most definitely interested in a sales position, preferably in the automotive field," one says.

"The financial sector is where I'd like to focus," says another.

Laughter comes from the cubicle across the hall. "Not reflexology," a woman says, "kinesiology."

I'm alone in the room for what seems like an eternity before a young woman strides in, ponytail swinging side to side. She takes a seat behind the small desk opposite me. "I'm Yuki," she says, offering me her hand.

I take it. It's ice cold and rock hard. "Hello," I say.

Yuki reviews the pages on the clipboard. I remind her that Helen invited me to come in to discuss the legal training job for the UK law firm.

"Oh, yes," she says. "That position is no longer available, but—"

"Excuse me?" I say.

"They called last week and pulled the listing. Too bad, because it was a nice position and a good salary, but we'll try to find you something else. Now, are you only interested in the legal profession?" she asks. "Because I have a lot of sales positions."

I wonder if she can hear me deflating.

"Why didn't you call me?" I ask, straining to keep my nostrils from flaring.

Yuki tilts her head to the side, her twenty-something Eurasian skin smooth and unblemished.

"Why would I have called you?" she asks.

"To tell me not to come in, that the position *you* called *me* about was no longer available," I say.

"I didn't call you," she says.

"I mean that Helen called me about," I say.

"Look," Yuki says, "do you want a job or not, because I have other people waiting to see me?"

A simple question, I know, but I can't seem to form any words. It's complicated, I want to say but Yuki won't understand. Tears begin to sting my eyes.

"Well?" she says.

"No," I say. "I'm sorry but there's been a misunderstanding."

Yuki's speechless as I mumble a goodbye. She's probably never had someone come to her office and say they don't want a job. I mean, what a waste. Why bother coming in at all if you don't want a job?

I jam my finger at the elevator button repeatedly, hoping the lift comes before anyone else joins me on the landing. Once outside, I curse my way down Queen's Road Central, my new sweater now unbearably tight, restricting my breathing. I retrieve my car from the car park at IFC, clenching the wheel, my red fingernails—so perfectly painted the day before—now taunting me.

It's nearing the lunch hour and traffic is thick. I fidget in my seat, dying to peel off this suit. How did I ever wear one of these things, day after day, week after week? It seems like a lifetime ago. I signal to cross right, making my way across Gloucester Road towards the Happy Valley turnoff. One more lane to go when a loud noise startles me. A police van's behind me, its siren light flashing. I can't move. Traffic's at a standstill in my lane. The van approaches on my right, inching toward my window. I roll it down as the van door opens, four, maybe five heads vying for a good look at me. The one closest, his hand on the door handle, says something I can't understand before the lot of them burst out laughing, me clearly the punch line to some joke about expat or blonde drivers.

"You crossed lanes in a no-cross zone," the officer finally says.

"Sorry," I say.

The group breaks out in laughter once again. I'm a regular comedian, it seems.

"Don't do it again," the officer says before pulling the door closed.

My lane is moving again and I accelerate forward. Happy Valley lies ahead, the hills of Tai Hang and Mid-Levels East rising above it. I'm teetering on an emotional cliff, unsure which way I'll go. I'm in the tunnel now, and I begin to laugh. Tentatively at first but then I can't restrain it. Laughter pours out of me, filling the car. I'm my own punchline now.

I pay the $5 toll and glide past Ocean Park, a smile on my lips as a nascent thought begins to take shape. I've got an unclaimed desk in my dining room and some good stories to tell. Maybe I'll write them down.

Coco Richter is from the US, where she practiced law for 18 years. She moved to Hong Kong in 2008 with her family and now writes fiction. She received an MFA in Creative Writing from the University of Hong Kong in 2011. Her writing has previously appeared in multiple editions of Imprint, the Annual Anthology of Women in Publishing Society Hong Kong.

CHARTING KOENJI

By Kathryn Hummel

SOMETIMES there are moments that catch in the flow of the everyday like a taped-up tear in a reel of film. Afterwards, there is an almost imperceptible change in the tension and projection of life, when I feel more than I see that Koenji is not my place. While I am closer than a stranger, I am still at a distance: this I measure from the inside out, since I can't get far enough away to see it as an onlooker, detached but still interested in how the scene rolls on. For the past two years, the everyday scenes of my life have had Japan as a setting: most of these have been concentrated in the district of Koenji-minami, Suginami Ward, Tokyo. During my first weeks here, I intoned that address so many times it became a mantra, a verbal talisman to guard against losing myself in the city. Although being an expatriate—a collection of syllables I don't often apply to myself—places me in a position of being both inside and outside, when I hear the wooden heels of my shoes clip the now familiar walkways of my neighbourhood, I am reminded only of this place, my present.

I. Arrival

Arrival is not signified by
the unburdening of suitcases
but the mechanics of realisation.
This is where I am, will be:
I have come now to the place
where before I was going.

Being present in a place means you inevitably paint yourself in the picture, draw the map around you. Slip outside these bounds and you are lost, or so I once thought. In 2004 I had stopped in Japan on my way from China to Australia and was delighted by my week-long visit. I knew that living and working in Japan would be harder than traveling through, when my only responsibility had been to find the best way to be happy before my set departure date. Still, I had friends in Japan and their phone numbers to call; a Japanese language certificate and alphabet flashcards; a few tatami mats' worth of rented space and a position, courtesy of an arts-exchange program, to write words for an intimate Koenji gallery wanting to commune with the English-speaking art world. If the present was a leafy bough, my future (as well as my literary imagery) would be heavy with the fruit of my Japanese incarnation.

I arrived in Osaka and rested for a few days at the home of Quentin, a university friend who had spent the last three years of his life traveling back to Japan to teach English, a compulsion he would spend another three years satisfying. At Quentin's suggestion, I made my way to Tokyo on a journey of acclimatisation and language practice. I took a slow train to Hamamatsu to go on a *gyoza* (dumpling) hunt and traveled on to Yaizu, where, walking to the beach to see the distant Fuji-san bathed in the light of sunset, I met and later made love to a fish-factory worker from Peru. Yet even this encounter had the day-seizing quality of one made on a transient journey only.

When I reached Tokyo, the city was so miserably wet I thought it would never dry out. As arranged, I was met at Koenji station by my landlord, whose easy graciousness flickered warmth over my arrival, and accompanied to the building where my first studio apartment was waiting. After giving me a tour, which consisted of opening the bathroom door and indicating to the rest of the open-plan space, diminished by a folded futon and my wet bags, my landlord retreated with a bow. I was not delighted by Tokyo so far but wanted to be, so I gave my wool scarf a tighter wind, armed myself with an umbrella and ventured out. During my walk, I found that the compass on my Bleu Bleuet watch was only for show—an incidental discovery, since instinct is the direction I rely on above all. At that particular moment, I had none, and the rain didn't help clarify my position. It leaked somehow through my umbrella and under my collar, where it remained without guiding me. As it usually happens when I walk the streets of a new place, I got lost.

The houses lost me. Or I lost myself in them. Every grey, dun, or cream-colored structure fit together in a maze of reinforced concrete. Some homes were irregularly shaped to sit correctly on their blocks; others had strange additions that seemed the architectural equivalent to tusks and antlers; oddly shaped, overgrown bonsai sprouting various thicknesses of branch and colors of foliage mingled with low electrical wires; antennas, rubbish bins, sometimes just inexplicable but neatly arranged collections of junk, assembled to give the impression that it was still of use, awaited their purpose. There was an element of seediness that did not feature in my memory of Japan: paint peeled from wooden walls and bald light globes had been left burning after midday. In the alleys behind restaurants, I was met with cardboard boxes, broken brooms and wooden pallets, rusty machinery and empty cans of cooking oil. The rain blurred the scenes without actually softening them, making greyer what was already dismal.

I told myself not to try to make sense of the maze. Tomorrow I would find my way to the gallery where I would be working and meet Kenzo-san, its owner, and all would be well if I believed all would be well. At the same time I thought, with naïveté or impatience, that I had to have a plan, that aimlessness would prevent me connecting to Koenji.

Before I left Osaka, Quentin studied my face as if trying to read its meaning. "You should have a Japanese name," he told me. "*Kat-san* isn't so easy to say."

To me it didn't seem as difficult as "Kassorin-san," but I already had thought of a name that sounded appropriately Japanese. "What about Katsu?" I asked. "It's a mixture of my first and second names: Kathryn Susannah."

Quentin shook his head. "No. It will make people think of *tonkatsu* (deep-fried pork). They'll think it's strange. Why not choose something that represents you—a tree, or an animal?"

Quentin's advice may have worked admirably for him in his various Japanese incarnations, but has never yielded the same results for me. I was then, and remain, "Kassorin-san," a woman who navigates her own way. On that first afternoon in Koenji, I continued to walk until I at last saw something that indicated my flat was not far off: a secondhand bookshop I never have learned the name of, though I did eventually begin to buy books there that I hope to read, one day, with ease. The bookshop is recognisable during the day by its awning of green-and-white stripes, at night, by its security doors. Each of the three doors is painted with a face: one with running mascara and a Clara Bow hairdo, one with a sweat-beaded forehead and a guilty laugh, the last with an angry eye and an imperious-looking nose.

These faces, which remain guarding the bookshop until 11:00 am each day, signal more than my location—they are signposts for my mood. Depending on whether my mind is full or empty as I walk past on my way to the gallery or language lessons or the house of a friend, I either ignore or sympathize with whatever I can read in their expressions: their moods always change. It seems charmingly whimsical to write that these faces were my first friends, though when I realised this, I knew it was time to stop observing and start finding my community in Koenji.

II. Kindred

*If, during the day, you fit the streets indelicately
and your shadow mattes the lustre of shop-shells,
follow, at night, the curve upstairs.
For those belonging to it, home does not float
but is part of the scene for consumption.*

Tokyo had lost its delightfulness. It seemed to be less of a city than a train-station-shopping-mall hybrid of concrete-cold efficiency. In Koenji the bustle had a softer edge, but people still moved in and out of their doors, through the streets, enclosed. Their enclosures and yours coexisted without colliding. People were often kind when it was really necessary to step outside of their allocated spaces, but until those times there were few nods, few smiles, only a lot of glances (discreet, to be sure, but noticeable) at anything unusual. Everything that made up a comfortable life was in place, except for the unpredictable pleasure of spontaneity. It was my task as the outsider to unfurl, to begin reaching out.

In a society where every door I enter seems to shut in a private clubroom, I have learned that there are always people who quickly calculate that you are worthwhile and allow you access; with this first step over the threshold begins the faint glow of a polite but unwavering connection. This I know because it happened with Kenzo-san, my *jou-shi* (boss), and his wife Reiko-san. My first and oldest friends, they invited me to their home within a week of my arrival in Tokyo and said, "Come again," with exactly that expectation. The crafting of the perfect moment is significant in the lore of Japanese hospitality, but as an outsider, I often upset this harmonious balance with a second entrance or invitation of my own.

Kenzo-san and Reiko-san not only accepted my hospitality but, after our second dinner together, introduced me to the Flamingo.

Where you drink in Japan is an important signifier of belonging and identity, though it's not such an easy process to find a kindred resting place. The entrance of the Flamingo is marked by three beach pebbles lying at the bottom of a narrow flight of stairs. If you know enough to know about what lies at the top, that detail is your passport. The walls, floors, and shelves are inlaid with wood that makes the bar resemble a sauna. Laid over that are the small touches of personality that make the Flamingo like no other place: the candle holders and Polaroid snapshots crowding the bar, the paper flower taped to the outstretched hand of a plastic marathon runner. Plants flourish at the window, reminding me of my grandmother's sitting room in Göteborg, though she never had fairy lights framing her panes. The decor of the Flamingo has a quirky daintiness rather like its specialty cocktail—a mixture of iced oolong tea and cherry liqueur—and is quintessentially Japanese even under its European influence. This combination creates the atmosphere of a salon, with the Flamingo attracting writers who leave behind copies of their books and articles and painters who donate miniature work to the barman, Ryo-san, a local celebrity who fronted a Koenji punk band in the 1980s. It was at the Flamingo that I met Kentaro-san, a retired book publisher, who joined me on a bar-hop of the district and shared the lovely, austere photographs he takes at his leisure—moving pictures of lace curtains in the wind, the tails of dogs, human forms shot through textured glass.

At my work I meet imminently talented beings whose creative practice follows a path of precision. The time I spend with these artists, talking to them about their vision, gathering critical responses to their work, and critiquing it myself, makes me aware of the generosity of their imagination and of the desire to share in return. The kindred feeling I have found in Koenji is not delineated by the culture of a country, but by creativity. The artists draw, paint, sculpt, shoot, move, play, use collage and computers; and I write. We communicate through a silent, common respect.

At the center of this wordless creative utopia is Kenzo-san's gallery: an intimate exhibition space, thoughtfully assembled with softly lit walls and simple furniture, with spare surfaces given over to displaying the work of friends, their business cards, exhibition brochures, and maps to their own galleries. The space Kenzo-san allocates me encourages my own creativity; on my first day, he invited me to sit at a long table and laid portfolio after portfolio before me, giving the reactions of my face closer attention than my words. "Instinct is never wrong," Kenzo-san told me. "It is only difficult to know."

Because Kenzo-san believed I could come to know my instinct, even in the confusion of my inside-outside space, I began to. His impeccable insight into people matches his sartorial style, but nothing comes close to his grace. I suspect people come to his gallery to partake of this quality, to stay and talk to him, to drink the tea he so carefully prepares and serves. "I wish you good days," he tells me every evening as I leave for home. For a good day, I seldom need to move beyond Kenzo-san's way of ordering the world and its art in the slender space we share.

With the discovery of such spaces, my life in Koenji began to radiate outwards, and the force moved me into the path of kindred company. One day, Fumi-san invited me to come to her studio and sit for a portrait. I had seen her work exhibited during my first autumn in Koenji and knew that she was a democratic portrait artist, feeling that every face deserved her close attention. There is, no doubt, an imbalance between cash and canvasses in Fumi-san's life; still, she paints, drinks beer freely, listens to cello concertos, and speaks in a loud, laughing voice.

Fumi-san tries to avoid writing in anything but *hiragana*, and her painting has the same considered simplicity. She works very fast and in hardly any time at all, blocks of color transform into my face with the addition of a few thoughtful strokes. Sitting cross-legged on the floor, she rests her canvas against a white wooden block daubed with her favoured palette, which echoes the tints of the neighbouring houses: brown, cream, flesh tones, slate shades of grey and green, some bright blue, edgings of black.

My Japanese language skills continue to hinder deep conversation, though they have improved slowly with regular language classes and a lot of unmusical practice. I can't remember exactly what Fumi-san and I talked about during my first sitting, or the next. It feels natural to sit and write while she paints and then, while the paint is still wet, leave the studio for dinner or a drink. After some sessions we sit back and listen to Fumi-san's sound recording of the painting: a microphone, attached to the back of her canvas, picks up the scrubbings and murmurings of the paint, brush, and palette knife. These mesmerising conversations are in a language neither of us recognise but are driven to interpret in more painting, more writing. Sometimes I abandon my pencil and simply sit straight on, waiting for Fumi-san's wry, bright eyes to capture my form and feeling. I never have asked her what she sees when she paints me, though her choice of color and the expression she applies to my face always seem right. Her eyes are the only parts of Fumi-san that are serious. She knows of the things inside me before I do, most of the time.

III. Mid-life

The streets are layered earth and memory.
Possibly regret makes up one of these.
New paint dries over old facades,
new globes cast light into old corners.

One day, the doubt came—and remained. Usually something as simple as company or coffee or the feeling of moving forward dispels any bad feeling I have, yet one year into my life in Koenji, doubt clung to me and dragged me down. I could not stop asking myself,

"Where will these years go and what do they count for? A few lines on my resume, a few trinkets and snapshots, a few notebooks full of memories?" Maybe these questions reveal me as a typical expatriate, who, when contemplating the end of her lifetime in one country, decides she cannot go back home—wherever that is—but must continue the life she started, even if it's not in her present place. I don't know if this is what starts off a perpetual expatriate life, but I do know that my life is not so meticulously planned.

My long period of doubt revealed the pointlessness of my existence. Usually there was meaning to each of my days but suddenly I couldn't recognise it. I went to the gallery, wrote, looked in shops and at cityscapes, talked feebly. Cynically I felt that all the connections I had made so far were only due to another person's pity or kindness. As the helpless recipient of someone else's compassion, there was no meaning to my presence except to smile broadly when someone cast a gaze or camera in my direction.

There is a restaurant I go to in Koenji whenever I feel an Anne Sexton mood coming on; normally I don't linger, lest my despondency become deeper. It is the kind of place that has special dishes for three hundred yen and only one out of the four light bulbs below the shop sign ever light up; lost souls tend to eat there. During my time of doubt, I would start each day unhappily and end each evening benumbed, full of cheap food that I consumed there, night after night. While I ate I counted all the weeks I had spent in Koenji and the weeks I had to go, feeling that the past was simply and hopelessly lost, while what lay in the future was impossible to grasp. At the same time I was aware that in the present, nothing was hurting me except the early onset of nostalgia. To cheer myself up, I fed myself words that had the opposite effect to the one intended: "It'll be over soon and then what? You'll miss it, like you do with everything else. You don't need to write a travelogue to remember because you're not traveling, you're living here."

My solution was to walk off the desperation. For a while I had the company of Hiroaki-san, a gentle young design student who had been living a starving-artist existence on the fringes of Koenji. His family, Hiroaki-san told me, did not approve of drawing as a job, and soon he would have to leave Tokyo, go back to his parents, and explain (again) why he didn't want to work in a bank. There were times when Hiroaki-san looked close to tears, though he always insisted everything was *daijoubu* (fine). Everything was certainly not fine; Hiroaki-san could not find the way out of his trouble, or even see it. Suddenly I had someone to get lost with.

There is something soothing about the normalcy of the lived-in city: the small twisting streets, bicycles, traffic, and congestion. The markings on the streets around Koenji are white, except for the yellow painted squares around the drains. The gutters are always clear of litter. Hiroaki-san and I walked where the light was warm, not cool. We would take the walkway under the Chūō line, walk the length of the path to Asagaya, and only feel at peace when the train rattled overhead. We walked the streets as we probably never would walk them again; we walked before knowing where we were, before our lives became too familiar with locations, vocations, and partners, before we realised we had to work harder at what we were talented at. In that moment of shared uncertainty, the suspicion of what lay before us was enough.

"Kassorin-san," Hiroaki-san would say as we walked side by side down an unknown street, tasting the air of our city, "please do not complicate this business."

IV. Chart

Amongst the pictures
We do not notice the cold
Inside it is warm.

When I have the chance, I walk the streets of Koenji at night to see the stamp of life on the tongue and groove of the streetscape. Sometimes I walk alone, to take in details, and sometimes in company, to share them. One night I came across an orange paper lantern outside a *yakitori* bar. The paper had split from the wire frame, and the light shining out was bold rather than muted. In fastidious Japan, you would think that the lantern would be taken down, thrown away—but there also exists, in Koenji at least, a sense of retaining and seeing beauty in what is worn out and breaking down. All around, the broken lantern cast jagged, surprisingly sharp shadows.

Some streetlights radiate a green glow. I come across an arrow that points one way but deliberately take the wrong direction. I have ground down my claws on these streets over so many nights that I now move with the sole intention to discover. The streets gleam, as if they have been washed especially for my wanderings; the blended tints of neon light reflect against the asphalt like slicked oil. I pass by the gates of a shrine and the park where Haruki Murakami imagined one of his characters sitting and gazing at the moon. I pass the coin laundry that is open every night to no customers, the racks of secondhand clothes protected by thick plastic slips. I notice little dirt but plenty of graffiti; I see where signs have been painted over and where the paint is chipping. Nothing is perfect here, including my approach.

I have started to take photographs rather than scribble words. I photograph the light and the shadows. I walk and wave at people I see behind windows, who smile at me but bow back. I also bow. I have remained silent and I have written about this silence. I have begun to gather my words and my life. I have a favourite drink at the Flamingo and can easily place an order for it. I know which chairs are the most comfortable in my favourite coffee shop, where

I can get the freshest vegetables on Saturday mornings, the best homemade miso paste, my preferred brand of tinned crab meat. I know at least part of Tokyo's subway map and attend parties where I recognise more than one face as friendly. I have charted the path I have taken through Koenji while knowing that what has passed may not prevent against loss, or getting lost, in the future.

I appreciate the freedom of Koenji, for the claim I have on life here is impermanent—or not quite permanent, not yet. Sometimes the realisation of my eventual departure allows me to throw off certain inhibitions, to take a risk and clasp the present experience. After all, can't the process of getting to know a place, or a person, sometimes be rushed? Why doesn't something rapid equate to something real? At whatever rate they come, the moments exist to be lived. The moment of relinquishing the self you knew in the old place, of tracing another identity in the new, of coming to a dead end, of losing yourself again. All the while, the place surrounding you expands, so the memory of it first draping folds over you is not forgotten, but continues, promising recovery. If you continue to walk, or even drift, along, charting the movement as you go, the more complex and colorful your creation becomes, even if it is something borrowed.

Kathryn Hummel's fiction, non-fiction, poetry, and photography have appeared in publications and anthologies from Australia, New Zealand, the US, Nepal, Bangladesh, and India. Recently she has completed a major work of narrative ethnography, drawing on memory and conversations with women in Bangladesh. Kathryn was a writer in residence in 2011 for the Cafe Poet Program (Australian Poetry) and for the Forever Now project (Aphids and Vitalstatistix), featured during Adhocracy 2013.

ACKNOWLEDGEMENTS

I would like to thank the many women whose work I read during the selection process for this anthology. There were far more wonderful stories than I could include here. Thank you for helping to create a collection that I hope represents the incredible variety of experiences we encounter in our lives abroad. I chose these stories because they capture deeply personal and specific moments in the lives of their authors. Thank you, writers, for sharing these moments with me.

I would also like to thank my grandmother, Donna Young. She is, for me, the original expat woman in Asia. She moved to Japan in the '50s to teach English, married my grandpa there, and then proceeded to live in Hong Kong, Thailand, South Korea, and the Philippines over the next forty years. I am grateful for her example of what it's like to live a full, varied, adventurous life, even on the other side of the globe.

I would like to thank Xu Xi for the idea for this anthology, and Marshall Moore and the team at Signal 8 Press for its publication. I am grateful to have had the opportunity to work on this project.

Of course, I must also thank my family back home in the US, my in-laws in Hong Kong, and my husband for their support and encouragement. You guys are the best.

CPSIA information can be obtained at www.ICGtesting.com
Printed in the USA
BVOW04s0611300614

357731BV00009B/200/P

9 789881 219527